STOP

THINK

Other Books by the Same Author

Agenda: A Plan for Action (1971)

Exit Inflation (1981)

Jobs For All: Capitalism on Trial (1984)

Canada at the Crossroads (1990)

Damn the Torpedoes (1990)

Funny Money:
A Common Sense Alternative to Mainline Economics (1994)

Surviving the Global Financial Crisis:
The Economics of Hope for Generation X (1996)

Arundel Lodge: A Little Bit of Old Muskoka (1996)

The Evil Empire: Globalization's Darker Side (1997)

STOP

THINK

PAUL HELLYER

Chimo Media

Canadian Cataloguing in Publication Data

Hellyer, Paul, 1923-
  Stop: Think

Includes bibliographical references and index.
ISBN 0-9694394-6-6

1. International economic relations. 2. International finance.
3. Neoclassical school of economics. I. Title.

HF1359.H444 1999   337   C99-930121-7

Printed and bound in Canada. The paper used in this book is acid free.

Chimo Media Inc.
99 Atlantic Ave., Suite 302
Toronto, ON M6K 3J8
Canada
Tel: (416) 535-7611
Fax: (416) 535-6325

CONTENTS

FOR

EVERYONE, EVERYWHERE

ACKNOWLEDGMENTS

A number of individuals and organizations have assisted in the preparation of this book.

I am indebted to Donald Champagne, Peter Hellyer, Wm. Hixson, Jim Jordan, Bruce Katz, Peter McCrindle, Doug Peters and W.H. Pope for reading the draft manuscript. Their insightful comments and suggestions were of immense value in preparing the final version. They also noted a number of errors and omissions. Responsibility for those that slipped through the net, and for the views expressed in the book, is mine alone.

Once again Andy Donato deserves a medal for capturing the essence of my thesis in his cartoon which appears on the cover. One picture is better than a thousand words in depicting the imminent danger posed by globalization.

My executive assistant, Nina Moskaliuk, deserves special mention. She was painstaking in her research and verification of facts and references as well an indefatigable in revising the text and preparing the pages for the printer.

I am grateful to Bob Olsen for keeping me up-to-date by e-mail and Edwin Durbin for preparing the index; also to the Toronto Metropolitan Library, the United States Consulate in Toronto, the Embassies of France, Italy, Japan, the United States and the United Kingdom High Commission in Ottawa for their cooperation. Each was most helpful.

Finally, I have to thank my family and especially my wife, Ellen, one more time. They are the ones who pay the price for my preoccupation with world affairs. I hope, at the end of the road, they will be able to look back and believe that it has all been worthwhile.

INTRODUCTION

Have you ever tried to write a column or a book to say to the vast majority of economists and opinion leaders that they have got it all wrong; that they have set the world on a collision course with disaster? It is presumptuous, of course, but those of us who are dissenters, and our ranks are growing daily, have a moral obligation to ourselves and others to sound the alarm before it is too late.

We seem to be hell bent toward a world without borders. Someone has decided to eradicate the nation state as an effective political entity and to rob it of much of its power by moving back to the corporatism of the medieval society; this is not forward-looking but a wish to move back to the pre-democratic era. Decisions that have been the prerogative of national governments are being transferred to outsiders including the World Trade Organization, the International Monetary Fund, the World Bank, the Bank for International Settlements and transnational corporations.

Apart from the dubious merit of such a massive transfer of power is the undeniable fact that it is being done without the advice or consent of the people whose lives are being affected. They, whoever they may be, are re-engineering the world without asking for our opinions and without giving us the opportunity to express them in any tangible way through the ballot box.

To add insult to injury, globalization is being pushed down our throats without the courtesy of any vision of what the world will look like when the revolution has run its course. Who will be in charge? To whom will they be accountable? How will changes be effected? What recourse will there be for the people who believe that they have been seriously disadvantaged in the process?

A skeptic might conclude that there are no satisfactory answers to these questions because globalization is, in reality, a gigantic smoke-screen for the biggest power grab in history. The wealthiest, most powerful, people in the world have become impatient with democracy which sets standards of conduct and taxes wealth to provide services for the common good. To paraphrase, their battle hymn is Arthur Christopher Benson's immortal line, "God who made us mighty, make us mightier yet."

This can be achieved by shackling the nation states; by taking away their right to determine the conditions upon which direct foreign investment is welcome; by insisting that they must admit goods produced under the most despicable of circumstances; by requiring that their land and assets be "for sale" to foreigners; and that their central banks be immune to political control.

The aim of the game is a world where nation states are powerless to protect their citizens from external shocks and developments, where governments are mere pawns in the hands of international banks, supranational corporations and world bureaucracies accountable to no one. To an extent considered inconceivable to many, the globalized world would be a world dominated by power and greed.

No one would deny that there are benefits to international action. Treaties to ban the use of land mines and a World Court to try persons accused of crimes against humanity may be steps in the right direction. Similarly, there can be benefits to liberalized and freer trade, but only if it does not undermine the viability of national economies and if the rules include acceptable safeguards and standards in areas such as labor and environmental protection.

Those standards do not yet exist, and the transnational corporations sponsoring globalization are determined that they never will exist, except on a purely voluntary and consequently ineffective basis. No mandatory restrictions on their freedom of action are on the negotiating table.

If liberalized trade may ultimately bring about some positive results the same cannot be said about globalized financial services and unrestricted capital flows. They are a recipe for international instability and chaos and there is no existing or potential financial watchdog that can prevent it. The principal beneficiaries of such a system are the parasitical currency traders and short-term money lenders who, like vampires, live by sucking the life-blood from one target of convenience after another.

Yet this kind of system has been the object of the negotiations for a Multilateral Treaty on Investment under the Organization for Economic Cooperation and Development, the proposed Free Trade Agreement for the Americas, the Article IV Amendment being pushed by the International Monetary Fund and other venues. The implications are far-reaching and exhaustive. They lead to a dead end that is difficult, almost impossible to reverse. Still the trend must be reversed!

The claim that globalization is the road to nirvana for a desperate world is false. It is the road that will lead inevitably to another financial meltdown, the impoverishment of millions of innocent people and the death of democracy in any meaningful sense. This book is dedicated to alternatives that would lead to a world of greater justice and opportunity for all.

It is not intended to be anti-American because, in truth, it is not. Yet it is impossible to write about globalization, and the imposition of a neo-classical economic system with a track record of failure, without holding the coach accountable for a game plan resulting in massive injuries to most of the players.

Readers familiar with my work will note that some of the arguments have been borrowed from earlier books. Everyone will find a certain amount of repetition. This is not inadvertent. Some of the principal points need to be emphasized over and over again.

Finally, it must be admitted that I am of a generation unschooled in the niceties of political correctness and inclusive language. I hope that I may be forgiven for expressing my hopes and concerns without fear or favor.

CHAPTER 1

SOMETHING HAS GONE
DESPERATELY WRONG

"Poverty is an anomaly to rich people. It is very difficult to make out why people who want dinner do not ring the bell."

Walter Bagehot

Almost daily when I skim the morning papers I find something that upsets me. Something, somewhere in our shrinking world, fills me with horror or dismay. People are starving, or they have just lost their jobs; their health care has been cut back or they have just lost their life savings on the stock market as a result of some pyramid scam or phony stock promotion like the Bre-X gold mine.

I tried to explain my increasing concern as a function of age, because I am well aware that the world has never been without poverty, ill health, turbulence and fraud. But this explanation won't wash when I compare the 1980s and 1990s to the more tranquil post-Korean War period. The incidence and severity of crises has been on the increase. Something has, in fact, gone desperately wrong.

Consider the state of affairs in Sub-Saharan Africa as a case in point. In the course of two decades the situation has gone from dismal to desperate. World Bank figures indicate that in 1980 their foreign debt was $84.1 billion equal to 34% of their Gross Domestic Product (GDP). In 1996, these countries, collectively, owed $227.2 billion, U.S., which was 78% of their GDP and far more than their export earnings will

1

allow them to service.[1] In addition they have had to cut back expenditures for health care and education, and find themselves in a state which, barring a miracle, leaves them without hope.

Latin American countries were very much in the news in the early 1980s when they suffered a debt crisis. Now they are back on the list of concerns as panicky investors retreat to the safe haven of American Treasury bonds and U.S. dollars. In late August 1998, for example, Venezuela faced a full-scale emergency as its foreign exchange reserves dropped and short-term interest rates soared to 120 percent.[2]

Brazil, considered the strongest of the South American economies, had its foreign currency bonds downgraded by Moody's Investors Services in early September, 1998.[3] To slow the outflow of capital, interest rates were allowed to soar to almost 40 percent.[4] Stop to consider what that does to the economy. If you want to borrow 10,000 Brazilian real to start a business, the carrying charge would be 4,000 real a year. How many small entrepreneurs can afford to take that kind of risk?

The high interest rates, however, were not enough to calm the nerves of skittish international investors so the International Monetary Fund (IMF) was obliged to cobble together a $42 billion rescue package comprising $18 billion in loans from the IMF itself, another $4.5 billion from the World Bank and a nearly equal amount from the Inter-American Development Bank, plus at least $15 billion more from the United States, Britain, France, Germany, Spain, Italy, Canada, Japan and several other countries. It was expected that the loans would be subject to the usual conditions like constraints on government spending and privatization of government-owned industry.[5] Even that was not enough to pacify international markets for long. The fourth assault on the real in 18 months forced the Brazilian government to devalue its currency in mid-January 1999, and then to let it float freely in the international market. Investors reacted nervously for fear the contagion would spread to Argentina and Mexico.

Mexico, too, was back in the news. On September 2, 1998, Mexico's Finance Minister José Gurría said he was concerned that prolonged high interest rates could deal new blows to the Mexican banking system.[6] This at a time when Mexican lawmakers were still deadlocked on the question of whether or not they should stiff the taxpayers for the earlier $50 billion international bailout in 1994.

The South-East Asian meltdown was so widespread that it defies synopsis. First Thailand then South Korea, the Philippines, Indonesia, and Malaysia had their currencies and their economies trashed. It was called the "Asian Flu" because it spread like a virus from one country to another.

It has also been called a crisis due to its worldwide effects. It was even cited as a significant factor in the landslide depreciation of the Australian, Canadian and New Zealand currencies, although one suspects that in this case cause and effect may have been exaggerated.

What is certain is that the taming of the "Asian Tigers" contributed to global instability. This conclusion was confirmed by U.S. Federal Reserve (FED) Chairman Alan Greenspan in his second day of congressional testimony in June, 1998 when he said: "The crisis ... has shown no evidence of stabilization at this point. We do not know how far it's going to carry or what its spillover will be."[7]

It is easy when talking about crises, interest rates, economic stalemate and debt overload to forget the impact these have on people — live human beings. The whole scene is bizarre in the extreme, but one set of figures released by Joseph Stiglitz, the recently appointed chief economist of the World Bank, hit me like a bolt of lightening. He estimated that 20 million Indonesians would lose their jobs and that a total of 50 million would be brought below the poverty line.[8]

These figures are beyond comprehension, yet they are real! And we, citizens of the world, have to face the fact that millions of innocents have been reduced to abject poverty due to circumstances over which they had no control. It is a sobering thought.

Equally sobering is Russia's new dark age. Ten years ago Russians had jobs and they had food. Today, millions of them have neither. In late 1998, the International Committee of the Red Cross planned to triple donations to cope with what they expected to be one of the coldest winters in years. "The situation has certainly worsened," the agency's information delegate told reporters in October. "We can't afford to underestimate the possibility of starvation in some regions." According to the Red Cross half of Russia's children are underdeveloped mentally and physically due to malnutrition.[9]

The transition from communism to capitalism has been a monumental failure and unhappiness has changed to bitterness. In the summer of 1998, when restless soldiers were about to have their rations cut to two meals a day and their officers hadn't been paid for five months, Alexander Lebed , himself a former general, warned of the possibility of a military uprising.[10] That immediate crisis passed but other politicians have since warned of the possibility of civil war if conditions do not improve.

With millions of Russians almost begging for bread and potatoes, there was something surrealistic about President Bill Clinton's summit encounter with Russian President Boris Yeltsin in Moscow in early September, 1998. Russia had to stay the course on the path of reform, the president admonished. There was no turning back the course of world history.

As I listened to a radio report of this little bit of gratuitous advice, the image that flashed across my mind was that of a man swept from the deck of an ocean liner by a giant tidal wave in the middle of the Atlantic. From the bridge the captain was yelling down at the drowning man, "Don't panic; just keep swimming and if you make it closer to shore we'll throw you a life-preserver." A nagging question arises. How can you characterize drowning in a sea of despair as "reform"?

Western Europe, with its free-market and democratic traditions has fared much better than its East European neighbors with their leap of faith from a system they knew and understood to one that is totally foreign to their culture and experience. Still there are pockets of discontent in countries like Germany and France which have been suffering unusually high unemployment rates and there is no doubt this was a significant factor in the defeat of Chancellor Helmut Kohl in the 1998 German general election. On the streets the rumblings of unemployed youth revive faded memories of the early 1930s.

American commentators tend to attribute this to the rigidity of European labor markets and social programs. Many Europeans I talk to are not convinced. They are more inclined to fault economic management and the stringent standards necessary to comply with the Maastrich treaty. For whatever reason, growth projections are now being scaled back to reflect what is perceived as the new world reality.

It is widely believed that Japan is the key to arresting a global slump. The protracted recession in that country has produced consumer belt-tightening. In early 1998 the government tried to stimulate spending with temporary tax cuts but to no avail. Skeptical consumers simply banked the savings and the economy remained paralyzed. Despite repeated prodding from Western leaders, an ironic demand for Keynesian interference in an era of market economics, a more comprehensive reform package became a political football between Prime Minister Kuzo Obushi's Liberal Democratic Party and opposition politicians.

Then there was the question of how to handle Japanese banks which were as weak as they are gigantic. The Japanese government insisted that they must be rescued because failure would create shock waves around the world. On the other side of the argument free market purists view the reluctance to let banks fail as one more sign that Japan's commitment to market solutions is less than total.

It was a dilemma compounded by the numbers. Estimates of bad loans on the books of Japanese banks ranged from $600 billion to $1 trillion U.S. dollar equivalent. Even the low estimate was a staggering figure which raised questions about the inevitable domino effect. When banks are allowed to fail, other businesses that can't get their money out in time, or have their credit cut off, go under and unemployment rises — not the kind of bad news the people of that troubled nation wanted. In the end the government put together the biggest rescue package in world history. Once again, however, it was taxpayers who had to pick up the tab for irresponsible bankers.

The United States has fared better than most other countries for reasons that will be discussed in future chapters. Still, beneath the apparently calm waters there are dangerous currents. U.S. corporations are loading up on debt at a rapid clip with the total increasing from about $2.5 trillion in 1990, to $3.7 trillion in September 1998.[11] U.S. consumer spending is at record heights and it is being financed, increasingly, through credit. The Federal Reserve Board estimates that Americans owe a staggering U.S. $1.24 trillion in automobile financing and revolving credit — double the debt load they carried in 1991.[12]

So it is not surprising that there has been an alarming increase in personal bankruptcies. About 1.94 million Americans declared bankruptcy in 1997. That marked a big increase over 1996 and surpassed even the worst year of the Great Depression.[13]

Even more worrisome for the long-range image and economic prosperity of the United States is the growing disparity of income between the rich and poor. During the period 1979 through the present, the growth in income has disproportionately flowed to the top. The bottom 60% of the population actually saw their real income decrease in 1990 dollars. The next 20% saw modest gains. The top twenty percent saw their income increase 18%. The wealthiest one percent saw their incomes explode over 80%.[14]

This is both a moral and an economic problem. It disturbs the pretence that all Americans are born equal. It also has a dampening effect on an economic engine fuelled, in large part, by consumer spending. Rich people can be conspicuous spenders but the day eventually comes when they cannot eat any more or drink any more and the number of cars and houses reaches the saturation point of gratification. If they then use their excess income to buy financial or other assets, that income is no longer available to provide jobs and income for others.

Canada has most of the advantages of the U.S. except that our central bank, the Bank of Canada, put the economy in low gear in 1989-90 and hasn't got it past second gear since. Excessively high real interest rates caused massive unemployment which still, at the end of 1998, remains at a stubbornly high 8.0% and economic forecasts indicate that it will remain close to that level well into the next century.

The high unemployment led to low productivity gains and this caused the Canadian dollar to fall relative to the U.S. dollar. It is great for the tourism industry but it is hard on national pride. By mid-1998 the decline had gone too far and our best assets became tempting bargains for foreign investors.

Canadians share the debt problem with the U.S. and the rest of the world. The Royal Bank, Canada's largest, estimated that average household debt would reach 100% of after tax income in 1998, which leaves little room for further growth of personal debt. Needless to say, bankruptcies have been occurring in record numbers.

In Canada, as in many other countries, politicians and commentators have become obsessed with the level of federal government debt. No one would deny its importance but it is only a fraction of the total debt, roughly one-third of the total $1.8 trillion (Cdn.). Smothering the economic outlook is the fact that the average interest rate is probably about twice as high as the growth rate of the economy. So I keep telling my friends that you don't need a Ph.D. in economics to know that if you owe 225% of your income, and the rate of interest on that debt is twice as high as your annual increase in salary, you have a problem. Canada has a problem in common with the United States (where total debt is about 190% of GDP), Australia, New Zealand, and virtually every other country in the world.

One of the most poignant stories of late 1998 was a November radio broadcast reporting that Ontario hog farmers were killing piglets because they couldn't afford to feed them. They had been selling pigs for $60 less than it cost to raise each of them, which couldn't continue. The reason I found the news so distressing, apart from the injustice, is because I hadn't heard anything like it since the Great Depression.

Another reminder of the Great Depression came from the International Labour Organization report which said that the vast army of the world's unemployed will be swollen by 10 million in 1998. "The global employment situation is grim and getting grimmer," Michel Hansenne, director-general of the agency, told a news conference. The report said that some 150 million workers are now unemployed and a total of one billion, or one-third of the world's labor force, are either out of work or underemployed.[15]

WHITE-KNUCKLE FINANCIAL MARKETS

It had to happen! With Asian currencies plunging, interest rates rising and former "tigers" being reduced to pussy cats you could tell instinctively that there was hurricane weather ahead. Too much hot, speculative money floating around. Too much International Monetary Fund interference. Too many previously robust economies either slipping or plunging into recession with the resulting effect on imports. The aftermath of the storm was destined to buffet distant shores. And it did!

By the end of August, 1998, the Dow Industrial index fell to 7,539.07 from its July 17 peak of 9,337.97, a decline of 19.26%; the Standard and Poors 500 dropped to 957.28 from 1,186.75 for the same period, a loss of 19.33%; the NASDAQ composite took an even bigger beating, falling to 1,449.25 from its July 20 peak of 2,014.25, a decline of 25.57%.[16] Other markets around the world suffered a comparable or greater battering.

Markets regained heart when President Bill Clinton suggested a coordinated interest rate cut. The Dow rose. A couple of days later when U.S. Federal Reserve Board Chairman Alan Greenspan and Hans Tietmeyer, president of the German Bundesbank, sat on their hands and demonstrated that they, and not politicians were in charge of the world economy, markets plunged again. Even a veiled hint of either lower or higher interest rates on the part of Federal Reserve Board Chairman Alan Greenspan is enough to set financial markets off on another roller-coaster ride.

The final straw was the IMF's year-end prediction of 2.2 percent growth for the world economy in 1999, the lowest since 1991. This was its forth downward revision since October 1997 and even this gloomy forecast was accompanied by warnings of several risks that could make things much worse.[17]

THE COMMON THREAD

Beginning in August, 1998, a few economists and commentators began to question the conventional wisdom. There had been a few brave prescient souls who had predicted trouble but they were generally discounted and found it difficult to obtain media coverage for their views. But by the time Japan had gone into recession, Russia had defaulted on some of its debt and decided to print money to rescue its banks, Indonesia had imposed capital controls, growth projections for Western economies had been reduced substantially and financial markets were in a perpetual state of flux, tentative dissenters began popping up like mushrooms in the basement. They were beginning to question the validity of the holy writ.

Is it possible to have financial stability in a world without boundaries? Is tight money and high interest rates the cure for Asian economies? Should the IMF use taxpayers' money to bail out imprudent financial institutions? Should speculators have the inalienable right to wreck national economies? Are derivatives an invitation to manipulate markets? How does cutting back on health care and education square with the demands of an emerging technological and information age?

Heresy has once again begun to raise its dormant head. Stephen F. Cohen, a professor of Russian studies and history at New York University, summed it up well in a column in *The Nation* entitled "Russia's new dark age". "Russian economists and politicians across the spectrum are now desperately trying to formulate alternative economic policies that might save their nation — one more akin to Franklin Roosevelt's New Deal than to the neo-liberal monetarist orthodoxies of the U.S. State and Treasury departments, the IMF, World Bank and legions of Western advisers, which have done so much to abet Russia's calamity."[18]

It is not just Russia's calamity that has been affected by

the neo-liberal monetarist orthodoxy. It is the common thread in the litany of despair that has affected the world. It has been a contributing factor, in varying degrees, to every bad news story I have recounted, and dozens more. The good news is that the set of economic principles widely known as the Washington consensus is now under serious attack, and not a moment too soon.

CHAPTER 2

THE WASHINGTON NONSENSUS

*"A national debt, if it is not excessive,
will be to us a national blessing."*

Alexander Hamilton

Some may consider me cheeky for re-naming the Washington Consensus the Washington Nonsensus. But I have always believed in calling a spade a spade and in my view that is what it is — nonsense! I say that notwithstanding the opinions of many learned friends who quote its alleged virtues and benefits with the same virtuosity and conviction with which Billy Graham quotes the Bible. To my mind the disciples of monetarism haven't taken time to stop and think through the dark consequences of returning to the pre-Great Depression system.

The Washington Consensus had its origin in what Nobel laureate Milton Friedman called the monetarist counter-revolution — a reversal of the revolutionary policies espoused by British economist John Maynard Keynes two generations earlier. Friedman would have preferred to label it Chicago School, in honor of the economics department of the University at which he taught. But it was "monetarism" which stuck. Whether known as monetarism, Chicago School or Friedmanism, it is all the same thing.

Milton Friedman's intentions were noble enough. He has been a champion of personal freedom within the framework of the rule of law. Liberty is his byword. But he must have drawn a distinction between law and lawmakers when he attributed the inflation of the 1970s to government intervention

11

on the Keynesian model and the apparent preoccupation with full employment at the expense of escalating prices. So the crusade began.

His starting point was an equation popularized in the 1930s by Yale economist Irving Fisher, MV = PT, which became known as the quantity equation. Money, multiplied by the velocity of turnover of that money, equals prices, multiplied by the volume of transactions. As Friedman pointed out in one of his books, *Monetarist Economics*, it is an equation that college students used to have to learn, then for a time did not, but with the monetarist counter-revolution, must again learn. It is quite ironic that Fisher's equation was the one that led me, more than twenty-five years earlier, to adopt quite different policy prescriptions from those that Prof. Friedman finally settled on.

It isn't the equation that is the problem. It is, like most economic theory, the way it is translated into the real world. In a conversation with an economics graduate one day I was abruptly reminded that Prof. Friedman had found that for 100 years in 100 countries there was a direct correlation between prices and increases in the money supply.

Yes, I replied, and in those same 100 countries, for the same 100 years, winter invariably followed summer. But that doesn't tell you how cold the winter was, or how hot the summer; whether rainfall was above or below average and whether crops were good or bad. A narrow interpretation of economics is like the blind man who, with his arms around the elephant's leg, thought the animal was like a tree. It was, alas, an incomplete appraisal.

Professor Friedman fell into a similar trap when he concluded that there was only one kind of inflation, i.e. the kind that results from too much money chasing too few goods. It is called classic inflation and it is the type economic historians are most familiar with.

It is not, however, the kind of inflation that has plagued most Organization for Economic Cooperation and Development (OECD) countries in the post-Korean war era. With few, and usually temporary exceptions, there have not been shortages of goods and services for several decades. The principal cause of inflation in the late '60s and '70s was wages rising out of sync with productivity, a development made possible by the market and monopoly power of big business and big labor.

In fact, wages rose by a multiple of productivity for 25 successive years, a phenomenon without precedent in the economic history of the world. It is this phenomenon which produced another precedent, dubbed stagflation. As wages rose, and then prices, central banks were put in an invidious position. If they allowed the money supply to grow fast enough to clear the market at the new higher price levels, there would be rampant inflation. If they didn't, there would be high unemployment. Most of them compromised which gave us too much inflation and too much unemployment at the same time. Hence, stagflation.

The arithmetic is simple enough. In the years 1964-1991 average wages and salaries in the United States increased 6.0 percent. Real output per member of the labor force rose 0.8% a year on average. Prices rose 5.2% which is the difference between the rate of increase in wages and the rate of increase in output. Similarly, in Canada, wages increased by 7.1%, output by 1.3% and prices 5.6 percent. The same approximation occurred in 15 OECD countries for the same time period.[1] Stated symbolically we have $\dot{P} = \dot{W} - \dot{Q}$ where $\dot{P}$ is the rate of change in the price level, $\dot{W}$ is the average rate of change in money wages, and $\dot{Q}$ is the average rate of increase in real output of goods and services per worker in the labor force.

While Prof. Friedman acknowledges the impact of wage gains in excess of productivity he rejects the significance of monopoly or market power. He makes the unsubstantiated claim that "wage increases in excess of increases in productivity are a result of inflation rather than the cause."[2] This proposition appears to fly in the face of the data. The Economic Report of the President, 1995, shows that wages outstripped productivity in the United States every year from 1964 to 1994. Therein lies the principal source of inflation for that period.

Not only did wages move up faster than productivity, they outpaced prices in 18 of the 21 years in advance of the time Milton and Rose Friedman first published *Free to Choose* in 1981 — the exceptions being '70, '74 and '79. For the entire 1964-1991 period the wage index kept ahead of the price index.[3]

THE FATAL FLAW

The failure to recognize the primary role of wage increases in excess of productivity as the principal initiator of inflation since the system settled down after the Korean War has been the fatal flaw in economic theory and, by extension, public policy. Professor Friedman and his colleagues accepted the conventional wisdom that the inflation of the late '60s and '70s began with the Vietnam War. President Johnson escalated the war and defence-generated incomes competed with other incomes for civilian goods. Congress and the White House did not drain off excess demand through higher taxes until 1968. Meanwhile, unions bargained, successfully, to compensate for past inflation and to hedge against future price increases.

This theory was endorsed by President Carter's Council of Economic Advisers, who wrote, "It was excess aggregate demand during the Vietnam War that drove up the underlying rate of inflation from 1 percent to 4 or 5 percent by the end of the 1960s."[4]

This conclusion was quickly accepted by economists and central bankers around the world. No one bothered to explain why even lower levels of unemployment in 1952 and 1953 — the lowest in more than a quarter of a century — were achieved without any comparable impact on prices. In fact, the inflation curve at that time was downward.

Even more disturbing is the lack of explanation for the fact that wages and prices began their steep ascent in Canada and the United Kingdom more than a year before they did in the United States.[5] Neither country was significantly affected by American involvement in South Asia; therefore, to conform with the conventional wisdom, their surge in prices should have followed rather than preceded the one in America.

The "it started with Vietnam" school was extended into a general theory in an attempt to explain the ratchet-like escalation of prices over the fifteen year period from 1965 to 1980. The Vietnam War was just the first of a series of explanations which included demand shock, the energy crisis, deficit spending by governments and inflationary expectations. While each of these rates a careful examination, I have argued in other books that none of them provides a valid explanation of the 1965-1980 phenomenon.[6]

The tragedy is that economists, including those of the Chicago School, came to the consensus that the post-Vietnam inflation was just one further case of too much money chasing too few goods. This conclusion implies that the United States economy and other Western economies are essentially pure market economies where all prices obey the law of supply and demand when, in fact, they are what I have long called "schizo" economies where some prices obey the law of supply and demand and others very definitely do not.

The difference in opinion is fundamental. If you believe that all prices obey the law of supply and demand then monetarism makes sense. If there are rigid prices resulting from the market power of big business and big labor, then pure monetarism becomes nonsense.

THE BANK BOONDOGGLE

Of all the advice that Milton Friedman has given us, none has been worse, or resulted in more hardship, than his recommendation that private banks be given back their virtual monopoly to create money, and that they be relieved of the necessity of maintaining cash reserves to back up their deposits.

It is an extreme irony that a spokesman from the Chicago School of Economics would propose a system of zero cash reserves when the Chicago School of the 1930s, closer to the consequences of economic devastation and more gifted with prescience, recommended that bank deposits be backed by 100% cash reserves. This would have prevented runs on the banks and ended the historic vacillation between too much credit and too little.

Milton Friedman initially supported the 100% solution. First in an article entitled "A Monetary and Fiscal Framework for Economic Stability", published in the *American Economic Review* in 1948,[7] and later in *A Program for Monetary Stability* published in 1959,[8] he makes the case for fundamental change. In the book he wrote: "As a student of Henry Simons and Lloyd Mints, I am naturally inclined to take the fractional reserve character of our commercial banking system as the focal point in a discussion of banking reform. I shall follow them also in recommending that the present system be replaced by one in which 100% reserves are required."[9]

In what appears to be a change of heart designed to neutralize the bankers' objections, Friedman proposed paying interest on the 100% reserves. In *A Program for Monetary Stability* he wrote: "I shall depart from the original 'Chicago Plan on Banking Reform' in only one respect, though one that I think is of great importance. I shall urge that interest be paid on the 100% reserves. This step will improve the economic results yielded by the 100% reserve system, and also, as a necessary consequence, render the system less subject to the difficulties of avoidance that were the bug-a-boo of the earlier proposals."[10]

It appears that this aspect of the proposal hadn't been adequately considered. Who would pay the interest on the cash? Presumably it would be the government. And how would the rate of interest be set? In Friedman's own words: "This problem of how to set the rate of interest is another issue that I feel most uncertain about and that requires more attention than I have given to it."[11] I can say amen to that, especially when I know how difficult it would be to ensure objectivity when banks are such generous supporters of the political system.

Although Friedman has not renounced his support for a 100% reserve system, it is no longer on his priority list as indicated in a footnote reply to a 1983 letter from William F. Hixson. "As good a reform as ever", Friedman wrote,

..."unfortunately with as little prospect of adoption as ever. I keep mentioning it but feel that tilting at windmills is not an effective way to spend my time."[12]

In a 1986 letter to Professor John H. Hotson, in reply to one on the subject of reserves and government-created money, he wrote: "In my opinion, either extreme is acceptable. I have not given up advocacy of one-hundred percent reserves. I would prefer one-hundred percent reserves to the alternative I set forth. However, I believe that getting the government out of the business altogether or zero percent reserves also makes sense. The virtue of either one is that it eliminates government meddling in the lending and investing activities of the financial markets."

"When I wrote in 1948, we were already halfway toward one-hundred percent reserves because so large a fraction of the assets of the banks consisted of either government bonds or high-powered money. One-hundred percent reserves at that time did not look impossible of achievement. We have moved so far since then that I am very skeptical indeed that there is any political possibility of achieving one-hundred percent reserves. That does not mean that it is not desirable."[13] Professor Friedman went on to say that the sole reason he stressed the zero percent reserves was "because it seemed to me at least to be within the imaginable range of political feasibility."[14]

If you happen to be unfamiliar with terms like "cash reserves", "fractional reserve system for banking" and "high-powered money", don't let it bother you. We will return to these in a later chapter. It is the significance of Professor Friedman's views that are important at this point. He has turned his back on the system that got us out of the Great Depression and then helped finance World War II and the early post-war years — a system where governments and private banks shared the money-creation function. In its place he has opted for the pre-Depression system when private banks had a virtual monopoly on money creation — the system that gave us the stock market crash of 1929 followed by nine years of misery and hardship until the outbreak of war rescued us.

THE WASHINGTON NONSENSUS

The Washington nonsensus, based on the theories of Milton Friedman and his colleagues at the University of the Chicago School of Economics is, above all, the resurrection of the system which failed us so miserably. It is a system under which private banks create almost all new money out of thin air with only a small capital reserve to back it. They do this every time they make a new loan. You, a business, or a foreign government, give them a note or a bond and, presto, with one flick of the computer a deposit in the agreed amount shows up in your account. Seconds earlier that "money" did not exist.

The problem is that all bank-created money is created as debt — and debt that is interest bearing. You have to pay interest on every cent you borrow. But if no one creates the money with which to pay the interest, what do you have to do? You have to borrow the money with which to pay the interest on what you already owe and go deeper and deeper into debt in the process.

It should be obvious to anyone who takes even a few minutes to stop and think about it that this system is not sustainable. Certainly it is not when the interest rate on all that debt is higher than the growth rate of the economy. The ratio of debt to income keeps rising until the burden is too great to carry. Then the crash comes. Values are deflated and a mass redistribution of wealth occurs bringing untold hardship to millions of innocents who have little notion of what is happening to them beyond the immediacy of the pain they feel.

A logical person might ask why, if all we have been doing is repeating past mistakes, so many of the world's most influential and powerful people have espoused the cause. In a word, it's "peer pressure". Everyone wants to be "with it", to be "trendy". It is so much easier and socially acceptable to ride with the current than to swim against it.

I learned one of my first lessons in mob psychology many years ago in the late '40s. My wife and I bought a ladies ready-to-wear shop because it had an apartment above it and we couldn't find any other accommodation due to the extreme post-war housing shortage. Although unfamiliar with the business, we had to learn fast that style was everything. A couple of designers in Paris or New York would send some models down a runway wearing skirts short enough to put half the cloth makers out of business. Then, within a few months, millions of women were wearing skirts that were magnets to the eyes. A couple of years later the same designers would dress their models in calf-length outfits and soon the mini-skirts were obsolete relics.

Regrettably, economists, too, follow the flock. I remember when there were just a few lonely Keynesians preaching the gospel of demand management. The idea was to even out the economic cycles by having governments borrow money and increase their spending when business is slack, and then raise taxes when the next boom arrives and use the money to pay off the earlier deficits. It was fascinating to watch the intelligentsia climb on the bandwagon one by one until, about 1970, "everyone was a Keynesian".

Then, along came Milton Friedman and his cohorts. Unable to fathom the origins of stagflation, they assumed that it was the product of government interference. So governments were out, and markets were in. Governments could do little that was right and markets could do nothing wrong. Adam Smith's invisible hand would guide the destiny of free spirits as they transformed the world economy into a seamless web of trade, commerce and investment. About the only role left for governments was to de-regulate the industries and dismantle the barriers to trade and investment necessary to give life to the process.

The dogma spread from school to school and government to government until it achieved the status of holy writ. Academic economists who spoke of other options could forget about tenure. Politicians who warned that the invisible hand might be the one that was picking your pocket were labelled left-wing loonies. Columnists submitting contrarian views found that access to the free press was much more open to those who shared the opinions of the publisher and the editor-in-chief and almost closed to those who disagreed.

The conventional wisdom, which soon abandoned pure monetarism when it proved to be technically flawed, and then substituted neo-classical economics, ignored two hundred years of economic history. There is nothing new about neo-classical economics. In fact, it should have been labelled retro-classical because it is the same old thing, recycled. It's the same decrepid old doctrine that gave capitalism a bad name, with its 45 recessions and depressions in 200 years, wrapped up in a glitzy new outfit.

THE FRUIT OF THE PUDDING IS IN THE EATING

If the Washington consensus had produced the kind of results you might reasonably expect from a good system critics wouldn't have a leg to stand on. Certainly the economic numbers and happiness quotients should be as good or better than the bad old days of regulation and government intervention. But that is not the case. The watershed occurred in 1974 when central banks adopted monetarism as their philosophical and operational textbook. Economic performance has been downhill ever since.

Not everyone agrees, of course, because those who have benefited most from "market economies" are quite happy with things the way they are. In New Zealand, for example, it is not difficult to find individuals who shout for joy at their liberation from the tentacles of government. It is, perhaps, the most extreme example because the level of bureaucratic red tape in that country was quite absurd. It was even necessary to get a permit for the foreign exchange required to subscribe to a foreign magazine. The level of government interference and control was what one would expect in an acute wartime emergency.

So, despite the enormous disruption and short-term suffering, business has benefitted enormously and hardly anyone, including those most disadvantaged by the revolution in its early stages, would want to go back to the old ways. Unemployment is low, inflation in check, and strikes, which were once commonplace, are relatively rare and by and large business confidence is high.

As in other countries the main debates are about adequate resources for health care and education. Also, there are continual worries about the economic underclass and inter-generational poverty. These problems, as in Canada, are especially acute among natives (Maoris) and Pacific Island immigrants and their descendants. It would appear that there are still some rough edges to be smoothed out and that perhaps the pendulum may have swung from one extreme just a little bit too far in the opposite direction.

Marcia Russell gives us her summation in the introduction to her book *Revolution: New Zealand from Fortress to Free Market*: "As we enter new political territory, we are forced to examine the balance sheet delivered by the revolution. The virtues of the 'market' are now being debated. By almost all measurements its rewards have been unevenly divided and there is a suspicion that in the rush to embrace the changes we trampled into near-oblivion some old hard-to-measure values, like ethics and morality. The notion of 'good for all' became a somewhat outmoded commodity."[15] It is this concept of the common good which seems to be taking such a drubbing in one country after another.

It will be difficult for me to forgive what monetarism and neo-classical economics has done to Canada. In the space of a few short years it has been reduced from a wonderfully endowed land of hope and promise to a fractious assembly of regions thrashing about in a sea of mediocrity. This has little to do with our two linguistic groups as some would pretend. It is almost exclusively due to the federal government's enthusiastic endorsement of the Washington consensus as to how countries should be run.

The Bank of Canada bought the Friedman line and aped every aspect of the U.S. Federal Reserve Board's carpet-bombing approach to inflation control. The 1981-82 recession was the genesis of huge deficits and subsequent debts. We hadn't fully recovered from that blow when we got it on the other chin in 1990 when Governor John Crow, an alumnus of the IMF school, decided that we should lead the world in inflation fighting. We did well on that score but at the expense of a decade of unconscionable high unemployment and unacceptably low productivity.

The federal budget of 1995 was the final straw — dictated, we were led to believe — by Wall Street. Since then we have seen the systematic dismantling of one of the world's best systems of health care, the substantial erosion of a first-class system of public education, a worrisome disregard of environmental priorities, a serious cut in the size and combat-readiness of the Canadian Armed Forces and a dramatic reduction in publicly-sponsored scientific research and development to the point where many of our best and brightest are looking elsewhere for the kind of career challenge that would otherwise have been available to them.

National unity has been affected too. The sovereignty movement in Québec which began as a linguistic and cultural imperative has been transformed into a predominantly economic contest. Québecers are being led to believe that they could run their own affairs more efficiently than Ottawa has been doing for the whole country and it's a difficult argument to refute. The saddest part of the whole tragedy is that none of it needed to happen. The whole unfortunate mess is the result of an abdication of independent power by Ottawa in favor of rule by international financial markets. It is enough to bring tears to the eyes.

While my anger at this turn of events is based on observation and experience, my case against monetarism and neo-classical economics is based on hard data from U.S. statistics. Again, the cutoff date is 1974 when central banks adopted the monetarist dogma, so I will compare two periods, the 26 years from 1948 to 1973 with the results of the 24 years from 1974 to 1997.

In the key area of economic growth, Gross National Product (GNP), in 1982 dollars, increased by an average of 3.70 percent from 1948 to 1973. For the subsequent 24 years Gross Domestic Product (GDP), in 1987 dollars, increased by an average of only 2.28 percent. Ignoring the small variation in measurement between GNP and GDP, output was down 38% in the monetarist era.[16]

The difference in average unemployment rates is even more startling. For the earlier period it averaged 4.8 percent. Since the monetarist counter-revolution began the average rate has been 6.8 percent. This is 41.7 percent more unemployed, on average, than in the Keynesian era.[17]

Then it is worthwhile to look at inflation. The average annual increase in the Consumer Price Index (CPI) in the earlier period was 2.67 percent. In the 24 years since the monetarist, neo-classical era began the average annual increase in the CPI has been 5.39 percent. The average inflation rate has been 102 percent higher since Friedmanism became the reigning philosophy.[18]

Most other key economic indicators are equally dismal by comparison. The rate of increase in per capita disposable income is down sharply as is average weekly earnings, median family income and increases in hourly and yearly output. Then, finally, there is the U.S. federal debt which was $266 billion in 1948, $466 billion in 1973 and $5.369 trillion in 1997. That represents a 78% increase in the 26 years before monetarism and a 1,052% increase in the 24 years since.[19]

The question is how can intelligent people trumpet a system which has produced more than 100 percent higher inflation, more than 40% more unemployment, a 38% reduction in output and a $5 trillion increase in federal debt and try to ram it down the collective throats of countries around the globe? Especially when the global statistics are even worse than those for the U.S. For the years 1950-1973 the average annual compound growth rate of per capita GDP was 2.90 percent. From 1973 to 1995 it was down to a disastrous 1.11 percent.[20]

I know that some defenders of the Washington nonsensus will argue that much of the poor performance of the early monetarist years resulted from trying to get a bad situation under control. It is an argument that doesn't hold water. If the disease had been diagnosed correctly it could have been brought under control by other means with none of the horrendous consequences I have recounted to date.

CHAPTER 3

THE IMF:
50 PLUS YEARS IS TOO LONG

*"The development of our financial oligarchy is by gradual
encroachment rather than by violent acts."*

U.S. Supreme Court Justice, Louis D. Brandies

I am somewhat ashamed to admit that for many years
I did not pay much attention to what the International Monetary
Fund (IMF) was doing. I knew of its origin, of course, as part
of the 1944 Bretton Woods agreement designed to stabilize the
post-World War II international financial system. The IMF's
role was to provide member governments with short-term
assistance when their foreign exchange reserves got too low as
a result of propping up their currency to maintain the fixed
exchange rate that had been agreed to.

Over the years, however, the system changed
dramatically. The gold standard was abandoned and many of
the world's leading currencies were deregulated. Floating,
rather than fixed exchange rates became the wave of the future.
That meant a reduced necessity for central banks to intervene
in currency markets and consequently little need to maintain
such large foreign exchange reserves. A logical consequence
was that the IMF lost its *raison d'être*. Its job was redundant.

With these vague images in mind it didn't surprise me
that the IMF was seldom in the news. All appeared quiet on
the journalistic front so I must have assumed that whatever the
IMF was doing was of minor consequence and not newsworthy.
This naive assumption ended like a dream interrupted by a clap

of thunder when, in 1995, I read Steven Solomon's frightening book *The Confidence Game: How Unelected Central Bankers Are Governing the Changed Global Economy*[1]. I found that the IMF, like most big bureaucracies without a real mandate, had been handed a new one, and a highly questionable one at that.

The story begins with President Jimmy Carter's appointment of Paul Volcker as Chairman of the Federal Reserve Board and his coronation as economic czar of the world financial system. Volcker, like most economists, misread the origin of the inflation of the late '60s and '70s and concluded that it was a monetary phenomenon which had to be tackled by monetary means. Although he may have entertained reservations about the monetarist formula he endorsed the philosophy and became a devout follower of Milton Friedman.

Volcker's early attempts to provide monetary restraint produced confused and unpredictable results so his next try was full brake. In 1981-82 the worst recession since the Great Depression of the 1930s was the predictable result. The social consequences were enormous. Millions of people worldwide lost their jobs, their homes, their farms and their businesses. It was a grim reminder of just how bad things can get when an economy goes berserk.

Most disappointing for me was the lack of discussion of alternative measures. A simple incomes policy that I had been proposing since the late '60s would have reduced inflation further and much faster and without any of the horrific social and economic consequences of the monetarist way. It was like waging atomic war on the whole society when a few well-placed shots from sharp shooters would have been sufficient.

This is a subject to be discussed later but for now let's stick to the economic consequences of Volcker's recession. Economies slowed, government deficits increased and these were rolled over into debt and compounded at high interest rates. In the United States the total government, corporate and personal debt, which had been remarkably stable at about 140% of GDP, suddenly took off and headed toward 190% in less than 2 decades — the highest since just before the Great Depression. Monetarism helped put the inflation genie back in the bottle but in doing so let the debt genie out of the bottle with a debt time bomb in its hands.

The effect on banks and banking was devastating. Led by Citicorp Chairman Walter Wriston, the big international banks had decided that lending vast amounts of money to Less Developed Countries (LDCs) was an easy way to get rich. Encouraged by the development of syndication and floating interest rates, which absolved them of interest rate risk, even small banks with no expertise climbed aboard the gravy train. Between 1970 and 1982 the profits on international operations (mostly LDC loans) of America's seven largest banks soared from 22% to 60% of total earnings.[2]

What the banks failed to anticipate was the effect of high interest rates on borrowers' ability to repay. All of a sudden the poor countries found they could not earn enough foreign exchange to pay the interest on their external debt. Poland and Hungary had to refinance debt, Mexico teetered on the brink of default and one Latin American country after another found itself in the same leaky boat and unable to meet its financial obligations. If markets had been allowed to reign supreme, virtually all of America's largest banks would have bit the dust. This didn't happen, however, thanks to the intervention of Paul Volcker and other members of the central bankers' club with an occasional nudge from concerned governments. The monetarist debt machine brought the entire international financial system within a hair's breadth of collapse and it is something of a miracle that catastrophe was averted.

Actually it wasn't a miracle. It was a wondrously complicated web of intrigue and deceit and anyone who has the stomach for it can read the gory details in *The Confidence Game*. The bottom line is that the public was kept blissfully unaware that their banks were technically insolvent until the IMF could ride to the rescue with taxpayers' money. Although there are many ordinary citizens who might applaud the bailout on the grounds that it was preferable to the alternative, it set a dreadful precedent. It telegraphed the message that banks could make irresponsible loans, willy-nilly, without undue fear of the consequences. They would know that taxpayers were always standing by at the ready with a life-preserver handy.

The IMF as lifeguard, however, does not ride to the rescue of the countries and people so negatively affected by the excesses of international capitalism. It is the foreign banks and financial institutions that are the objects of its largesse. They are the ones who pick up their welfare cheques from the taxpayers of the world.

In addition, and in a sense even worse, the IMF attaches conditions to its loan agreements requiring recipient countries to adjust their macro-economic policies in order to conform with the ideological imperatives of the Washington consensus. Almost always these changes are tailored to the interests of official and commercial creditors and almost always to the considerable discomfort and impoverishment of the majority of the people living in debtor countries.

As I admitted at the beginning of this chapter I was not as *au courant* as someone interested in public policy should have been. Like most people in developed countries I was too busy and too pre-occupied to keep informed. My five daily newspapers smother me with information overload but seldom provide in-depth analyses of Third World problems. Fortunately, friends recommended that I read *The Globalisation of Poverty: Impacts of IMF and World Bank Reforms*, by Michel Chossudovsky[3], professor of economics at the University of Ottawa, and *50 Years is Enough: The Case Against the World Bank and the International Monetary Fund*, edited by Kevin Donaher.[4]

The case histories are enough to bring tears to the eyes of anyone whose heart is not made of granite. I asked one of my sons, your average MBA, to read *50 Years is Enough*. Obviously affected, his bravest retort was "It does go on and on." That is the truth. It goes on and on from one country to another to another recounting in painful detail the economic and human carnage in the wake of IMF "reforms". In reality, an IMF reform is a synonym for deform.

The devaluation of a nation's currency has often been a pre-condition for IMF "help". The social impact is immediate and brutal. Prices of food staples, essential drugs, fuel and other necessities increase overnight. Government subsidies for the basics have to be reduced or eliminated. IMF packages often specifically prohibit domestic wage increases to compensate for the rapid decline in purchasing power.

Borders must be opened to foreign products. Domestic industries, unable to compete with imports, must be allowed to fail. This is the exact opposite of the protectionism that allowed countries like the United States, Japan, France and Germany to build a powerful domestic industrial base.

Open borders and unrestricted imports create balance of payments problems. So the IMF encourages Third World countries to concentrate on growing food and specialty crops for export instead of food for their own people. Millions of additional people are subject to starvation diets as a result.

IMF encouragement for many developing countries to concentrate on commodity exports, to earn the U.S. dollars with which to pay the interest on their debts, led to a world over-supply and consequently lower prices. That means LDCs have even more trouble earning enough to service their existing debt so they have to borrow extra to pay the interest on what they already owe and go further into debt — an inadvertent contribution to the world debt crisis.

Another condition of IMF "help" is "central bank independence from political power" as a remedy against the alleged inflationary bias of governments. The IMF prevents the funding of government expenditures by the central bank, through money creation — as Canada, the United States and other countries did to escape the Great Depression, help finance World War II and post-war development. The IMF effectively assumes monetary sovereignty in the countries that it "aids".

As Michel Chossudovsky points out: "The IMF, on behalf of the (international) creditors, is in a position virtually to paralyze the financing of real economic development. Incapable of using domestic monetary policy to mobilize its internal resources, the country becomes increasingly dependent on international sources of funding which has the added consequence of increasing the level of external indebtedness."[5]

What we see here is a level of meddling in domestic

affairs unequalled in modern history. Intolerable intervention with negative consequences. If the Sub-Saharan countries had achieved higher growth, better health, higher education and better environmental protection some applause would be in order. But the converse is true. With the IMF, as with the Washington consensus, it is "promises, promises." Instead of short-term pain bringing long-term gain, as solemnly promised, all it has delivered is long-term pain.

ALL THE SAME MISTAKES IN SOUTH-EAST ASIA

When the IMF had wreaked such havoc worldwide you would think a different approach might have been tried in South-East Asia. No such luck! U.S. Treasury officials had regained confidence from their experience with Mexico in 1994. By July, 1997, the Mexican peso had been stable for a year and this was considered a triumph for American policy. It didn't seem to matter that Mexico had endured a painful recession and that the peasants were really suffering. The money was okay, the international investors were secure, and that's all that mattered.

The situation in Thailand was similar but less severe when it devalued its currency in June, 1997, after running out of foreign exchange. When it turned to the U.S. for help the till was dry but Thailand would get a $17 billion loan package for promising to impose high interest rates, restrain government spending, close floundering banks and let its currency fall in order to boost exports and reduce imports. It was the same old bitter medicine that had failed so miserably so often.

What became clear, however, was the extent to which the IMF had been reduced to a tool of U.S. foreign policy as determined in the Treasury Department. Long suspected to be the case, any pretence that the IMF was acting independently ceased to matter. Treasury Secretary Robert Rubin and Deputy Treasury Secretary Lawrence Summers call the shots with a little private advice from Federal Reserve Board Chairman Alan Greenspan and the enthusiastic collaboration of International Monetary Fund chief Michel Camdessus and his deputy Stanley

Fischer, the Massachusetts Institute of Technology (MIT) economist that had been hand picked by Mr. Summers. These five men must be one of the most fearsome collection of ideologues the world has known.

They say that power corrupts so it is not too surprising that the U.S. scuttled a Japanese proposal for an Asian Monetary Fund of about $100 billion to cope with regional crises. Mr. Rubin and Mr. Summers opposed the idea because they feared the fund would offer big loans with less stringent conditions than the IMF demanded. That was their stated objection. Skeptics suggest that the real objection was loss of power and control.

The IMF has served American interests well. It has imposed the Washington consensus on proud but helpless nations. Thus it was to be expected when it was South Korea's turn, that previously proud Asian Tiger was told to toe the line. Deputy U.S. Treasury Secretary Lawrence Summers boasted that the IMF package did more to promote the U.S. trade agenda in South Korea than decades of bilateral negotiations.[6] Summers did not underline the fact that of the $58 billion rescue package that the IMF and the U.S. assembled, much of the money flowed right back out to pay Korean banks' debts to foreign banks. Once again the financial gods were appeased with a sacrificial offering of peoples' money.

Indonesia was one of the most extreme examples yet of outside meddling. The IMF package was so detailed that it set the price at which rice should be sold and how plywood sales should be handled. The Indonesian government was forced to slash spending at a time when the economy was already reeling and President Clinton personally told then President Suharto to toe the IMF line, which, loosely translated, meant the American line. When this line led to widespread rioting the best that IMF chief Michel Camdessus could do was express concern. He said he was worried about the social impact of economic reforms.[7]

Camdessus went on to defend IMF policy as he told a conference in Melbourne, Australia, that Asian nations being nursed back to economic health under IMF bailouts —

Indonesia, Thailand and South Korea — were each responsible for their own plight. "Sometimes a medicine creates even more pain", he said.[8] Some of us would say it was the IMF medicine that created more pain. Harvard economist Jeffrey Sachs was on target when he said: "This crisis didn't have to happen. It was not an inevitable feature of the weakness of Asia. It's a bad accident that simply keeps getting worse and worse."[9]

WHAT NEXT FOR THE IMF

As the Asia crisis deepened, calls for IMF reform became widespread. Many observers called for greater transparency and accountability. Others, myself included, thought that the total package of medicine being forced down countries' throats was more likely to kill than cure. Perhaps long-term and serious disability would be more precise. This lender of last resort has been exacerbating crises with its tight money, high interest rate policies. That may attract foreign capital but it risks bankrupting otherwise viable Asian businesses.

A GLOBAL REGULATOR

Amongst the wild ideas circulated in the aftermath of the Asian spill-over effect was a proposal to amalgamate the IMF and World Bank into one giant lender of last resort with trillions in capital — enough to cope with crises as large or larger than those encountered in South-East Asia. But if the charge sticks that the IMF has become little more than a fire brigade for private banks that make imprudent loans, increasing its capital sounds like pouring gasoline on a fire.

This fear cannot be dismissed lightly. To quote J. Richard Finlay, chairman of the Centre for Corporate & Public Governance, a Toronto-based think tank: "As things stand now, the IMF can always count on the support and lobbying clout of the global banking community. And the world's top bankers can always count on the old boys at the IMF to make them 'whole' as U.S. Treasury Secretary Robert Rubin so quaintly put it recently."[10]

THE IMF AS WATCHDOG

One of the least tenable roles for the IMF is that of global financial watchdog, a kind of "supervisor of supervisors" with authority that transcends national boundaries and treats the world as one financial entity. This idea, put forward by Canada's Finance Minister Paul Martin, and endorsed by the Group of Seven (G7) countries in London, in May 1998, was overtaken by time and reality.

The IMF's record in forecasting is dismal at best. It failed to anticipate the Mexican crisis in 1994 but was ready, indeed anxious, to help after the fact as the bail-out action provided a new impetus for its continued existence.

With its global antennae tested by the distress signal from Mexico, the IMF was still incapable of detecting any SOS from a whole series of sinking ships in South-East Asia. It, like the rest of the world, was taken by surprise. The best it could do was to say, after the fact, that the Asian crisis would have little spill-over on the rest of the world. This prediction would have been better left unsaid.

IMF economists may have recognized that any attempt to put together a rescue package big enough to rescue the Russian economy would be difficult at best. But here again there was a monumental underestimation of the magnitude of the problem. Similarly the huge $42 billion package assembled for Brazil may not prevent the financial contagion from spreading. The cost of compliance is high and the benefit to the average Brazilian largely negative.

The real naïveté of Finance Minister Martin and those politicians and officials who endorsed his plan to give the IMF a watchdog role revolves around the assumption that it is possible to forecast financial crises in a fully global, unregulated financial system. It is not possible! So rather than spend taxpayers money to establish or enhance a bureaucracy whose role is "mission impossible", it is far better to consider a means of changing the system in a way that will provide stability and some predictability.

WIND UP THE IMF

As for the IMF, it should be wound up and the sooner the better. All the big words used by those who would reform it, words like transparency, enhanced supervision, better monitoring and greater sensitivity, are simply words. You can paint a leopard's spots but that won't change the nature of the beast. Its voracious appetite to interfere cannot be contained so it must go.

This position is now supported by some very experienced people. Former Secretary of the Treasury, George Shultz, laid out the intellectual case in congressional testimony. He objected to "a pattern of escalation of ambition of the IMF" which would only grow if its request for increased capital was granted. The world financial system would be better off without the IMF, he argued, "because creditors would learn certain lessons. "Don't loan money when there are questionable risks. Realize you'll be held accountable for your mistakes."[11]

In his appearance at a hearing of Congress's joint economic committee in May, 1998, Shultz repeated and elaborated on arguments he had made earlier in an op-ed piece in the *Wall Street Journal* which he co-wrote with former treasury secretary William Simon and former Citicorp Chairman Walter Wriston. "The IMF is ineffective, unnecessary and obsolete. We do not need another IMF ... Once the Asian crisis is over we should abolish the one we have."[12]

A surprising ally in this conclusion is Milton Friedman who endorsed this conclusion in his own op-ed article in the *Wall Street Journal* on October 13, 1998. While not blaming private lenders for accepting the IMF's implicit offer of insurance against currency risk, he did blame the international agency for offering it. Friedman shared my conviction that the U.S. and its allies are derelict in allowing taxpayers' money to be used to subsidize private banks and other financial institutions.

Other critics of the IMF include Harvard economist Jeffrey Sachs and Henry Kissinger, former U.S. Secretary of State in the Nixon era. In an article he wrote for the French newspaper *Le Monde* under the title "The IMF does more harm than good", Kissinger said: "It almost always pushes austerity measures that result in a brutal fall in standard of living, an explosive increase in unemployment and poverty." Furthermore, for him, the IMF "is always blind to the consequences of its decisions."[13]

Neither Sachs nor Kissinger recommends abolition of the IMF settling instead for a modified and considerably reduced role. It is a conclusion I might have reached if the decision were taken in isolation from other urgently needed reforms. But what the world needs now is not a reformed IMF, even if that were possible; it needs a massive relief from unsustainable debt. Certainly, it does not need an IMF whose principal function is to pass the tin cup for needy banks and financial institutions. The time has come for a clean start without the IMF and without any of the conditions it has imposed on the poorest of the poor.

CHAPTER 4

WORLD BANK —
WORLD DISASTER

*"They no longer use bullets and ropes.
They use the World Bank and IMF."*

Reverend Jesse Jackson

As with the IMF, I did not monitor the activities of the World Bank as closely as I should have. Regrettably this applies equally to many of my friends and colleagues. It is not a subject widely discussed in social circles yet it should be because the influence of its policies and actions on the world economy has been profound beyond belief.

I was familiar with the Bank's origin as part of the 1944 Bretton Woods agreement and that its name was The International Bank for Reconstruction and Development (IBRD). But I had lost touch with how it was carrying out its mandate and it required a little reading to "put me in the picture."

The World Bank: Its First Half Century[1], by Devesh Kapur, John P. Lewis, and Richard Webb seemed a good place to start. This was followed by *Masters of Illusion: The World Bank and the Poverty of Nations*[2], by Catherine Caufield, a brilliantly written and extremely well documented exposé. This in addition to the two books mentioned in the previous chapter, *The Globalisation of Poverty* and *50 Years is Enough* comprising a number of monographs written by people familiar with the experience in their own country. These provided a pretty good overview of the Bank's activity.

While the Bank has grown from its small beginnings,

and has financed myriad projects, there are few, if any, that can be rated as an unqualified success. As you will see in the following pages, the more I read the more I sided with the critics in their view that the social and environmental damage, in addition to major interference in local affairs and the extension of intolerable debt, outweighed the benefits by a wide margin. A brief review of the Bank's early days and ever-changing role is illustrative.

The IBRD, soon universally known as the World Bank, had objects that were clear and admirable. It was not intended to compete with private banks but would guarantee their loans. There was little demand, however, because private banks were reluctant to make overseas loans and the Bank soon found that it could make loans at lower interest rates on its own account once it had convinced Wall Street and the financial world that its bonds, guaranteed by the most powerful countries, were a safe and good investment.

This took time, however, as the Bank got off to a slow start. Its first president, Eugene Meyer, a 70 year old former investment banker, resigned after only six months in office without having made a single loan. His successor John J. McCloy, a former assistant U.S. secretary of war, was most reluctant to take the job and only did so after assurances that he, rather than its International Board, would run the Bank. It was a pattern that would continue with his close friend and successor Eugene Black and subsequent presidents.

It was Black's thirteen-year reign that really made the Bank a formidable force in world affairs. By the time he left in January 1963, the institution had made 370 loans worth $7 billion without suffering a default. It was piling up profits and its balance sheet was strong and exemplary.

The Bank literally changed the face of the Third World with its highways, railways, ports, mines, factories and dams. For this it was greatly admired and became the most respected, as well as the most profitable, of international agencies. To all intents and purposes it was fulfilling its mission of helping the needy nations to climb the ladder of success and enjoy the benefits of a better life.

In retrospect, however, the Bank suffered from a fatal flaw. The decisions were all made by people who had little, if any, knowledge of the history, geography, climate or culture of the areas and people being affected. It was primarily a numbers game, played by bright young economists whose mandate was to lend money for big projects.

BIG DAMS

Almost from the outset big dams became the World Bank's stock in trade. It provided $80 million for the construction of the Kariba Dam, on the Zambezi River, the first great dam in Africa. When it was completed, in 1963, fifty thousand people were displaced from their homes. Violence erupted and several Africans were killed and others wounded by gunfire.

The purpose of the dam was to provide power for two huge copper companies and looked at from this narrow perspective the project was a success. There was no provision, however, for rural electrification or irrigation for farming communities. People problems were ignored with the human and environmental consequences excluded from the equation.

As Catherine Caufield points out in *Masters of Illusion*: "Thayer Scudder, a Cal Tech socioeconomist and frequent Bank consultant, has studied the Kariba oustees for nearly thirty years. In a 1993 interview he said, that in 1963, five years after being moved, many were 'beginning to get back on their feet.' During the next decade, the living standard for the majority rose every year. Since then, however, things have gotten worse, due to the collapsing fertility of the poor farmland they were given and the antagonism of the people on whose land they were settled. 'The majority — and their children — are now definitely worse off than if they had not moved,' said Scudder, adding that the dam has also been 'disastrous' for farming and fisheries well over 1,000 kilometers downstream."[3]

The Akosombo dam on the Volta River in Ghana was an even more questionable project. But at the same time it was seen as a passport to the kind of industrialization every developing country dreams of. So when Kwame Nkrumah became prime minister, after Ghana gained independence from Britain in 1957, he became a passionate supporter of the giant project. Giant is the only word for it because the 8,500 square-kilometer reservoir would be the largest man-made lake in the world.

There was also a giant problem connected to the dam. It would generate far more power than Ghana required. So it would only be economically viable with a big customer like an aluminum smelter. The United States, eager to demonstrate its friendship toward Africa's first newly independent country, and anxious that it would not turn to the Soviet Bloc for help, agreed to help finance a study by the Henry J. Kaiser Company whose business was aluminum.

The completed study recommended building the dam but not the railways, ports and irrigation systems that were part of the grand plan of Nkrumah and his advisers. In 1957 a World Bank mission to Ghana concluded that "the sheer size of the project itself is a problem." The fact that there would be so much excess power would put the country at the mercy of Kaiser or any other major consumer and "the project would not necessarily bring outstanding benefits to Ghana." A second Bank mission in 1960 was equally unenthusiastic and reported that "the Volta Project" is not very attractive.

By this time, however, world politics and the Cold War became active ingredients in the decision-making process. Nkrumah, who was as ingenious as he was ruthless, decided to go to Moscow. When the U.S. State Department learned of the end run they told Black to sew up the Ghana loan in advance without waiting for the Bank to finish its study. Black complied. The Bank lent Ghana $47 million and construction on the dam began at once.

The plan did not include resettlement provisions for the eighty thousand persons who would be displaced. This was left until the waters began to rise when each family was promised twelve acres but without the social amenities they previously enjoyed. A shortage of suitable land forced an experiment in Western style agriculture but without the tools to make it work.

Starvation threatened and United Nations relief was required.

The huge new reservoir created new breeding grounds for infectious diseases including river blindness transmitted by a fly that breeds around the periphery. "By 1980, 100,000 people in the region were afflicted with river blindness, and 70 percent of them were completely blind. According to a Bank study, 'massive dosing of the river with DDT, and later, dieldrin, gave only temporary relief to the people residing within five miles of the reservoir. Fear of river blindness caused the abandonment of 40 percent of the land area of northeastern Ghana. In the early 1980s, the newly built Kpong Dam, downstream of Akosombo, flooded some of the breeding grounds of the river-blindness fly, thus easing the problem in certain areas."[4]

Meanwhile the major beneficiary of the project was Kaiser, operating as the Volta Aluminum Company (Valco for short). It negotiated a contract to buy as much electricity as it needed at a price below cost. It was also exempted from duties and taxes while the people of Ghana paid about twenty times the company's preferred rate for power. Even after the Valco contract was renegotiated in 1985 its rate was only a fraction of the local rate.

Ghana didn't get many of the benefits it might have expected from the Kaiser deal. To avoid being hostage to fortune the company imported bauxite from Jamaica rather than use Ghana's rich reserves. And instead of building a processing plant in Ghana it shipped the alumina to the United States to be turned into finished aluminum while its benefactor was forced to import all of the aluminum it used.

In fact Ghana got the short end of the stick all around. None of the related projects such as irrigation and lake transportation were developed. And even though a U.S. government study found that water from the Volta could be at least as profitably used for irrigation as for power, this option had been effectively foreclosed by Kaiser's engineers who had deliberately designed a dam that could not be used for irrigation. It was also one of the most inefficient dams on earth, ranking thirty-seventh out of forty in a survey of the worlds biggest dams.

"C.K. Annan, former head of the Ghana Water Supply Industry, calls the dam 'a short-sighted and prodigiously narrow-minded project.' He and others argue that a series of smaller dams would have been cheaper, caused less social and environmental upheaval, kept the river open to navigation, and generated power even in the droughts that have recently brought Akosombo power production to a near halt."[5]

A NEW DIMENSION

When New York investment banker George Woods succeeded Eugene Black as president he inherited an organization which was solvent, profitable and superficially successful. The Bank had not bothered to monitor its projects once they were completed, however, so most of the social and environmental damage which subsequently came to light was not documented and not discussed, so there was no mechanism by which the Bank could learn from its mistakes.

One problem that Woods did discover was that Third World countries were taking on debt faster than their capacity to cope. Their gross domestic products were increasing by 4.8 percent a year but their foreign debt was growing three times as fast. Quite obviously the door for further lending was closing, fast.

Woods appointed my former boss, Lester B. "Mike" Pearson, to head a high-level international commission to study, among other matters, the debt burdens of developing countries. Pearson, who had just retired as Canadian prime minister a year earlier, welcomed the challenge in the field of international relations that he knew so well.

I recall him summarizing the commission report, *Partners in Development*, when it was released in 1969. The increase in Third World debt in the previous fifteen years had been explosive and the rate of increase could not be maintained. Too great a proportion of the foreign loans was simply being recycled to pay the interest on existing loans. A straight line projection showed that if borrowing continued unabated at then existing levels, by 1977 South Asia would be spending all its new foreign loans to service existing debt; Africa's debt service payments would be 120 percent of new borrowing and Latin American's would be 130 percent.[6]

The report should have set off alarm bells and warned both the Bank and the international financial community that the saturation point had been reached. Instead, the Bank applied greater ingenuity in order to justify its continued existence. Loan repayments were rescheduled and the reasons for loans extended in order to assist Third World countries to adjust their economies to the Western model.

Woods moved away from the near-exclusive infrastructure funding of his predecessors to include social lending on the assumption that it would increase growth and consequently the creditworthiness of the borrower. It was a fond hope which was destined to fail. Money was spent for projects which were not self-liquidating while recipient countries went further and further into debt. Before he left office he called for a reassessment of the Bank's work and the development process in general.

McNAMARA's THRUST

Any uncertainty or uneasiness that Bank officials may have had about their mission was soon set to rest after Robert S. McNamara took over the presidency in June, 1968. Although there had been both contradictory and controversial aspects of his stewardship as C.E.O. of the Ford Motor Company, and later as Secretary of Defense, he was a "take charge" man wherever he happened to be. He was also a numbers man, so it is not surprising that he spent his first days at the Bank to pore over figures on bank lending and world poverty.

When he had finished there were two conclusions. First, that the Bank should be lending much more. So he instructed his staff to bring forward all the projects they would consider approving if money were no object. Second, he would invest more in social services for the poor in the hope that the well documented income disparity could be narrowed. In this sense, McNamara was something of a social crusader who felt deeply for the hundreds of millions of impoverished people on planet earth and who desperately wanted to use his power and influence to help them.

I know Bob McNamara well enough from the almost five years we collaborated regularly on North American and European defence issues that I am totally convinced his objectives were sincere and idealistic. I also know him well enough to be equally convinced that macro economics was not his forte. So I am not surprised that he ordered the Bank to steam full speed ahead even though many rocks and shoals had been observed and identified by previous captains — Woods, in particular.

Many of McNamara's reforms had the opposite effect to the one intended. The Bank began to lend much more for agriculture and by the end of his term a third of Bank financing was agriculture. The money, however, was not tailored to the needs of small and subsistence farmers but to the wealthy two percent who controlled three-quarters of the developing world's farmland. In much of Latin America, for example, it was the big ranchers who were encouraged to clear rain forests to provide the ten acres or more of grazing land required for each animal.

The road to chaos is paved with good intentions and the trip for the Bank was never-ending. Instead of its much touted "trickle down" theory working to close the gap between rich and poor, that McNamara had counted on when he made the loans to promote Western-style agro-business, the disparity of income between classes increased. About the only thing rich and poor had in common was that their country was mortgaged to the hilt and the only way to avoid foreclosure was to negotiate new loans to pay the interest outstanding.

STRATEGIC ADJUSTMENT LOANS TO THE RESCUE?

Strategic Adjustment Loans (SALs) were not tied to any one specific project. Instead these new multi-million dollar loans were contingent on a Third World government's agreement to introduce drastic economic reforms in order to conform to the Washington consensus. "This included reducing the state's role in the economy, lowering barriers to imports, removing restrictions on foreign investments, eliminating subsidies for local industries, reducing spending for social welfare, cutting wages, devaluing the currency and emphasizing production for export rather than for local consumption."[7] In effect, the World Bank, like the IMF, was attempting to impose the monetarist, neo-classical counter-revolution on that vulnerable part of the world that comprised its client base.

Understandably such a monumental interference in national sovereignty was enough to deter takers at the outset. But the Paul Volcker initiated debt crisis of the early 1980s made it increasingly impossible for Third World countries to service the huge loans made to them by Northern banks in the 1970s. One by one debtor countries capitulated. Additional private financing was not available without the World Bank imprimatur. So countries were driven to accept SALs. By 1985, 12 of the 15 top-priority debtors including Argentina, Mexico and the Philippines were hooked. (Bank economists would probably say "rescued").

"Over the next seven years, SALs proliferated as the economies of more and more Third World countries came under the surveillance and control of the Bank. About 187 SALs had been administered by the end of the decade, many of them coordinated with equally stringent standby programs administered by the IMF. Whereas in the previous division of labor between the two institutions, the World Bank was supposed to promote growth and the IMF was supposed to monitor financial restraint, their roles now became indistinguishable. Both became the enforcers of the North's economic rollback strategy.[8]

The effects of this economic counter-revolution have been ghastly. "The average Gross National Product for nations in sub-Saharan Africa fell by 2.2 percent per year in the 1980s; by 1990, per capita income on the continent was back down to its level at the time of independence in the 1960s. A United

Nations advisory group reported that throughout the continent, 'health systems are collapsing for lack of medicines, schools have no books, and universities suffer from a debilitating lack of library and laboratory facilities.' Structural adjustment programs have also promoted massive environmental damage, as many African countries were forced to cut down forests rapidly and exploit other natural resources more intensively to gain the foreign exchange they needed to make mounting interest payments.

"Latin Americans regard the reverse financial flow from their continent as the 'worst plunder since Cortez' and refer to the 1980s as the 'lost decade'. Per capita income in 1990 was at virtually the same level as ten years earlier. Severe malnutrition stalks the countryside, paving the way for the return of cholera, which people thought had been eradicated."[9]

POLLUTE THE SOUTH

Even a casual reading of the World Bank's history is enough to conclude that environmental concerns were never high on its list of priorities. Perhaps there were other urgent issues but there may have been an attitudinal problem, as well.

Laurence Summers, who later became President Clinton's top international economist at the Treasury Department, was the World Bank's chief economist responsible for the 1992 *World Development Report* devoted to the economics of the environment. He suggested that it made economic sense to shift polluting industries to the Third World countries. In a December 12, 1991 memo to senior World Bank staff he wrote: "'Just between you and me, shouldn't the World Bank be encouraging more migration of the dirty industries to the LDCs?'

"Summers has justified his economic logic of increasing pollution in the Third World on the following grounds. Firstly, since wages are low in the Third World, economic costs of pollution arising from increased illness and death are lowest in the poorest countries. Summers thinks 'that the economic logic behind dumping a load of toxic waste in the lowest wage country is impeccable, and we should face up to that.'

"Secondly, since in large parts of the Third World pollution, is still low, it makes economic sense to Summers to introduce pollution. 'I've always thought,' he says, that 'under-populated countries in Africa are vastly under-polluted; their air quality is probably vastly inefficiently low compared to Los Angeles or Mexico City.'

"Finally, since the poor are poor, they cannot possibly worry about environmental problems. 'The concern over an agent that causes a one-in-a million change in the odds of prostate cancer is obviously going to be much higher in a country where people survive to get prostate cancer than in a country where under-five mortality is 200 per thousand.'"[10]

The World Bank apologized for Summers' memo but the record shows that it has, in fact, been financing pollution intensive industries in the Third World. It has funded steel plants, pesticides and chemical fertilizer producers, for example. In addition, the use of the dangerous chemical, Agent Orange, was authorized to defoliate part of the Amazon basin for a dam of doubtful necessity.

ENVIRONMENTAL HAVOC IN THE AMAZON BASIN

The Bank was always ready to cooperate with Latin American dictators. Their regimes often appeared more stable and consequently more trustworthy, if not creditworthy, than the democracies. In the 1970s the military dictatorship in Brazil used World Bank loans to invest in huge infrastructure projects to stimulate private investment. It appears, as often happens, that the bulk of the costs wound up as public debt while the benefits accrued primarily to private investors. Marcos Arruda, professor of philosophy of education at the Institute of Advanced Studies in Education, Getulio Vargas Foundation in Rio, tells one story from his perspective.

"The state projects were intended to serve as radiators of development. The idea behind creating an enormous hydroelectric dam and plant in the middle of the Amazon, for example, was to produce aluminum for export to the North.

The project involved the use of subsidized energy from the hydroelectric facility, minerals from Para (a state in northern Brazil) and a plant set up by transnational companies, including Alcan and Alcoa, in connection with a Brazilian state company. The government took out huge loans and invested billions of dollars in building the Tucuri dam in the late 1970s, destroying native forests and removing masses of native peoples and poor rural people who had lived there for generations.

"The government would have razed the forests, but deadlines were so short that they used Agent Orange to defoliate the region and then submerged the leafless tree trunks under water. Now the trees are rotting, and we have to pay millions of dollars to clean up the excessive amount of organic matter that is decomposing under water.

"The hydroelectric plant's energy is sold at $13 to $20 per megawatt when the actual price of production is $48. So the public sector of Brazil — meaning taxpayers — is providing subsidies of $28 to $35 per megawatt. We are financing cheap energy for transnational corporations to sell our aluminum in the international market, often to themselves; Alcoa in the United States or Alcan in Canada buy what Alcoa sells from Brazil, a product with very little value added.

"We think these sorts of projects are destructive to the environment and financially irrational for the Brazilian government. The government is now responding to this irrationality with the magic word 'privatize.'"[11]

A SCAR ON THE PLANET

Catherine Caufield, in *Masters of Illusion*, says: "It was another Brazilian project — the Northwest Region Integrated Development Program, or Polonoroeste — that dealt the most severe blow to the Bank's reputation for honesty and competence. Beginning in 1981, the Bank lent more than half a billion dollars for this massive highway-building and colonization project covering 150,000 square miles of the Amazon. From its inception, Polonoroeste had many critics — in Brazil and outside. They predicted that there would be violent clashes between colonists and the Indians whose land they would clear, and warned that much of the soil would be unsuitable for farming. The Bank took these concerns seriously enough to make its loans conditional on Brazil's implementing an impressive array of measures designed to protect the environment and the rights of the indigenous people. The measures included the establishment of fifteen Indian reserves with health facilities, two biological reserves, four research stations, and a national park. In addition, there would be no settlements on soils that were unsuitable or of unknown quality. Thanks to its influence, the Bank boasted, Polonoroeste was a model of ecological and social planning.

"By 1984, reports from the project region indicated that matters were not proceeding in line with the Bank's plans. Hundreds of thousands of eager settlers had poured into the area, many attracted by a government-sponsored ad campaign, only to find that the schools, health clinics, water wells, and other promised services were not in place. After clearing thousands of square miles of forest with axes and fire, the colonists had discovered that the soils were unsuitable for farming. They moved on, clearing more forest and then abandoning it, and then clearing more, so that in just a few years 50,000 square miles, an area roughly the size of the state of Wisconsin, had been devastated.

"NASA called the burned forest, which was visible from space, the largest man-made change to the earth's surface. Meanwhile, the indigenous population was being pushed off its land by colonization and killed by newly introduced diseases; the Catholic church estimated that by the end of the decade 85 percent of the region's native people had died through violence or disease. The ecological breakdown also resulted in an epidemic of malaria, which by 1984 was infecting 150,000 people in the project area every year — and spreading from there to the rest of the country. (By 1988, the infection rate had nearly doubled; the following year the Bank lent Brazil $99 million so that it could spray the project area with 3,000 tons of DDT.)"[12]

The examples are legion and the books I mentioned

describe many of them in detail. Two unhappy themes emerge from the case histories. Almost every large project produces major social or ecological devastation — often, both: and the introduction of Strategic Adjustment Loans played a key role in the incessant attempt to homogenize the world economy.

THE SOVIETIZATION OF THE SOUTH

In reflecting on the process I realized that the North, and more particularly the United States, has copied all the mistakes of the Soviet Union. It is trying to remake the world in its own image in accordance with the strongly held dogma of its own intellectual elite. Thus the IMF and the World Bank have been telling nation states that they must open their borders to imports, they must sell their state owned enterprises, they must grow shrimp, or coffee or cocoa for export even if it means the destruction of their domestic food production and the starvation of their people, they must reduce government expenditures even if health and education are badly affected, they must impose consumption taxes that siphon off disposable income and slow economic growth and they must not use their central banks to finance health, education and full employment. Instead, they must rely on "assistance" from abroad.

I doubt if there is any precedent in world history of such massive and minute central management of allegedly independent nation states by outsiders. It is the Soviet system enlarged to a global scale. Bureaucrats in the Kremlin would decide how much jam, marmalade and peanut butter would be shipped to each restaurant, regardless of local tastes or preferences for one over the other. They would order an increase in production quotas of cloth that no-one would wear — shades of IMF and World Bank bureaucrats pushing the production of primary products which cannot be sold at a profit.

The problem is the same. It is the arrogance of pampered officials who think they know what is the best for people whose interests, needs, tastes and cultures they do not understand. But "father knows best" so decisions ranging from ill-considered to disastrous are imposed on the helpless by the secret service in one case and the power of the purse in another. The result, however, is the same. One evil empire is replaced by another at least as bad and probably worse. And just as the first collapsed under its own dead weight, so will the second. Centralized planning is just as inefficient globally as it was in Northern and Eastern Europe.

GOODBYE WORLD BANK

When I began to write this book it was my intention to recommend that the Bank be continued but on a vastly reduced scale with more limited terms of reference. Indeed, that is what the original "promo" for the book said. On reflection, however, I have concluded that it has distorted its mission and outlived its usefulness. It is too set in its ways and incapable of serious reform.

The Bank's deeply-entrenched policy of promoting a capital-intensive, energy-intensive, unsustainable Western model of development has, either by design or by accident, been primarily beneficial to Third World elites, Northern banks and transnational corporations. For ordinary citizens the legacy is unsustainable debt. Social activist Susan George puts this in perspective.

"Every single month, from the outset of the debt crisis in 1982 until the end of 1990, debtor countries in the South remitted to their creditors in the North an average $6.5 billion in interest payments alone. If payments of the principal are included, then debtor countries paid creditors at a rate of almost $12.5 billion per month — as much as the entire Third World spends each month on health and education. ...

"Debtor countries have deprived their people of basic necessities in order to provide the private banks and the public agencies of the rich countries with the equivalent of six Marshall Plans (the program of assistance offered by the U.S. to Europe after the Second World War).

"Have these extraordinary outflows served to reduce the absolute size of the debt burden? Not a bit: in spite of paying out more than $1.3 trillion between 1982 and 1990, the debtor

countries as a group began the 1990s with a full 61 percent
more debt than in 1982. Sub-Saharan Africa's debt increased
by 113 percent during this period."[13]

A brief ray of sunshine did break through the clouds at
the joint annual meeting of the IMF and the World Bank in
October, 1998, when Bank president James D. Wolfensohn
broke with the IMF and U.S. Treasury Department line
emphasizing currency stabilization and an acceleration of
"reforms". "If you do not have greater equity and social
justice, there will be no political stability," Wolfensohn said,
"and without political stability, no amount of money put
together in financial packages will give us financial stability."[14]

Truer words were never spoken and it is good to have
someone in high office who actually cares about people and who
comprehends the inevitable consequences of interminably
ignoring their interests. Wolfensohn is fortunate to have as his
chief economist Joseph Stiglitz who was one of the first to
question the "party line" when he expressed concern for the
unemployed and poor in Indonesia.

It was also encouraging, but highly ironic in view of the
devastating negative effect of IMF and Bank policies on health
and education, that the Bank's 1998 World Development Report
would stress knowledge as the key to development. "Discarding
its one-time belief that markets alone can achieve development,
the World Bank says both developing countries and foreign-aid
donors must make the creation and flow of knowledge —
ranging from seed varieties and birth-control methods, to
consumer standards and accounting procedures — their primary
concern."[15]

When you read the fine print, however, questions arise.
For example, the report suggests that developing countries put
a much greater emphasis on private educational institutions
notwithstanding the fact that thousands of students have been
dropping out of schools because they can't afford the modest
fees countries have been imposing in sheer desperation as a
result of Bank and IMF policies. In a nutshell, the report
reflects the ideology of homogenization and confirms my fears.
I don't think that Wolfensohn and Stiglitz, for all their good

intentions, have the power and ability to transform an old toad into Prince Charming.

The Bank's bureaucracy is too big, too cumbersome, too pampered and too ideological to change. Its best and brightest, as the Bank's economists are known, are the ones who fervently believe that the U.S. model is right for the world even if it is imposed from the top down rather than allowed to develop from the bottom up in myriad permutations and combinations more suitable to the history, geography, culture and state of development of each individual country.

So, rather than attempt the impossible, the best solution is to wind-down and then wind-up the World Bank. With the package of reforms I will be recommending it will no longer be needed. We can leave the regional development banks in existence for a while just in case there should be some need. Perhaps they could support micro-banking which would be a useful function.

CHAPTER 5

THE MAI —
GLOBALIZATION GONE MAD

"When all government, domestic and foreign, in little as in great things, shall be drawn to Washington as the center of all power, it will render powerless the checks provided of one government on another, and will become as venal and oppressive as the government from which we separated."

Thomas Jefferson

It is disappointing in the extreme that the G7 leaders who have recently discovered the word transparency, and who plan to impose it in areas where they have no jurisdiction, were not, themselves, more open about negotiations for a Multilateral Agreement on Investment (MAI) between the 29 nations of the OECD. Detailed discussions had been underway for two years before anyone I knew was really aware of it.

It might have remained in the shadows of international diplomacy if a leaked copy of the draft hadn't appeared on the internet in early 1997. When I finished reading the hefty draft I was stunned. It was obviously one of the most important treaties in the history of the world and it was scheduled to be signed within a few months without the advice or consent of the millions of people whose lives would be affected.

I was so concerned that I wrote a book entitled *The Evil Empire: Globalization's Darker Side* and began to promote it as my contribution to a public debate that had barely begun. My first stop, in December 1997, was Halifax, Nova Scotia. The way the treaty was drafted the offshore fishery would be opened wide to foreign fishermen and I knew this would come as unacceptable news to the people of that province.

At the end of a busy day, which included a noontime meeting at Dalhousie University and the usual radio and TV interviews, I headed for the airport by cab. For some reason I decided to get in the front seat beside the driver. He asked the reason for my visit and when I said it was to discuss the MAI his response was limited to one word, "colonization". He had been listening to the discussion on his cab radio and that was his conclusion.

On the flight home I thought about what the man had said. He was right. The net effect of globalization is colonization on a scale never before dreamed of. What is involved is the biggest power, wealth and land grab in the history of the world. The benefits do not accrue exclusively to any one country but it is the wealthiest power elites of the half dozen largest industrialized countries who are the principal beneficiaries. The middle class and the poor of all countries are the losers.

To succeed, of course, the systematic dismantling of economic boundaries must continue and the power of nation states to protect the interests of their citizens curbed. It is a continuous process that began with trade in goods, followed by a freer flow of services, including financial services, all leading to the ultimate prize — unlimited access to other people's land, resources, factories and financial institutions — in effect, a world without economic borders.

THE BIG TRAIN

In theory, free or freer trade is supposed to bring benefits to all parties involved. Each party is able to capitalize on its natural advantages, i.e. Canadian ice cubes for American oranges. So everyone gains and there have been a number of learned studies supporting the theory. One of my most erudite economist friends says there are no comparable studies for investment. In any event, there are serious reservations in respect of both. A look at the origin and rationale of the big globalization train illuminates both the impetus and the danger.

The impetus for the big globalization train began with unrealistically high expectations. Rates of return on investment of 10 to 15 percent a year create expectations of continued success of the same order of magnitude. Obviously, however, that cannot be achieved by every bank and every company competing for business in an economy that is only growing by 2 or 3 percent annually. Attempts to maintain the momentum resulted first in a rash of leveraged buyouts, takeovers and mergers. The top dogs, including senior officers and participating banks, as well as shareholders, were well rewarded. The negative benefits were usually higher costs, resulting from the price of the acquisition, and reduced employment as jobs were eliminated by the streamlining necessary to restore cost competitiveness.

There are only so many companies to be bought in each industry so it wasn't long before new strategies for growth became essential. In effect, the mergermania which produced mixed but sometimes spectacular results internally had to be extended internationally. With nearly all the big fish in the local pool already hooked the only solution is to fish in other people's pools. That is only possible if you can first get a license.

INVESTMENT DISGUISED AS TRADE

Although the "bigger is better" phenomenon has by no means been limited to the United States, it has the most transnational corporations and the most powerful banks so it is not surprising that the global investment thrust had its origin there. It probably began with the United States Council for International Business which recruited the Washington establishment as its stalking horse. Free trade, which initially meant unrestricted access for U.S. exports, became the nirvana of eternal hope for a new and wonderful world.

The first bi-lateral treaty was negotiated with Israel. One can only speculate that Israel was chosen as the target because America's financial aid gives it incredible leverage in negotiations with that state. Next on the list was Canada, America's neighbor and largest trading partner.

CANADA-U.S. FREE TRADE AGREEMENT

This carefully orchestrated treaty appeared as a Canadian initiative at the outset and it was only years later we learned that U.S. Ambassador Thomas Niles had been a power behind the throne. A series of dinners with fine food and fine wine for Canadian bigwigs provided the fertile soil for the seeds to be planted. They spread the message that Canada should take the initiative in negotiating a deal with the U.S. and that Washington could be counted on to respond positively.

Somehow the Canadian big business moguls managed to get through to the government of Prime Minister Brian Mulroney despite his recorded views in total opposition to such an arrangement. A secret government memorandum set out a strategy of telling the Canadian people as little as possible on the assumption that the less they knew the less opposition there would be. Points to be stressed were that there would be no loss of sovereignty and that the big benefit for Canada would be guaranteed access to U.S. markets.

Canadians assumed that their government would protect their interests and were blithely unaware that the "Free Trade Agreement" — after all that is what it was called — was not primarily about trade. It was, above all, an investment treaty. The U.S. insisted on the inclusion of a new principle of international law called "national standing" under which U.S. investors were given the same rights in Canada as Canadians citizens. The Canadian negotiators, more generously endowed with bluster than foresight, were asleep at the switch and allowed the globalization train to roar through.

It was a coup for the U.S. Immediately after signing the agreement on October 3, 1987, Clayton Yeutter, U.S. trade representative remarked: "We've signed a stunning new trade pact with Canada. The Canadians don't know what they have signed. In twenty years they will be sucked into the U.S. economy."[1] Yeutter was correct, and his 20 year time frame will probably prove prophetic in the absence of a dramatic reversal.

Confidential briefing papers prepared for Treasury Secretary James Baker and Trade Representative Yeutter were leaked and published in the U.S. They reflected the American government's internal assessment of its achievements. "We have achieved a major liberalization of the investment climate in Canada and imbedded it permanently so that in future Canada's investment policies cannot retrogress to the old policies of NEP (National Energy Program) and FIRA (The Foreign Investment Review Act) ... The vast bulk of U.S. direct investment in Canada now will go forward with no Canadian government interference whatsoever." The briefing paper concluded: "Essentially, in the text we got everything we wanted."[2]

While technically the U.S. and Canada each gave up sovereignty under the deal the consequences are virtually inconsequential for one, at least in the short run, while they are probably life-threatening for the other. At the time Canada was already the most foreign-dominated of any industrialized country in the world; 100 percent of its tobacco industry, 98 percent of the rubber industry, 92 percent of the automobile industry, 84 percent of the transportation, 78 percent of electrical apparatus industry, 78 percent of the petroleum and coal industry, 76 percent of the chemical industry and 75 percent of heavy manufacturing were foreign, largely American, owned. In contrast, foreign ownership of the U.S. economy was only 3 percent; of Britain's 3 percent; Japan's less than 2 percent and 3 percent in France. If the U.S. and Canadian figures on foreign ownership had been reversed there is no way the deal would have been acceptable south of the border.

NAFTA AND STATES' RIGHTS

With unfettered access to Canadian industry and resources locked up, the next country target was Mexico. Again, a misleading title was used to obfuscate the real nature of the project. Basically the same provisions that applied in the

Canada-U.S. Free Trade Agreement were rolled over into the North American Free Trade Agreement (NAFTA). Of the new provisions the most significant was the addition of a dispute settlement mechanism under which corporations could sue a country directly in the event of any action which affected profits or future profits, without the necessity of using the good offices of its home government.

The disputes would be settled by a three-person panel established under the rules set out in the treaty. The decision reached by this panel is final and not subject to appeal in any court, which seems out of joint with the rule of law.

In effect, corporations are elevated to nation state status which gives them greater rights than ordinary citizens. They can sue any host country that changes its labor, environmental, land use and other laws in a way which reduces the profit or *future* profit of the foreign investor. This means that an investment may only be in the planning stage but if those plans are frustrated by changes in the rules then this is considered to be "expropriation" and grounds for suit.

Citizens of the world soon got a foretaste of what is likely to happen to them by observing the experience of first Canada, then Mexico and later the United States under the provisions of NAFTA. It is this same provision that was included in the draft Multilateral Agreement on Investment. After the Canadian province of Ontario elected the New Democratic Party (NDP) in September 1990 it planned to implement provincial automobile insurance which had been one of the planks in its platform.[3] News of this was enough to bring a threat of a $2 billion lawsuit by State Farm Mutual Insurance if the plan was implemented. The government backed down and decided not to proceed.

Personally, I am not a fan of provincially operated auto insurance but that is not the point. The NDP had made a promise during the election campaign and the voters had elected that party so presumably it had been given a mandate which couldn't be fulfilled without prohibitive cost. The will of the electors was frustrated by the commercial interests of a foreign corporation.

In 1998 Canada suffered a much more humiliating experience under this same provision of NAFTA.   The Parliament of Canada had passed a law banning the importation into Canada and the distribution within Canada of the gasoline additive methylcyclopentadienyl manganese tricarbonyl (MMT). The Ethyl Corporation of the U.S. sued the Canadian government on the grounds of lost profits and damaged reputation.   The case would be heard by a three-person panel whose decision would be final.

When its lawyers advised that it would likely lose the case, the Canadian government settled.   It paid $13 million (U.S.) in compensation for legal fees and lost profits.   Far worse, as part of the settlement agreement, two ministers of the crown made statements that said MMT was neither harmful to the health nor the environment, and this despite increasing evidence that low-level exposure to airborne manganese is linked to nervous-system problems and attention-deficit disorder among children.

Another American corporation, S.D. Myers Inc. of Tallmadge, Ohio, launched a suit against Canada claiming compensation for a 15-month ban on the export of polychlorinated biphenyls (PCB's) dating back to 1995.

Until November, 1998, all of the actions under NAFTA were launched by U.S. corporations.   Then the Canadian funeral giant Loewen Group Inc., of Burnaby, British Columbia, billed the U.S. government for losses sustained in a Mississippi court which ordered it to pay $500 million (U.S.) in damages in a contract dispute with the O'Keefe family, operators of a small funeral and insurance business in the state.

The suit was subsequently settled for $150 million but the case left the company financially crippled.   Now Loewen argues that Mississippi violated accepted standards of justice by forcing it to post a bond equal to 125 percent of the damage award.

Reaction was swift, and predictable.   "This case is an all-out attack on democracy," Joan Claybrook, president of Public Citizen, a Washington-based consumer advocacy group founded by Ralph Nader, charged.   "It would open a huge, back-door way for corporations to get protection from their liabilities in a way they have been unable to win in two decades of lobbying in Congress."[4]

The claim for damages constitutes an attempted "end run" around U.S. jury verdicts, Ms. Claybrook said. "We cannot stand by and allow NAFTA to be used as a broom for a sore loser to sweep justice aside."[5]

Without commentating on the merits of the case which appeared, at a distance, to be anything but just, one must agree with Ms. Claybrook's concerns. The issue, in reality, is sovereignty. The provisions of NAFTA constitute a serious intrusion on national sovereignty and regardless of the outcome of these cases they will be just the first of hundreds if the same "right" is entrenched in other multilateral treaties.

The case which causes greatest alarm for people concerned about states' or provincial rights is Metalclad vs. Mexico. In January, 1997, this U.S.-based waste disposal company filed a complaint with the International Center for the Settlement of Investment Disputes (ICSID), alleging that the Mexican state of San Luis Potosi violated a number of provisions of NAFTA when it prevented the company from opening its waste disposal plant. Metalclad took over the facility, which had a history of contaminating local ground water, with the obligation that it clean up pre-existing contaminants. After an environmental impact assessment revealed that the site was over an ecologically sensitive underground alluvial stream, the governor refused to allow Metalclad to re-open the facility. Eventually the site was declared part of a 600,000 acre ecological zone. Metalclad claims that this action effectively expropriated its future expected profits and sought $90 million in damages. By way of contrast this figure is larger than the combined annual income of every family in the county where Metalclad's facility is located.[6]

Environmental zoning has been attacked, especially in the United States, by "property rights" activists — also known as the "takings" movement — which seeks compensation for complying with environmental regulations. In a manner similar to the Ethyl Corporation's claim, Metalclad claims that the zoning law constitutes an effective seizure of the company's property — seizure that, under the property rights extended by NAFTA, requires that the offending government compensate the company. While Metalclad would have a very difficult time convincing a U.S. court that the "taking" is compensable, and it is inconceivable that a Canadian company would be rewarded in Canadian courts, the broad language of the NAFTA expropriation provision sets a higher standard for investor rights.[7]

This case demonstrates how responsibility for certain non-market-related risks of investment could be shifted from companies to governments. Without the NAFTA's strong provision on expropriation, Metalclad alone would be forced to assume the risks of investment and would have learned a valuable lesson about conducting a proper environmental assessment before committing significant resources. Under the rights conferred by NAFTA the government of Mexico could be forced to shoulder the risks and costs of Metalclad's investment should the company win its suit.[8]

The Metalclad case raises other alarming questions. Metalclad claims the Mexican federal government is, unofficially, encouraging the company's NAFTA lawsuit so that it can deflect the political fall-out from forcing the state to open its facility. The local community, still reeling from water contamination resulting from the illegal storage procedures of the facility's previous owners, was never consulted about the possibility of re-opening the facility by either the federal or state governments or Metalclad, and vehemently opposes locating a toxic waste dump in this area.[9]

If Metalclad's claim that the Mexican federal government supports the suit is indeed correct, it raises the disturbing possibility that investors can use their right to collude with governments to force unwanted or even dangerous investments on unwilling populations. A spokesman for Metalclad stated: "I don't know of anything the federal government could have done and didn't do, short of sending the army in."[10] States' rightists beware! "The MAI could have profound implications on state lawmaking in the areas of the environment and labor, especially since state and local governments cannot defend their own laws from investors' challenges, but must rely on the federal government, which may or may not be committed to the local legislation."[11]

THE MAI — RHETORIC AND REALITY

For almost four years the treaty was being sold as just another international treaty to tidy up some loose ends from a plethora of bi-national treaties and provide a level playing field for investors worldwide. This was a monstrous deception. It was and is about power and control. The issue, bluntly, is whether the world will be run by supranational corporations and international banks or by elected representatives of the people. It is corporatism versus democracy.

In effect the MAI was drafted as a Bill of Rights for corporations without any corresponding obligation to the people of the host country or any obligation to act as good corporate citizens. Nor was there any obligation to employ local labor, share technology or operate in a people-friendly and environmentally acceptable manner. Furthermore, corporations would be entitled to sue if anyone changes the rules — anyone.

The MAI, as distinct from NAFTA, was a much broader agreement in that its terms applied to all levels of government without exception — federal, state or provincial, district and municipal.[12] Investors would be entitled to dispute all government measures. These measures would not be limited to legislation, but would extend to all acts attributable to governments including regulations, policies and practices. In essence, foreign investors would be provided with a better legal remedy than citizens under these rules.[13]

GLOBALIZATION WITHOUT CLOTHES

Most of us learn the hard way that it is important to read the fine print. What does free trade mean for most Canadians? What does free unrestricted capital flows mean in terms of the ability to govern? What does unfettered capitalism, and a world without borders, mean for the majority and the minority?

To begin, unrestricted free trade is being pushed by the half-dozen biggest, most powerful, most industrialized countries in the world. It is curious that every one of them became big, wealthy and powerful by protecting their own industries against foreign competition. So what they are really saying to the less-developed countries of the world is "now that we have it made we intend to see that you will never be able to claw your way up the ladder in similar fashion."

Now, all of a sudden, neo-classicists are saying protectionism is wrong, almost evil. The net result will be Third World countries buying manufactured goods from First World countries and trying in vain to pay for them by exporting primary products which, thanks to IMF and World Bank policies, have created a glut on the market.

Of course First World countries demand the right to locate manufacturing facilities in Third World countries. But why? In the majority of cases it is to enjoy the cheapest labor, the lowest environmental standards and the least regulation. To make sure it stays that way the MAI, or whatever reincarnation First World countries attempt to push down Third World throats, will guarantee that any democratic attempt to raise wages or environmental standards will lead to compensation for lost profits.

The investment provisions also guarantee that in the event a locally owned company grows to the point where it begins to cut into the market share of one of the big multinationals it can be bought and either integrated into big brother's business or shut down and the competition eliminated.

Free uninhibited capital movements on a globalized basis has to be one of the most ill-considered tenets of the capitalist manifesto. Take Mexico's experience as a case in point. "The value of existing U.S. direct investment, before inflation adjustment, fell between 1982 and 1987. But it took off in the late 1980s, rising 133 percent between 1988 and 1992. Yearly direct investment flows into Mexico from all countries followed a more dramatic pattern, falling 86 percent between 1981 and 1984, then rising 1,305 percent since. During the days of heavy debt service and capital flight, financial resources drained out of the country — a net drain of $26 billion from 1983 to 1988. However, the capital-friendly policies of the Salinas regime have since lured a remarkable influx of money — $73 billion in financial inflows plus $21 billion in direct investment between 1989 and 1993. The euphoria over Mexico and other 'emerging markets' has a very bubble-like feel to it, with expectations levitating far above present realities."[14]

No country can control its own economic future with that kind of feast or famine from outside investors. It creates an impossible situation. In fact free capital flows are like living on a street with twenty houses where the rules are that any of the people can move into anyone else's house at any time without notice and later leave just as abruptly leaving their garbage behind for someone else to pick up.

There are countries big enough and powerful enough to allow free capital flows although even these have to beware of the possibility of raiders. There are many other countries that can *normally* operate without capital controls of any kind. But most and probably all of these are vulnerable to the kind of sustained attack we have seen too often in recent years. They absolutely must be allowed to invoke capital controls in times of extreme volatility.

If nation states are to play any significant role whatsoever they must be able to protect themselves from international arbitragers jumping from currency to currency to pick up a few basis points additional yield. It should be within the power of individual countries to raise or lower their interest rates somewhat to fit their own particular needs without triggering a massive capital outflow or inflow as the case may be.

THE MYTH OF FREE TRADE

While unrestricted capital flows can undermine the stability of any economy, unfettered free trade can also pose major problems. In fact, there is no such thing as free trade. Just ask Manitoba farmers who have had their trucks loaded with grain stopped by barricades at the U.S. border; and Canadian lumber producers who have been subjected to punitive measures to prevent them from gaining a larger share of the American market. Or, on the other side, consult U.S. dairy and poultry producers whose access to the Canadian market has been limited by regulations that have been an integral part of our marketing system.

A dramatic photo in the *New York Times* on December 10, 1998, topped an article entitled "American Steel At the Barricades: With Prices Low, Companies and Labor Unite in a Campaign to Limit Imports."[15] I must admit that if I were an American steelworker, and both my pay and my job were threatened, I would be an energetic booster of that campaign. It wouldn't really matter to me that someone, far away, who was paid a fraction of what I got, could make steel cheaper. This is the reality President Clinton had in mind when he proclaimed, that same month, that he wouldn't allow the U.S. to be flooded with cheap foreign imports.

The President's statement was confirmation of the fickle nature of "free trade". It is good when it is good for us and bad when it works to our disadvantage. No politician can survive with electors who have been personally touched by the "globalization pinch". This political reality raises again the whole question of whether or not the notion of one global economy — a world without borders — is really practical or just theoretical pie in the sky.

Free trade has been the cornerstone of Western policy since World War II. It has been considered good until proven otherwise and this has been the foundation on which the General Agreement on Tariffs and Trade (GATT) and its successor the World Trade Organization (WTO) were built. Trade was promoted as the panacea which supplemented economic growth when it was feared that national economies would eventually run out of steam. There have been dissenting voices, however, which appear in retrospect to have been prescient.

In 1993, Herman E. Daly who was at that time the senior

economist in the environmental department of the World Bank, wrote an article for the *Scientific American* which was captioned "The Perils of Free Trade: Economists routinely ignore its hidden costs to the environment and the community". Daly challenged the assumption that free trade was, by definition, inevitably good. He said: "That presumption should be reversed. The default position should favor domestic production for domestic markets. When convenient, balanced international trade should be used, but it should not be allowed to govern a country's affairs at the risk of environmental and social disaster. The domestic economy should be the dog and international trade its tail. GATT seeks to tie all the dogs' tails together so tightly that the international knot would wag the separate national dogs."[16]

Daly when on to say that a wiser course had been well expressed in the overlooked words of John Maynard Keynes, who wrote: "I sympathize, therefore, with those who would minimize, rather than those who would maximize, economic entanglement between nations. Ideas, knowledge, art, hospitality, travel — these are the things which should of their nature be international. But let goods be homespun whenever it is reasonably and conveniently possible; and, above all, let finance be primarily national."

If you stop to reflect on Keynes' advice you may conclude, as I have, that nearly all of the economic and especially financial turmoil we now face could have been avoided if we had listened to him.

THE MAI AND GLOBALIZATION

The MAI was designed to cast in stone a kind of globalized neo-classical chaos where power rules and people suffer. It represents the kind of unfettered capitalism that George Soros, the Hungarian-born American financier, now considers a greater threat to the world than either fascism or communism. Indeed, it is the kind of capitalism that produced both of these extremes in the 1930s and is destined to do so again in the absence of radical change.

The MAI, under the aegis of the OECD, may indeed be dead thanks to an international network of concerned citizens and Prime Minister Lionel Jospin of France . But its provisions are not. Attempts will be made to resurrect the essential parts under the World Trade Organization, the Free Trade Agreement of the Americas and other treaties.   The MAI represented capitalism's darker side.   It and its myriad cousins and look-alikes *must* be stopped!

CHAPTER 6

ECONOMISTS NEVER LEARN

*"People are wrong when they say is isn't what it used to be.
It is what is used to be. That's what's wrong with it."*

Noel Coward

Fifty years ago, at university, I asked my economics professors if recessions and depressions were really necessary. It was not an academic question. I was a child of the depression and I couldn't understand a system where unemployed carpenters had neither enough food nor adequate clothing for their families; unemployed needleworkers were hungry and needed their roofs repaired; and farmers, with repair jobs to be done and whose wives and children were in need of new clothing, were pouring milk down the drain and letting tomatoes rot in the field because there were no buyers. It didn't make any sense to me that people were unable to provide for each other's needs when they had the capability to do so. The professors' answers were far from satisfactory. In effect, they were recitations from economic history. There had been a long series of booms and busts and so, by extension, there would continue to be. In essence, these cycles of good times and bad times were inherent to the system.

To emphasize the point, they were predicting another full scale depression for 1950. I was so upset at the prospect, and so convinced that the disaster could be avoided, that I ran for parliament in what was considered to be a hopeless constituency for my party.[1] As proof of the existence of miracles, I was elected.

Then political reality set in. When I arrived in Ottawa I found that not only could back-bench members of parliament not influence economic policy, they couldn't influence anything of significance. But, fortunately, and I use the word cautiously and reluctantly, because lives were lost, the Korean war broke out in 1950 and, once again, what was impossible in peacetime suddenly became possible out of necessity. The dreaded depression never occurred.

By the time the war was over nearly everyone had adopted the ideas of British economist John Maynard Keynes. A maverick and free thinker, Keynes had broken with the pack of classical economists and written a *General Theory of Employment, Interest and Money*.[2] In it he expressed what was, at the time, the heretical view that there was indeed a periodic shortage of "aggregate demand", as the economists call it, and that when that occurs governments should spend money to "prime the pump" and level off the business cycle. Then, when times improve, raise taxes to siphon off excess purchasing power and replenish the treasury.

Inadequate aggregate demand just means insufficient purchasing power or, in the vernacular, not enough money in the hands of people able and willing to spend it. A periodic shortage of demand is something that ordinary laymen had observed for generations. But this idea was vigorously denied by economists who based their case on a law invented by Jean Baptiste Say. Say's law says that all production creates an equal and opposite demand. Consequently, there could be no such thing as a periodic shortage of aggregate demand.

The problem is that the real political economy doesn't work that way, and Keynes' heresy merely confirmed the obvious. The fact that he was a member of the economics club, however, gave his ideas more currency than those of outsiders who had been ignored. Still, it is interesting to note, that it was about fifteen years after Keynes had written his general theory before his ideas were generally accepted. This gives you some sense of the snail's pace at which one orthodoxy is supplanted by another.

In any event Keynes reigned supreme for about 15 years

after the Korean War and these were widely recognized as the "golden" years of economics. Thousands of farmers moved to the cities and found jobs. Millions of immigrants did the same thing. Sure they often started out washing dishes and cleaning toilets but it didn't take long to get established and many became entrepreneurs and capitalists in their own right. In those years both capital and labor did well. Productivity was high, wage settlements were not unreasonable, and very low interest rates kept the total debt to GDP ratio more or less constant.

This was all thanks to an era of demand management and it is somewhat bewildering to see the revisionists now referring to the bad old days. This in spite of both the data and anecdotal evidence showing that they were better days than any days we have had since. It was an era of genuine "trickle down" when even the poor could expect their lot to improve with the general level of prosperity. The mood, as I remember well, was generally optimistic and upbeat.

The era began to go into decline in the mid-sixties for reasons which a few of us considered easily observable. In the post-war period business had been consolidating to the point where in many industries there was "market power." Four or five companies controlled more than 50% of the market so they didn't engage in price competition. Efforts to increase their share of the market were by means of advertising, service and the development of new products. Price wars became increasingly rare because they were almost always self-defeating. Nobody won — except the consumer!

At the same time trade unions were consolidating their power, building up huge war chests to finance strike pay and learning strategy from business. They learned where and when to make demands on vulnerable companies least able to afford a lengthy strike. Often it was in the interests of oligopolistic industries to settle because they knew they could pass on the higher costs to their customers by way of higher prices. Of course when one company agreed to wage increases in excess of productivity there was tremendous pressure on other companies to follow suit. It was called "wage leadership".

I saw this phenomenon at work in my own country. In Montréal, Mayor Jean Drapeau was vigorously pushing everyone involved to get on with preparations for Expo '67, the World Exhibition which proved to be Canada's most magnificent collaboration between its English and French-speaking peoples. Progress was steady but, long before the fair was ready, trouble appeared. Construction workers said, "Mr. Mayor, if you want your party to be ready when your guests arrive you will have to give us a very large raise in pay." Give the strategy any label you want, but it worked. The raise was granted and in the following two years, as contracts came open for negotiation, construction workers all across Canada demanded and were granted comparable increases.

A year after Mayor Drapeau's ordeal, a Canadian government of which I was a member made one of the silliest decisions imaginable. Workers on the St. Lawrence Seaway demanded an increase of 30 percent to give them wage parity with U.S. seaway workers. A commission chaired by Norman Mackenzie, former president of the University of British Columbia, was set up to review the case. It recommended that the increase be granted over two years.

When the recommendation came before cabinet every minister who spoke, with one exception, was against accepting the commissioner's recommendation. Some were adamantly opposed. I did a quick calculation and said compliance would cost the department of national defence at least $70 million the following year. Still, the settlement was approved because the prime minister didn't want to let his "dear old friend", the commissioner, down. Cabinet, whether parliamentary or presidential, works on the basis of consensus where consensus is defined as "one or more of whom the chairman is one."

Well, the cat was amongst the pigeons and the inflationary wage-push spiral took off. And, as I mentioned earlier, this occurred more than a year before it did in the United States due to the alleged impact of the Vietnam War. It took years to wrestle inflation to the ground which again, as I said before, could have been accomplished in 12 months with the correct diagnosis followed by the correct medicine.

There were a number of incomes policies tried in various countries during this period. Some worked reasonably well for a while but, in the end, all failed because the design was faulty. Some plans were voluntary which can't possibly succeed for long because it just takes one breach of the agreed norm to send the whole "social contract" up in flames.

Other plans had public officials setting wages and prices. Again, it is a system which cannot work for long, except in a wartime emergency, because the data used in making decisions can be stale within weeks, or even days, in some cases. Still other plans rewarded workers in high productivity industries more generously than workers in low productivity or zero productivity — as we measure it — service industries. The perceived and real sense of injustice was more than enough to bring any such system to a jarring end.

None of the plans were designed to address the real problems which were market power and monopoly power. It was this combination of big business, big government and big labor that first permitted, and then perpetuated a system under which wages rose faster than productivity. As a result, costs rose and then prices. Higher prices led to even larger wage demands, which in turn led to higher prices and so the dog chased its tail 'round and 'round without ever quite catching it for long.

OUT OF THE FRYING PAN AND INTO THE FIRE

It was against this backdrop that the winds of change shifted direction. Government interference was cited as the origin of all manner of problems and Milton Friedman and his colleagues at the University of Chicago recommended that markets replace governments as the regulators of all things social and commercial. This was advertised as something new and wonderful whereas in truth it was a plan to dismantle the cage and let the wild beast of unfettered capitalism loose to prey on all the other species in the economic jungle.

It is a plan for economic Darwinism under which governments systematically withdraw from ownership, regulation and, most important of all, responsibility for the economic welfare of the citizens who elected it. Responsibility would be delegated to that all-seeing, all-knowing invisible hand which would provide for the welfare of humankind by the imposition of a ruthless discipline of efficiency and productivity.

The only problem is that the implied promise of a better life for all is a lie. The system won't produce grand results for the vast majority. It can't and it won't. The speed at which desperate human needs are met will be slower — for millions, too slow to maintain life itself.

PRIVATIZATION

I am no great fan of government-owned enterprise and I speak with some personal experience of the subject. When I was in government the Canadian National Railways and Air Canada reported to parliament through me as did Central (now Canada) Mortgage and Housing Corporation, which encouraged and participated in the construction of millions of houses in the post-World War II period. I was also responsible for most of Canada's major ports and for numerous smaller crown corporations of various sorts. I would not attempt to make the case that Canadian National and Air Canada should not have been privatized. I agree with the decisions that were taken. But I would remind myself, and others, that there was a time when Canada would not have had a transcontinental railway or a national airline without government.

And sure there was government interference from time to time and some of it increased costs. But not all of it was bad. Service was provided to people who would have been without service otherwise. Markets would not and, in many cases, have not maintained services previously provided in the absence of direct subsidies — which is just meeting the social cost from another pocket.

What I am saying is that privatization should be considered on its merits rather than as an imperative by royal decree. This applies in all countries but especially in underdeveloped countries where they are not yet ready to privatize because potential buyers are limited to domestic rogues or foreign vultures. The IMF and the World Bank have done the developing world an incredible disservice by applying and enforcing conditions which are far more relevant to the United States and Europe than they are to less-developed countries.

WHERE DOES PRIVATIZATION END?

In general, it should end at the point where it ceases to make sense to the people of that country, which means that every country will be different at any particular point in time and that the line may shift in one direction or the other in the course of time. In my own country I am extremely uneasy about attempts to privatize education, health care, highways, municipal water supplies, jails and so on. We appear to be aping U.S. trends rather than following the dictates of our own desires. Regrettably our governments act on our behalf through incremental change and without any specific mandate to do so.

In Ontario, for example, our public education system is being systematically stripped of its vitality. Cutbacks at the primary and secondary levels are eliminating "frills" like swimming pools, art and music. Demands that teachers instruct more classes have resulted in a severe cutback in extracurricular activity like drama, bands and sports. At the university level reduced funding has led to a substantial increase in tuition fees and an ever more dramatic increase in students' debt load on graduation. Increasingly it is becoming a system for the rich.

I feel very strongly on this point because my fees were paid by government under the Veterans Charter. Literally thousands of veterans were educated at public expense and most contributed enough in future years to repay the investment many times over. Because people are born with different gifts I have never believed that equality was anything more than a revolutionary slogan; but I do think that a certain equality of opportunity should be a hallmark of any civilized society.

For that reason I strongly believe that access to post-secondary education should be universal for qualified applicants. By any measurement other than "pure market" it has to be one of the best investments any country can make. This same logic applies to elementary and secondary schooling in developing countries. The imposition of user fees on people who haven't enough money to buy bread due to the government frugality demanded by the Bretton Woods institutions has to be one of the gravest crimes to be listed on their docket.

One of the greatest concerns of Canadians is their health care. Market driven initiatives have resulted in critical cuts in government funding. At first the changes were subtle but later more pronounced. Hospitals were closed, nurses fired and replaced with less qualified persons, as queues for elective surgery lengthened. Signs of a two-tiered system, one for the rich and one for the rest, began to appear.

Rumours are rife. Early in his career Ontario's Conservative premier went fishing with former U.S. president George Bush and soon things American began to happen. Our health care system which, despite the propaganda of George Bush and the U.S. health lobby, was, arguably, the world's best health care system is being systematically dismantled in order to be replaced with the American market system which is, arguably, the worst — except for the rich. I had lunch with an official in the Ontario government and asked him if he thought that was the aim of the game. He nodded "yes".

But is it the system Canadians want? Washington evangelist Tom Skinner, who had never been sick a day in his life, arrived home one day with a pain and not feeling well. At his wife Barbara's insistence he sought medical help.[3] He died 65 days later after running up medical and hospital bills of $215,000. In Canada that sort of financial disaster simply could not happen — at least until now. But for how much longer?

There are other areas of concern including highways and water systems. I have no intrinsic objection to toll roads, and use them from time to time at home and in the U.S. But I am not wild about them and vastly prefer roads to be part of the public infrastructure, available to all. At the same time reports from England about the horrific loss of service when the municipal water supply was privatized simply signals the need to proceed with great caution to ensure that the benefits exceed the cost.   The point is that no set of rules applies to all situations in all countries at all times.   Consequently, any ideology which imposes rigidities and denies innovation and indigenous solutions becomes a straight-jacket on the market of ideas.

DEREGULATION AND MARKET MADNESS

It is mildly ironic that I am writing in defence of regulation when I must premise what I want to say with the admission that public officials, attempting and usually succeeding in enforcing inappropriate regulations, have been driving me crazy all of my life.   At the same time I am extremely apprehensive about living in a deregulated world; so in this, as in so many other things, I seek the never-static course midway between too much and too little.

I worry about wages and working conditions in a deregulated world.   I remember reading that a hundred years ago children were working 10 to 12 hours a day in the mines and factories under the most unsatisfactory conditions and that it took decades of dedicated statesmanship to pass laws outlawing these practices.   And now they are back as transnational corporations move production to countries with nineteenth century rules.

The National Labor Committee in New York sent me a 17-page fax outlining the results of an investigation into sweat-shop working conditions in a Nicaraguan factory.   It revealed that child workers as young as 15 were working up to 13 hour days, seven days a week for a base pay of 15 cents an hour producing garments including brands such as Faded Glory for Wal-Mart, Arizona for JC Penny, and Route 66 for K-Mart.[4]

"Once they arrive at work, employees allege they are subjected to verbal, physical, and sexual abuse. One worker, Jolena Rodriguez, states, 'They hit you ... they hit you on the head ... to make you work faster.'"[5] ... "Workers are paid hourly, but they have daily quotas of production they must meet. Overtime is mandatory and does not pay time and a half.

One worker, Olga Maria Condoza, says, 'They make us work overtime. They make us stay. Anybody who doesn't stay gets a warning, three warnings and you are fired.'"[6]

Business friends reply to these revelations by saying that they are providing jobs for these poor women who wouldn't have jobs otherwise. This rebuttal would gain some credence if the women were paid a living wage, but they were not. They live in substandard conditions, work in a barb-wire enclosure, are transported in overcrowded buses and are so malnourished that many have to use some of their meagre wages to buy megadoses of vitamins to keep them going.[7] Some transnational corporations ape dear old Scrooge in demanding the last mite of work for the least mite of pay.

Safety conditions are another concern. I know that in the construction business Canadian contractors used to take risks with workers' lives. Largely as a result of trade union pressure safety in the workplace has taken on a higher priority. But what about countries without strong unions and government enforced regulations? The Guatemalan women complained that their hands were burned from the bleach and chemicals used to make stone washed jeans. Worse, and it's an image that will be burned in my mind forever, was a picture of Indian men lined up on the beach dismantling the worn-out ships of the world, steel plate by steel plate, for 10 cents an hour. They had no shoes and no helmets and the report indicated that skulls were sometimes crushed and sometimes toes cut off when one of the plates was dropped.[8] This is market capitalism at its worst and the tragedy is that the men have no alternative but to accept the jobs on the market's terms.

Governments have played a crucial role in setting standards for the cars we drive, the airplanes we fly in, the food we eat and the water we drink. Market enthusiasts are pressing to have more and more responsibility for setting and maintaining standards turned over to industry itself on the assumption that the industry knows its own business and will act responsibly in its own interests.

It is an unrealistic assumption. There have been too many cases of cheating in food quality. There have been too many cases of unsatisfactory maintenance in underfunded airlines. There have been too many cases of pesticides and chemicals that are banned in the U.S. and Canada being shipped to Third World countries. And why do you think that the gasoline Exxon sells in my home province of Ontario contains as much as 520 parts per million of sulphur content whereas the gasoline it sells in California only has 30 parts per million?[9]

It is simply that California has had the highest standards and the oil companies are kicking and screaming because environmentalists want them to match California's requirement. The case is just one more dramatic example of the constant tug-of-war between market-oriented economics and the public good. Experience has shown that these seemingly intractable problems are quite capable of resolution and accommodation when necessary.

GOVERNMENT'S RESPONSIBILITY FOR FULL EMPLOYMENT

I hesitate to use this sub-title when it is so repugnant to classical economists but I must because that is the way I was raised. The cabinet ministers I met in the early post-World War II years were absolutely determined that there would be jobs available for all of the returning servicemen and women and that nothing would be allowed to stand in the way of achieving it. One of the greatest ministers was an American-born engineer, the Right Honourable C.D. Howe, whose attitude toward public servants was "I didn't invite you into my office to tell me it can't be done. I brought you here to tell me how to do it."[10] Oh that there were more like him around today.

Throughout my active political life full employment was taken for granted as a top priority for any government — almost anywhere in the Western world. Then came the monetarist counter-revolution and the priorities changed. And the brain-washing began. Not only was price-stability elevated to number one priority, economists and their echoes increasingly led people to believe that full employment was no longer a realistic goal. Machines would be doing the work of people and making them expendable.

Political parties, including the one I belonged to at the time, attempted to redefine "full employment" so that it would mean something less than full employment. Milton Friedman invented the term "natural rate of unemployment" in an attempt to explain the higher levels of unemployment that his counter-revolution had produced. And even though he couldn't explain how you could determine the "natural rate of unemployment", the concept was accepted uncritically by the academy along with his other theories.

On one occasion when I was giving a lecture at the University of Waterloo, in which I included the concept of an incomes policy designed to produce full employment and low inflation simultaneously, an exceedingly brash young man, with the same assured self- confidence that I had had at the same age, jumped up and demanded, "Haven't you ever heard of the natural rate of unemployment?" I had, but in my opinion there was nothing "natural" about it. There is only high unemployment or low unemployment and the former, to my mind is not acceptable.

Governments give all kinds of excuses as to why there are often not enough jobs to go around. If it is not the influence of technology and the transition from an industrial age to an information age, it's due to foreign competition and the effects of world markets. It is always the fault of something or somebody beyond the government's control — never the fault of the government itself. It's what Canadian writer Linda McQuaig calls "The Cult of Impotence". Governments refuse to act because they claim they have no power to act. Instead, they talk about shorter hours, work sharing and other non-solutions.

Professor Friedman blames unemployment on govern-ment. During a May 19, 1994 question and answer period at the Fraser Institute, a Vancouver-based think tank made in his own image, he was asked: "If you had been invited to the G7 meeting on employment, what advice would you have provided to the ministers"? Answer: "I wouldn't have attended, ha, ha, but the answer is quite simple. The problem that they were dealing with is — unemployment is a government-created problem, created by excessive regulation of the terms and conditions under which people can be employed ..."[11]

It was a cop-out if I ever heard one, and I have heard many. Of course excessive regulation is an impediment to enterprise and I have known hundreds of people who were better off on Unemployment Insurance or welfare than they would have been working for the minimum wage. Obviously these conditions must be addressed for economic systems to operate at their highest level; but they don't come close to explaining why the OECD countries projected 35 million unemployed in 1995[12] or why world unemployment is projected at 150 million in 1999.[13]

The principal reason, stripped of all the rhetoric of political and academic excuses, is the same one that has plagued Western economies periodically for two hundred years, i.e. a shortage of aggregate demand.

IT IS A SHORTAGE OF AGGREGATE DEMAND, STUPID!

It is a lesson I thought economists would never forget. During the Great Depression there were those millions of unemployed men riding the rails and looking for jobs that didn't exist. Why? Because there wasn't enough money being spent. Banks wouldn't lend to most of the people who wanted to borrow because they had no collateral. And people who had collateral were reluctant to borrow because profitable investment opportunities were rare. Governments did launch a few projects but the number of jobs created was woefully inadequate.

Then Hitler invaded Poland and the whole scene changed. In Canada the government began letting contracts for ships, planes and guns. The U.S. received defence orders from Britain and later, after the Japanese attacked Pearl Harbour, declared war and went all out to win it. Soon all of those unemployed millions were either in the armed forces or employed in defence industries. There were jobs begging to be filled and this provided an unprecedented opportunity for women to join the labor force.

How was it all possible? Central banks began to print money and make it available to government at negligible interest. Central banks, including the Federal Reserve, printed money to buy government bonds. Governments paid the central banks interest on the bonds which was later returned to governments by the banks. The net cost was between zero and one percent — just the cost of administration.

The new cash, which was spent into circulation by governments, was deposited in private banks where it acted as the "high-powered money" which enabled them to increase their loans both to government and private industry. Gross national product sky-rocketed as the money supply grew. And the factor that was unique in modern times was the low cost as governments and private banks shared the money-creation function and central banks conspired to keep interest rates low, so that the cost of servicing wartime debt was manageable.

The system continued through the '50s and '60s and worked so well that when people asked me if we would ever have another depression like the Great Depression I would say "Definitely not. We have learned too much about demand management to let that happen." I would never have guessed how wrong that answer was. But then I would never have guessed how little we had learned from experience and that we would fumble into repeating the same old mistakes all over again.   The one problem that all of the worlds' high unemployment countries have in common is a shortage of aggregate demand.

IT'S THE BANKING SYSTEM

The monetarist counter-revolution, followed by the reincarnation of classical economics, created two monumental problems. The first was the mountain of debt caused by slow growth and high interest rates. With debt in most countries growing much faster than the economy it became just a question of time until the inverted pyramid would collapse. The second problem was the return of the private bank monopoly on money creation.

For an economy to grow and provide new jobs the money supply has to increase. One of the things most economists agree on is that nominal GDP grows in parallel with the rate of the nominal increase in the money supply. But under our system the money supply only grows when someone borrows more from the banks. It can be government, industry or individuals — or all three — but someone has to be willing to go further into debt.

As the end of the twentieth century approaches most governments are so deeply in debt that there is voter resistance, in addition to ideology, preventing them from assuming more. Some companies are taking on more debt but others are trying to reduce their existing burden and the level of household debt is the highest ever. So where are the potential borrowers needed to keep the economy afloat and growing? Lower interest rates reduce the cost of servicing existing debt, and encourage some borrowers to assume more, but there is a finite limit.

You would think that economists would take a leaf from history and recommend the creation of limited amounts of zero cost money to help finance urgent needs of various sorts. Especially in underdeveloped countries where health, educational, social and environmental needs are acute, or worse. But no, the IMF and World Bank, egged on by the U.S. Treasury Department, are specifically forbidding developing countries the use of the most powerful economic tool available to them for their own welfare. Instead they are required to keep on borrowing foreign currency which they can never hope to repay.

The whole worldwide financial mess, and its consequent social distress, is the child of two academic fantasies. The first is one that Milton Friedman and the late John Maynard Keynes hold in common, namely, that the system is self-correcting. They differ as to whether governments should enter or exit the stage of economic management but they both attribute properties to the system that it doesn't possess. The booms Keynes counted on will never allow the repayment of debt accumulated to keep an economy growing. Neither will Friedman's assumption that market economics will produce an economic equilibrium ever square with the real world of excess debt that plagues all nations.

The second fantasy is that fine tuning, greater transparency, standard accounting practices, early warning indicators or some other kind of wishful thinking can restore the vitality of the system and keep it healthy into the twenty-first century. It isn't possible with a highly leveraged, fractional reserve or zero reserve banking system. As long as banks are allowed to blow up "credit" money like a balloon, a day will inevitably come when someone sticks a pin in the balloon and the system starts to collapse.

Two hundred years ago the engineers did their job by designing the machinery that would turn out goods in abundance. But the economists didn't design a fair system for the distribution of those goods. Two hundred years later, they still haven't.

Even the handful of good economists who haven't been sucked in by the monetarist counter-revolution and retro-classical theories, still speak and write about business cycles as though they were as natural as summer and winter. But is that really true, or is there a fundamental flaw in a system that was never designed but just grew like Topsy?

Stop and think about it. Ask yourself this question. If a country — any industrialized country you choose — has as many factories as the year before, as many machines with as good or better technology and as many people, or more, who are as well educated and motivated as the year before, why should that country produce less goods and services than it did the year before? The physical plant and capacity is there but all of a sudden it is under-utilized.

Consider this analogy. You own a powerful motorcar. Usually it zooms along the highway effortlessly at the speed limit. But every once in a while it slows down appreciably as if the carburetter was suffering a spasm and refused to let enough gas into the powerful engine. (Someone may say that this is the era of fuel-injectors. Yes, but carburettor is more appropriate to a story about classical economics.) You consult a mechanic who says "sorry, the car was built that way and there is nothing I can do about it," while not even bothering to check under the hood to see if the carburetter needs replacing. Mainline economists are just like that mechanic.

In fact, there is no logical reason for business cycles in industrialized economies. They are as artificial as falsies. They are and always have been monetary phenomena directly attributable to the operation of the banking system. I know a few economists who recognize and understand the problem totally. The majority, including many of the most famous, do not. They stoutly defend the right of private banks to create credit money out of thin air when there is no existing mechanism by which it can all be repaid with interest. I say this after reviewing several books on macroeconomics to reconfirm my recollection that not one of them comes to grip with these fundamentals.

If, after two hundred years, mainline economists remain charter members of the flat earth society it is not at all surprising that most publishers, editors, editorial writers, financial columnists and business men and women are equally mystified. Obviously laymen will have to do their own research as they are unlikely to be enlightened by any of the five daily newspapers I read. On the contrary, they are just loaded with articles outlining various methods of patching up the old system.

Succeeding chapters will deal with two aspects of the same problem. The extent to which the love of money is the root of all evil, and the extent to which the lack of understanding of money, what it is and where it comes from, is directly responsible for the world financial crisis.

CHAPTER 7

THE FIRST COMMANDMENT

*"When they arrived, we had the land and they had the Bible
and they told us to close our eyes to pray. When we opened
our eyes, they had the land and we had the Bible."*

Desmund Tutu

When Moses came down from Mt. Sinai with the two
tablets of stone setting out the Ten Commandments the first and
primordial one was "You shall have no other gods before Me."
It was clear enough in the Biblical stories that when the law was
observed the Children of Israel prospered, and when it was
forgotten calamity of one sort or another inevitably followed.

Western civilization, which has its roots in this tradition,
seems to have forgotten the precepts on which it was founded.
Few could deny that it has made gold its number one god. The
near-worship of money has become the driving force of
economic life and organization. Shareholders' value, recently
adopted by the OECD as the primary responsibility of
corporations worldwide, is to be achieved at the expense of fair
wages, safe working conditions and protecting planet earth as
a safe haven for generations yet unborn. Efficiency overrides
all other considerations such as justice and compassion.

The whole purpose of corporations was to allow
individuals or groups to take investment risks without being
personally liable in the event of failure and bankruptcy. This
would permit the production of a greater volume and variety
of goods and services and serve a wider band of human need.
It was never intended that these legal fictions would be afforded
greater rights and protection than natural persons. Certainly

it was not envisioned that they be given the elevated status of nation states with power to usurp the functions of democratically elected governments.

Yet all of this has been happening. Natural persons are not allowed to move to any country they like without first being screened as desirable and then subject to any quotas which may be in existence at the time. Yet under NAFTA, the draft MAI and other treaties currently under negotiation, corporations are demanding the right to invest in any country without any screening* and not subject to any limit. If that were not chutzpah enough they then demand the right, through financial arm-twisting, to force their hosts to repeal or abstain from passing laws that might be in the public interest but which interfere with their profits. This is an abominable intrusion on democratic rights.

THE ASCENDANCY OF MARKET POWER ECONOMICS

In the summer of 1997 Federal Reserve Board Chairman Alan Greenspan told a luncheon meeting of the Washington Press Club[1] that what they were seeing was the ascendancy of market economics. I smiled when I read that and wondered if he was being serious or speaking tongue in cheek. What he should have told them is that what they were seeing was the ascendancy of market power economics, but on a global as opposed to a national scale.

It is a repeat of what happened in the latter part of the nineteenth century when John D. Rockefeller achieved a stranglehold on the oil business because he didn't like "vicious competition." For a while, in the 20th century, anti-trust laws stopped and reversed this trend toward monopoly in favor of oligopoly which has the merit of imposing the discipline of fighting for market share though usually by means other than price competition. An attempt is now underway to extend market power across the globe because big companies are no more sanguine about competition from foreigners than they are from fellow countrymen.

On February 14, 1995, at the suggestion of the editor

of Toronto's *Financial Post*, I submitted four articles outlining some of the perils of neo-liberal economics and where it was likely to lead. In the final column I wrote: "As the so-called globalization process continues, the big monopoly players in one country will gobble up or be gobbled up by the big players in the trading area. Access to credit will be the key factor as we head toward a world hegemony of all key financial and industrial sectors. Such a concentration of power will not only be able to move production from one part of the globe to another, in search of lower costs and taxes, it will be able to eliminate price competition by stamping out new entrants to the market place with the ease of an elephant standing on a seedling plant."[2] None of the articles were published because they were too avant garde for the *Post* which was a guardian of the New Right.

Usually when oligopolies conspire to agree on prices they avoid a paper trail and, as the great nineteenth century liberal philosopher and political economist John Stuart Mill pointed out, they do it over tea. Sometimes, however, the agreements are more specific and sometimes, though rarely, they get caught. Such was the case with three former executives of the Archer Daniels Midland Corporation — the self-proclaimed "Supermarket to the World" — who were found guilty of engaging in an international conspiracy to fix the prices of a widely used additive for animal feed. Evidence at the trial indicated that price fixing was widespread and had been going on for a long while.

It was an important victory for prosecutors especially in light of the history of Archer Daniels. As the *New York Times* reported: "For decades, the grain giant has been run as a virtual family fief under the iron-fisted control of Dwayne Andreas, one of the nation's most politically powerful executives who is known by presidents and prime ministers alike. Despite that influence, Mr. Andreas was unable to stop the weight of the judicial system from falling upon his son and one-time heir apparent, Michael."[3]

Another international case involved Pharmacia & Upjohn Inc., the Rhone-Poulenc SA drug unit Rhone-Poulenc Rorer and the Hoechst Marion Roussel drug unit of Hoechst AG. P&U, the Swedish-U.S. drug maker based in Bridgewater, New Jersey, agreed to pay $102.5 million, U.S., to settle a class-action suit filed in 1993 on behalf of all U.S. retail pharmacies. "P&U said it had acted 'ethically and lawfully in its selling practices,' but was settling the lawsuit in order 'to limit its financial exposure and to avoid a lengthy, costly and uncertain jury trial.'"[4]

There is undoubtedly more to this international iceberg than merely the tip.

POWER CORRUPTS

The old saw that power corrupts and absolute power corrupts absolutely can apply to business as well as politics. As restraints are relaxed and removed the temptation to abuse increases. This applies in myriad ways and right across the spectrum. Highly paid executives know they can "earn" huge bonuses if they slash the number of employees on the payroll so there is a temptation to do it whether or not it is essential to company welfare.

When Robert E. Allen, AT & T's chairman, ordered 40,000 jobs cut from the payroll at a time when the company appeared to be doing very well financially, his action struck a hornets nest of opposition. Stung by the criticism of his compensation package, Allen responded with a testy letter to all employees.[5] Allen was apparently unaware of the fact that employees resent what they perceive as gross injustice.

"Al Dunlap was the CEO of Scott Paper Co., for two years. During that time he eliminated the jobs of 11,000 people and put them out on the street with no prospects of any future. He cut research and development in half, sharply cut back expenditures on staff training and cut out all contributions to any kind of community charity. He also told the managers of the company that they were not to participate in any sort of voluntary community service because if they had any extra time and energy available it should go into the company. The value of Scott Paper shares went up roughly 220%; added something on the order of $6 billion to the shareholder value of the company. For two years work he walked off with $100 million in compensation.[6]

The sequel to the story has been described as poetic justice. Dunlap, who had earned the nickname "Chainsaw Al", was hired by Sunbeam Corp. to revive its fortunes. But Sunbeam's stock sank and sales lagged so Dunlap was sacked in a one minute conference call which he said left him "personally, financially and professionally devastated." In the course of an interview with the *Wall Street Journal* Dunlap's eyes filled with tears.[7] It is a moot question how many ex-employees of Scott Paper wept with him.

It was left to Victor Rice, chief executive officer of Lucas Varity PLC, to tell his fellow moguls at the exclusive Davos forum on economics what the bottom line, on acquisitions and mergers that result in streamlining and downsizing, should be, "Don't hesitate about people decisions," he said. Rice, who cut almost 60,000 jobs from Massey-Ferguson after he took over in 1978, was then in the process of eliminating 3,000 jobs at Lucas Varity, the company formed when Varity, formerly Massey-Ferguson, merged with Lucas Industries in 1996.[8]

Of course there are many executives who disagree and most of them did at the Davos conclave. But the overall impression created by globalized mergermania is one reminiscent of nineteenth century capitalism. People are assumed to be a commodity. So when you need them you hire them. When you don't need them any longer you dump them like so many overripe cabbages.

It is all a question of ethics and morality in the workplace. In September, 1998, a leading activist against garment industry "sweatshops" accused American luxury clothing company Liz Claiborne of exploiting female workers in El Salvador even as it co-chaired a White House panel intended to curb abuses. In a factory called DoAll, workers sewing Liz Claiborne garments were being paid below subsistence wages of 60 cents an hour, denied health care and forced to work as long as 84 hours a week, according to a report by the New York based National Labor Committee. It said that the women were subject to pregnancy tests and allowed only two bathroom breaks a day that were monitored by supervisors.

In response, Liz Claiborne said it had been working with factory owners and management to address problems. "Our regular inspections of DoAll have led to certain improvements, including in fire safety. But certain problems common to the region, such as pregnancy testing, cannot be solved by one company alone."[9]

Ethical questions in business know no national or industry boundaries. Certainly sweatshops for garment workers have a near universal dimension. They can be found in Canada and the U.S. as well as Third World countries. The scale of wages may be different but the aspect of exploitation is universal.

Other questionable practices abound. The directors of Bre-X Minerals Ltd. learned that 148 of 150 core samples from their Indonesian Busang mine site tested by potential partner Barrick Gold Corp. had showed no gold. Company minutes show that they decided to set up an offshore indemnity fund for themselves. This was before shareholders became aware of the results and that consequently their shares were worthless.[10]

In December, 1998, Northern Brands, an affiliate of RJR-Macdonald Inc. which is the Canadian subsidiary of U.S. tobacco giant R.J. Reynolds, pleaded guilty and was ordered to pay $15 million for its role in a massive smuggling operation that exported cigarettes from Canada and smuggled them back into Canada through the Akwesasne Mohawk reserve near Montréal. It was the first time a major tobacco company has been convicted of a federal crime in the United States.[11]

Another worrisome area is the relationship between drug companies and the doctors and hospitals that undertake clinical trials for them. There have been several publicized cases of test results being suppressed through confidentiality agreements. One involved Dr. Nancy Olivieri, a highly competent researcher at Toronto's world famous Hospital for Sick Children, who signed a confidentiality agreement with Toronto-based Apotex

Inc. when she agreed to test deferiprone in clinical trials on her young patients with thalassemia, an inherited blood disorder.

When it became apparent that the drug had potentially harmful side effects she decided to inform her patients, the research community and regulating agencies. That brought threats of legal action by Apotex and a disheartening lack of support from the hospital which turned down her request for legal assistance.[12] In early January, 1999, Dr. Olivieri was demoted by the hospital, allegedly for reasons other than the Apotex controversy. At the end of the month she was reinstated but the while episode raises uneasy questions about the relationship between corporations and clinical research.[13]

While much industry-funded medical research has no strings attached, documented exceptions and statistical sampling is quite disturbing. A Harvard Medical School survey of 2,000 members of science faculties found that "43 percent had received a gift — biological material such as pieces of DNA, medical equipment, trips and money — in the past three years. Half of those who received the gifts acknowledged that there were strings attached, including the right to review the academic's work before it was published. The survey also showed how academics see industry as a necessary sugar daddy. Two-thirds of those who received them said the gifts were very important to their work."[14]

Assuming that the volume of privately-sponsored research is likely to increase in the 21st century something is required to ease the public mind in respect of this conflict between power and money on the one hand and truth on the other. Perhaps the Federal Drug Administration in the U.S. and equivalent bodies in other countries should enact regulations which would deny approval of any drug which had been tested by scientists subject to any unreasonable or unacceptable restrictions involving confidentiality, delay or review before publication.

In some of the cases where scientists have been conscience driven to break confidentiality agreements in the public interest they have suffered some of the negative consequences attached to whistle-blowing generally. When

Dr. David Kern from Memorial Hospital in Pawtucket, Rhode Island, revealed that his research discovered a higher-than-normal incidence of lung disease among the employees of Microfibres, his sponsor, trouble began. Not only was his contract with Memorial Hospital's occupational and environmental health service not renewed, its academic affiliate, Brown University, terminated its program in occupational health, of which he had been director, one week after he presented his findings at a scientific conference.

A Business Ethics and Fraud Survey undertaken by KPMG, an international accounting and consultant's group, discovered that about two-thirds of its business respondents have a written policy requiring employees to report fraud or misconduct in the workplace. Failure to report was viewed by almost 90% of respondents to be unlikely; and failure to protect their whistleblowers from retaliation was ranked least likely of all the items measured by the Business Ethics survey. So far, so good.

On the other hand only 40% of businesses reported having formal systems designed to protect internal whistleblowers from retaliation. The rest rely on informal measures which may not be adequate. "Studies show that job loss, significant in reduction in wealth or status, harassment by co-workers, divorce and even suicide all take place as a direct result of blowing the whistle. Over 80% of whistleblowers reported having suffered from physical deterioration and emotional stress including anxiety, depression, powerlessness, and isolation as a result of their actions. In this regard, the KPMG surveys reveal that corporate self-interest is taking precedence over obligations to employees due to faulty assumptions about the likelihood of retaliation, and by ignoring harm to others.

"Central to the issue is the notion of loyalty. Companies expect their employees to demonstrate loyalty to them by internal whistleblowing. However, the same degree of loyalty is not reciprocated as most companies provide very few protections from the possible negative consequences of such actions."[15] The double standard is obvious and one that applies in many areas of corporate and political life.

THE DOUBLE STANDARD

The great tragedy of the quarter-century ascendance of neo-classical economics has been another divorce between the financial economy and the real economy — between Wall Street and Main Street. Mergermania has provided glorious opportunity for a few people to get rich quick. Up front fees for bankers and deal makers replaced the discovery of oil deposits and gold mines as the gold pot at the end of the rainbow. Complex derivative instruments and currency trading have enabled bright young college graduates to earn millions in bonuses and establish themselves as the nouveau riche. Stock markets soared as paper profits multiplied.

Chief executive officers reaped handsome rewards. A Reuters dispatch from New York in May, 1998, quoted *Forbes* magazine to the effect that Travelers Group chairman Sanford Weill received $228 million in compensation in 1997 — more than George Lucas, Oprah Winfrey or Michael Jordan — making him the highest-paid boss in the United States. Behind Weill on the list were insurer Conseco's CEO Stephen Hilbert, with $125 million, HealthSouth Corp's Richard Scrushy, $107 million, Occidental Petroleum Corp's Ray Irani, $105 million and industrial powerhouse AlliedSignal Inc.'s Lawrence Bossidy, $58 million.[16]

Having the top salary doesn't necessarily make you the richest. Microsoft's Bill Gates only received $591,000 in compensation, putting him at No. 749 on the Forbes 800 — but whose stock in the company was valued at $49.5 billion.[17] Salaries at the top of the *Forbes* list are really obscene especially when you compare them to the U.S. low and minimum wage earners who have difficulty keeping a roof over their heads.

"The economy is booming for select people, but for the needy the gap gets wider," said Tom Lyons, executive director of the New England Shelter for Homeless Veterans, who estimated the average stay at his shelter has stretched from eight months to more than fourteen months over the past two years. We are constantly encouraging men and women to rebuild their lives with work, but at the end of the road we aren't finding housing for them, Mr. Lyons said."[18]

According to U.S. federal statistics a worker earning the minimum $5.15 an hour would have to work an estimated 88 hours a week to afford a one-bedroom in Miami, while in Westchester County, N.Y., a minimum-wage earner would have to work 150 hours a week to afford an average-priced two-bedroom apartment. Market driven economics provide neither the income nor the basics to sustain life for marginalized workers.

Perhaps nowhere is the double-standard as grotesque as in who qualifies for welfare and who does not. For several years now most governments infected by the Washington consensus have been making life increasingly difficult for people at the bottom of the economic ladder. Entitlements have been cut back and thresholds raised in an effort to force people off welfare and into active employment. It would be a logical as well as a humane strategy if there were jobs available at pay rates which would at least provide adequate food, clothing and shelter. In the absence of such jobs it's out of the frying pan and into the fire, which includes living on the streets in some cases.

Contrast this treatment of low-skilled workers with that provided for the banks. When Third World countries couldn't afford to pay their interest on international bank loans in 1981-82 many of America's largest and best known banks faced possible bankruptcy. In some cases the loans that were about to go into default exceeded the total capital of the banks. Instead of letting them go broke — a solution totally compatible with free market economics — Federal Reserve Board chairman Paul Volcker persuaded the IMF to ride to the rescue with loans sufficient to pay the interest owing on existing loans.

Emboldened by the success of this emergency bailout international banks made irresponsibly large loans to Mexico and once again their faith in Santa Claus was rewarded. The IMF and the United States Treasury, with taxpayers' money, moved into place for a cliff-hanging rescue of the Mexican economy.   Again, however, it was neither the Mexican economy nor the Mexican people who were rescued. Both were about to go into a state of shock. It was the international banks who were saved from the consequences of their own folly.

It is almost comical to watch this demand for government assistance — or interference, depending on the purity of one's ideology — from the wealthiest, most powerful people on earth.   Their appetite for aid has extended to Thailand, Korea, Indonesia, Malaysia, Russia and Brazil — everywhere they had tried to make a fast buck without considering the risk.

It is important to understand what has been going on. International banks, which are not required to maintain cash reserves and only a minimum capital base, create billions and billions of dollars, usually, although not always, denominated in U.S. funds, to lend to countries and some businesses all over the world. They do this knowing that the countries involved can never pay it back. Sufficient real money does not exist. Chart No. 1 illustrates the dramatic increase in international bank lending which is the root cause of the world debt crisis.

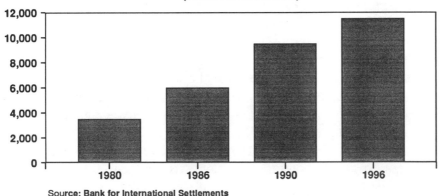

International Bank Lending
(billions of U.S. dollars)

Source: Bank for International Settlements

Chart No. 1

To keep the pyramid from collapsing requires a constant flow of new money from the World Bank and the IMF. This has two results. Debtor nations have the cash to pay the interest on their foreign loans. Debtor nations keep going further and further into debt. So you can see the picture. Michel Camdessus, president of the IMF, dressed in his Santa suit, going from one First World country to the next with his tin cup asking for handouts of taxpayers' money to provide relief for their biggest banks.

Of course the shell game can't go on forever. That is obvious after even a cursory look at the numbers. What is frightening is that the G7 world leaders would like us to believe that their package of reforms as announced in the Fall of 1998[19] will resolve the problem and lead to a stable financial system and a more prosperous world. On the contrary. Their plan which relies heavily on the IMF doing more of the same is simply setting us up for a bigger fall. In order of magnitude, instead of just the roof caving in the whole financial superstructure will collapse.

We were given a peek through the veil of secrecy surrounding international finance when we learned about the 911 call John Meriwether, CEO of Long-Term Capital, made to William J. McDonough, president of the New York Federal Reserve Bank, in late August 1998. Meriwether was in trouble with his hedge fund which gambled on the differentials between bond prices using computer models developed by two Nobel Prize winning economists.

Meriwether's problem was that the computer models were not infallible and whereas his millionaire clients had made 30 percent return on their investments for a couple of years a big bet went wrong. Long-Term lost $4 billion and the rich clients, faced with losing their bundle, were apoplectic. Fortunately, for them, some big financial houses including Merrill Lynch & Co., Goldman Sachs & Co., Bear, Stearns & Co., and Bankers Trust Corp. were in bed with them. They had lent Meriwether's company big bucks and they, too, were begging for a bailout.

"These companies were of course seeking to save their

own skin. But McDonough put forth the official spin before a House of Representatives Committee. 'Everyone I spoke to that day volunteered concern about the serious effect the deteriorating situation of Long-Term Capital could have on world markets,' McDonough said. Ah yes, world markets. And so McDonough calls Fed Chairman Alan Greenspan and Treasury Secretary Robert Rubin and a bailout is arranged.

"Former Lehman Brothers partner and current financial columnist Michael Thomas is right — it was improper for the Federal Reserve to arrange a private bailout. If Merrill Lynch and Goldman Sachs want to protect their behinds by arranging a private bailout, fine. But the Fed should have stayed out of it. Or, as former Fed Chairman Paul Volcker asked in a speech, 'Why should the weight of the Federal Government be brought to bear to help out a private investor?' [He must have forgotten where it all began.]

"'Capitalists now all want it one way,' Thomas says. 'They want to do whatever the hell they feel like, but let someone else pay. It's called privatizing the profits and socializing the risks.'"[20]

It's not all capitalists who get the red carpet treatment when they go cap in hand looking for a bailout. It's just the big ones who can claim they are too big to fail — the ones for whom failure would affect all sorts of people far and wide. The magnitude of the double-standard is great indeed as I know from personal observation.

I am, to my wife's dismay, an auction buff. And one of the saddest experiences of my long career was to go to auctions for small and medium sized companies of all sorts who went bankrupt when Paul Volcker and the Fed pulled the plug on the U.S. and world economies in 1981-82 and his successor Alan Greenspan did again in 1990-91. The bankrupt companies usually represented the life savings and lost dreams of energetic young entrepreneurs in their 20s, 30s or 40s. Their beautiful desks, the works of art, everything they owned going for less than 20 cents on the dollar to pay off part of the bank loans that had been arbitrarily called when central banks tightened the money supply. There was no bailout for the young and struggling — most of whom were doing just fine until they had the rug pulled out from under them. They were victims of the market — or was it the bureaucratic interference of arrogant and unaccountable central bankers?

Just before it recessed for the elections in November, 1998, Congress was wrestling with legislation designed to make it more difficult for people who declare bankruptcy to escape their responsibilities. There is a case to be made for tighter rules. But Americans will know they live in a just society when Congress bills the banks for the billions of taxpayers' dollars that have accrued to their benefit.

AMERICAN VALUES

As I was driving to work one morning I heard Ambassador Richard Holbrook say that not only did the U.S. have a responsibility to intervene in world hot-spots, like the former Yugoslavia where he has been so deeply involved, there was also a necessity for America to "stand up for its values." Two thoughts occurred. There are skeptics who wonder if the IMF had not attempted to impose the Washington consensus, resulting in the cut-back of transfer payments to the Yugoslav provinces, the federation might have remained intact. That, of course, cannot be proven one way or another but it seems to me that the world has the right to pick and choose from the marketplace of ideas without being forced to accept one particular set of solutions — especially if they are people-unfriendly solutions.

For example there may be some countries which would prefer to have a fairer distribution of income. Since Canada has been emulating the American model our distribution of income has become increasingly unjust. Not as bad as the U.S. yet, mind you, but headed in the same direction. In 1973, just before monetarism assumed the academic throne, the richest 10 percent of American families with children made 21 times more than the poorest. By 1996 the richest 10 percent made 314 times more than the poorest.[21] To the extent that American "values" conquer the world this trend is bound to continue. The spread between executive compensation packages and ordinary wages is simply illustrative.

"Rose Gerrit Huy was a fast-rising executive at Daimler-Benz A.G., the German industrial giant that makes Mercedes-Benz automobiles. A Harvard-educated economist, she was in charge of developing cars like the SLK roadster before she was promoted to head the company's finance and tele-communications subsidiary. But in 1997, Ms. Huy, 43, quit Daimler after 11 years to become the Compaq Computer Corporation's managing director in Germany. Not that her Daimler salary was skimpy, but the Texas computer maker offered something that could catapult her into vastly greater riches: stock options."[22]

With the advent of a reincarnated classical economics, or "unfettered capitalism", the gap in executive pay between America and the rest of the world has widened dramatically. "This is largely because the political cultures of many European and Asian countries recoiled at the idea of lavishing vast riches on capitalist chieftains for a single year's work. Pay packages like the $49.9 million that Sanford I. Weill, the chairman of Travelers Group Inc., collected in 1997, or the more than $556 million that Michael D. Eisner, the chairman of the Walt Disney Company, made in 1997 by exercising fewer than half of his stock options left many people in Europe aghast.

"Now, though, that attitude is changing, albeit slowly. To stem a drain of executive talent to their American rivals, big European and Asian corporations have begun pressing their governments to modify securities laws and accounting practices that discourage jumbo pay packages.

"'The rest of the world is moving to our pay model,' said Kevin J. Murphy, a University of Southern California finance professor and a leading expert on worldwide executive pay. 'Maybe that movement is out of efficiency, maybe it is out of greed — we don't know which yet — but the trend is clear.'"[23]

To make up your own mind as to whether it is efficiency or greed just look at the data for worldwide economic output. Despite the spectacular performance of a few companies, usually through the takeover or merger route with its inevitable downside of closed facilities and displaced workers, most national economies including the U.S. economy, have not done nearly as well as the world economy did before the Age of Aquarius in the 1960s was supplanted by the Age of Greed in the 1980s and '90s.

Two other aspects of American society that are viewed with some apprehension by outsiders are health care and culture. With such a huge disparity of incomes it is easy to understand why the wealthy would be content with a system of health care for profit. They can afford to buy the most comprehensive insurance packages available and pay personally for any service that isn't covered.

At the other end of the income scale the poor can't afford to get sick. And if they do they risk having their life savings wiped out. This in spite of the fact that America's total bill for health care represents a larger proportion of GDP than anywhere else in the world. So the system can't be any more efficient than it is fair in meeting one of society's greatest social needs.

When it comes to culture the U.S. offers the best of worlds and the worst of worlds. It possesses many of the best opera and ballet companies and finest symphony orchestras. Its art galleries and museums radiate excellence and the scope and variety of its many attractions is beyond compare. Still, there are some cultural exports that are not universally welcome.

It may be a function of age but I detect a marked increase in the incidence of sex and violence in American movies and video games. Years ago when Hollywood allowed the Hays office to set and enforce industry-wide standards it was far more fun guessing what the lovers were doing underneath the sheets. It didn't require a lot of imagination but there was an element of intrigue that has been lost in the process of exposing everything. Perhaps the imposition of standards is impossible in a globalized system but one longs for a little restraint.

Much more worrisome is the degree of violence. It is difficult to pick a movie where no one gets killed, and one with less than a half dozen homicides is considered tame. This trend has spilled over into video games that are getting painfully ugly. The Fall 1998 generation of software titles allowed players to indulge in masochism, mutilation — even prostitution. As for violence, try this for size. Duke Nukem runs forward, grabs the shotgun and pumps a round into the chamber. "Groovy," intones the video-game hero in his gravelly voice, just before he starts blasting alien scum into a gory pulp.[24]

Is this the kind of "inspiration" young people should be exposed to? Is there any correlation between the incidence of violence in television, movies and video games and the incidence of violent crimes committed by children and young people in real life? The questions are valid even if the answers are complex. But one wonders about unseemly products that serve no social good except to make money for their producers. One wonders, too, about trade agreements that say this kind of product must be admitted in any country that is party to the treaty. If not, the country can be sued for damages by the company in question.

Speaking of money reminds me of an interesting story about values. The Canadian comedy team of Johnny Wayne and Frank Shuster began their routine at college and polished it a bit every time an opportunity came along. Their big break came when they were invited to New York to appear on the immensely popular Ed Sullivan show. They never looked back. They were Ed's guests on numerous occasions and eventually got their own TV show produced in New York.

They developed the habit of flying back and forth from Toronto to New York weekly and were quite content with their comfortable lifestyle. Their New York agent, however, had more ambitious plans for them. He wanted them to do the circuit of major night clubs including Las Vegas. Frank and Johnny said they were perfectly happy. The agent persisted and the pair stoutly maintained that they were quite happy with things as they were. "Ah yes," the agent replied, "but there is more to life than happiness."

THE TEMPLE MONEY

There is an extreme irony in the fact that Americans are the most church-going people in the world and yet when you start talking economics to them, with a few absolutely marvellous exceptions, it is as if their leader and role model never existed. They are not alone in this. The same attitude can be found in most Western countries including Canada. There is an inexplicable hardness of heart that appears to me to be much more pronounced now than it was twenty-five years ago.

Today there is a temptation to emulate the money-changers in the temple in Jerusalem where all money had to be converted into temple money to be acceptable. This creates an almost irresistible temptation for Americans because the U.S. dollar has become the equivalent of temple money. It is the standard by which all other currencies are measured. The U.S. dollar has also replaced gold as the safe-haven for the wealthy and become the currency of choice for many of the largest international banks. They manufacture tens of billions in credit denominated in U.S. Dollars and lend it to emerging economies and Third World countries until they are all drowning in debt. When they are about to go down for the third time the IMF throws a lifeline with another loan. All too often the lifeline has been conditional on a devaluation of the local currency — sometimes to an absolutely ridiculous extent. This is the signal for the ghouls and money-changers to step in and make a killing.

Of course the path had been cleared for them as the IMF and World Bank had already demanded that public enterprises be privatized and that restrictions on foreign investment in land, resources, industries and enterprises be removed. The result has been the biggest fire sale and expropriation of assets in world history.

Confiscation is really a more appropriate word and the magnitude is so great that it makes what Fidel Castro did to the United States look like lifting a dime from a Sunday School collection plate by way of comparison.

It should be noted that not all of the booty has gone to American nationals. It has gone to anyone with access to U.S. dollars or U.S. credit and most of the transnational corporations are in that fortunate position. They and their bed-fellows, the high priests of international finance, have been on a shopping spree that should lead to even greater stock options in the days ahead.

Money is the name of the game and whereas the love of money may indeed be the root of all evil, it is the lack of understanding of what money is and where it comes from that has transformed our world from its beautiful natural state to one in bondage.

CHAPTER 8

WHERE DOES MONEY
COME FROM?

*"The manufacturing process to make money consists of
making an entry in a book. That is all."*

*Graham Towers
First Governor of the Bank of Canada*

It would be interesting to know whether money or sex
is the most talked about subject. Rarely can you read a
newspaper or listen to a radio or TV broadcast without being
lectured about one or the other, or both. In one case, however,
there is so much explicit material that few secrets remain. Even
adolescents know where babies come from. They may have
witnessed a live birth on the TV program Murphy Brown, or
on one of the education channels. The origin of money,
however, is a different matter. It is still shrouded in mystery
for the vast majority of young and old alike.

In the course of writing an earlier book I asked more
than 100 friends and associates — not including my economist
friends — if they knew where money comes from. The sample
included newspaper publishers, editors-in-chief, financial
columnists, doctors, lawyers, clergymen and professors, as well
as business men and women — all people with wide experience
and much common sense. Not one of them had what I would
call a working knowledge of the monetary system.

To begin, they were uncomfortable with the question.
But with encouragement the answers came: "the government
prints it", they would say. When a follow-up question asked

what percentage of the money was printed by government the answers ranged from a low of 60 percent to a high of 100 percent. If that were true we would have a totally different system than the one that actually exists. Furthermore the world would not be facing a financial crisis of uncertain proportions. In fact, nearly all of the new money created each year results from a tap on the computer of one of the world's privately-owned banks, and therein lies the problem. If Graham Towers, the first governor of the Bank of Canada, were alive today he would say: "The manufacturing process to create money consists of making an entry in a computer. That is all."

More alarming than the average person's lack of understanding is the fact that most of our political leaders are in the same boat. There are only about half-a-dozen members of the Canadian parliament, out of 301, who really understand, and I am reliably informed that the proportion in the U.S. Congress is not too different. Yet they are the people who draft and pass the laws that control our destiny.

I am positive that President Bill Clinton, Prime Ministers Tony Blair, Jean Chrétien and the other leaders of the G7 countries do not understand. If this were not so they would not have endorsed a package of "reforms" which can most charitably be described as band-aids for a patient requiring radical surgery. So a top political priority must be to expose world leaders, and their advisers, to the rudiments of an unstable and unsustainable system and the banking reforms necessary to make capitalism the positive force that it can and should be.

A LITTLE MONETARY HISTORY

For most of the world's history, commerce was conducted either by means of barter or by the payment of money for goods and services. Through the years money has taken many forms with the most predominant, until the nineteenth and twentieth centuries, being coins of gold, silver, copper and iron. As the volume of commerce grew dramatically, however, there were insufficient coins available to accommodate the growth and new forms of money had to be invented. This is the point at which economists began to let us down and a monetary vacuum was created. It was a vacuum the banking fraternity willingly volunteered to fill.

Although European banking can be traced back to Roman times, my launching point is the introduction of paper money to England which appears to have begun with the London goldsmiths in the latter half of the 17th century. Until 1640 it was the custom for wealthy merchants to deposit their excess cash – gold and silver – in the Mint of the Tower of London for safe-keeping. In that year Charles I seized the privately owned money and destroyed the Mint's reputation as a safe place. This action forced merchants and traders to seek alternatives and, subsequently, to store their excess money with the goldsmiths of Lombard Street who had already built strong, fire-proof boxes for the storage of their own valuables.[1]

The goldsmiths accepted gold deposits for which they issued receipts which were redeemable on demand. These receipts were passed from hand to hand and were known as goldsmiths notes, the predecessors of banknotes. The goldsmiths paid interest of 5 percent on their customers' deposits and then lent the money to their more needy customers at exorbitant rates becoming, in fact, pawnbrokers who advanced money against the collateral of valuable property.[2] The goldsmiths soon learned that it was possible to make loans in excess of the gold actually held in their vaults because only a small fraction of their depositors attempted to convert their receipts into gold at any one time. Thus began the "fractional reserve system", the practice of lending "money" that doesn't really exist. It was to become the most profitable scam in the history of mankind. It was also the quicksand on which the Bank of England was subsequently founded, in 1694 – more than three hundred years ago.

THE BANK OF ENGLAND'S SCAM

The Bank of England was conceived as a solution to a dilemma. King William's War, 1688-1697, had been extremely costly and this resulted in much of England's gold and silver going to the continent in payment of debt. As a result, the money supply was sorely depleted and something had to be done to keep the wheels of commerce turning. Someone got the bright idea that establishing a bank might help to fill the void.

At the time the Bank was chartered the scheme involved an initial subscription by its shareholders of £1,200,000 in gold and silver which would be lent to the government at 8 percent. That seems fair enough, although the interest rate was more than ample for a government-guaranteed investment. It was only the beginning, however, because in addition to a £4,000 management fee, the Bank of England was granted an advantage only available to banks and bankers. It was granted authority to issue "banknotes" in an amount equal to its capital and lend the notes into circulation. This was not the first case of paper money issued by private banks in the modern era but it was the first of great and lasting significance in the English-speaking world.[3]

It was the same system developed by the goldsmiths. By lending the same money twice the Bank could double the interest received on its capital. Nice work if you can get it and you can with a bank charter. It is not too surprising, then, that discussions of this advantage encouraged some members of parliament to become shareholders in the Bank. Money lenders learned early, and have never forgotten, that it pays to have friends in parliament.[4]

The first Bank of England banknotes lent into circulation were, in fact, bank-created money. Public acceptance was based on the assumption that the notes were "as good as gold". Even when the Bank was subsequently authorized to increase the number of banknotes outstanding in proportion to the gold in its vaults, the public seemed blithely unaware that the promise "to redeem in gold" was really a sham. The bankers got away with the deception because they knew, like the goldsmiths before them, that only a small fraction of banknote holders would attempt to redeem those notes at the same time. What had begun as a fraud had been legalized and legitimized, but that wasn't enough to protect the beneficiaries from the consequences of their own greed.

There were times when the Bank of England did not have enough gold in reserve to meet the day-to-day demands for conversion and within two years of operation an early "run" on the bank forced it to suspend payments in specie, that is, in coins as opposed to paper.[5] This was a situation that was to recur periodically through the next three centuries every time a "crisis" occurred.

"By the year 1725 all the basic essentials of the modern financial mechanism were in being" in England.[6] The Bank had increased its capital, its loans to the government, its issues of banknotes, and reduced the ratio of gold in its vaults to the number of banknotes in circulation. By this time most of the start-up problems had been disposed of, and its status as a going concern firmly established. The Bank of England's unique charter gave it a virtual monopoly on banking in London.

Meanwhile, on the other side of the Atlantic Ocean both French and English colonies encountered money supply problems, and had to innovate as best possible. The French government neglected to meet the monetary needs of New France, as part of Canada was then known, and it was impossible to balance the budget with its heavy naval and military expenditures. Inflation began in 1685 when Intendant de Meulles, in great need of funds, cut playing-cards in four and signed them to serve as cash, and this card money increased in volume.[7]

GOVERNMENT-CREATED MONEY

The English colonial settlers faced comparable problems. Few were independently wealthy and the colonies suffered a chronic and often acute shortage of gold and silver coins. To make matters worse, Britain routinely banned the export of silver and gold to the colonies because it was desperately required as a base for the expansion of the money supply in the mother country. Deprived of support from "mother" England, necessity became the mother of invention.[8]

In 1690, four years before the Bank of England was chartered, the Massachusetts Bay Colony issued its first colonial notes.   This, according to an American friend, the late Professor John Hotson, was a consequence of their part in King William's war. Soldiers had been dispatched to invade Canada on the promise that the French had lots of silver, "Beat 'em and get paid that way", is how he told the story. But Québec did not fall, and the Yanks went back to Boston sore, mean, and unpaid. Something had to be done, so the Massachusetts Bay Note, redeemable in gold "sometime", was born. "This was, if not the very first, one of the first cases of government-created paper money (GCM) of the modern age."[9]

Early in the 18th century, in May 1723, Pennsylvania loaned into circulation, with real estate as security, notes to the amount of £15,000; and another £30,000 was issued in December. It was enacted that, "counterfeiters were to be punished by having both their 'ears cut off', being whipped on the 'bare back with thirty lashes well laid on,' and fined or sold into servitude."[10] While the punishment for counterfeiters seems somewhat extreme by 20th-century standards, the issue of notes accomplished its purpose and sparked a revival of the colony's economy.   Ship-building prospered and both exports and imports increased markedly.[11]

The experiment was so successful that the number of notes in circulation was increased from £15,000 in early 1723, to £81,500 in 1754 – a growth rate during the thirty-one years of a moderate 5.6 percent. Even Adam Smith, who was not a fan of government-created money, admitted that Pennsylvania's paper currency "is said never to have sunk below the value of the gold and silver which was current in the colony before the first issue of paper money."[12]

Paper money had been used by the Chinese centuries earlier but for our part of the world, as Curtis Nettles points out: "Paper currency issued under government auspices originated in the thirteen colonies; and during the 18th century they were the laboratories in which many currency experiments were performed."[13] There were no banks at that time in any of the 13 colonies so all the paper money was created under the authority of the colonial legislatures. In all there were about 250 separate issues of colonial notes between 1690 and 1775 and the system worked just fine when they avoided over or under issue. It also had distinct advantages over bank or coin money. The legislature could spend, lend or transfer the money into circulation, while banks could only lend (or spend their interest earnings back into circulation) and the coin money was always leaving the colonies to pay for imports.

There is no doubt that the 13 colonies were the Western pioneers in GCM which has often been labelled "funny money" by skeptics and cynics. Why they consider it any funnier than bank-created (computer) money I will never understand. Perhaps they just suffer from a peculiar sense of humour.

Historians usually play down the role of money creation as a causal factor in bringing about the War for Independence. On the other hand, "[Benjamin] Franklin cited restrictions upon paper money as one of the main reasons for the alienation of the American provinces from the mother country."[14] "To a significant extent, the war was fought over the right of the Colonists to create their own money supply. When the Continental Congress and the states brought forth large issues of their own legal-tender money in 1775, they committed acts so contrary to British laws governing the colonies, and so contemptuous and insulting to British sovereignty, as to make war inevitable."[15] (The U.S. Treasury Department, the IMF and the World Bank must have been tutored in the George III school. They would be wise to note the consequences of his policies.)

When the war began the United Colonies, or the United States, as they came to be called, were really strapped for gold and silver. Their difficulty was compounded by the blockade imposed by the British Navy. At the same time the war had to be financed by one means or another so the separate states, and the United States, acting through the Continental Congress in an act of defiance against King and parliament, continued the policy that they had previously followed when gold was in short supply – they issued paper money.

But now there was a difference. Instead of just printing

enough to meet the needs of a moderate growth in trade, they had to print an amount which, when added to foreign borrowing and the receipts from taxation, was sufficient to finance the war. Inevitably that amount ceased to have any relation to the increase in output of goods and services and the paper began to lose its value. In 1784 Benjamin Franklin, after defending the necessity of what was done, went on to explain the consequences of excess. "It has been long and often observed, that when the current money of a country is augmented beyond the occasions for money as a medium of commerce, its value as money diminishes...."[16] It is a truism to which one can say Amen! The amount of money created was so great that its worthlessness was inevitable.

It is noteworthy, however, that much of the hyperinflation of the later years of the Revolution was caused by British counterfeiting in a deliberate attempt to discredit the Continental currency. If that was their aim they succeeded brilliantly, but in this particular round of the war over money it was the colonies that had the last laugh. They paid for much of their war effort by issuing GCM and the total cost, including interest, until the debt was liquidated, has been estimated as about $250 million. Britain, on the other hand, relied almost entirely on bank-created borrowed money.

By 1783, the British national debt was roughly $500 million greater than in 1774. But here is the really interesting fact: since 1783 Britain's national debt has never been less than it was at the end of that year. The conclusion that William Hixson draws in his excellent book the *Triumph of the Bankers*, is that "Britain has not even yet finished paying for the war it lost attempting to suppress the emerging United States."[17] Hixson goes on to say that in the intervening 200 years British taxpayers have paid over $4 billion in interest to their moneylending class of 1783 and its heirs. To add injury to insult, the original $500 million is still outstanding.[18]

While the Americans won that round, future historians may speculate about who "lost" the next one. As a result of the hyperinflation, and the discredited "Continental", Alexander Hamilton, who seemed determined to model the United States monetary and banking system on that of England, was able to get a federal charter for the first Bank of the United States (BUS) and several state banks were chartered. This despite the strongly expressed views of Benjamin Franklin, John Adams and Thomas Jefferson. The Jeffersonians hated the BUS and had it killed after 20 years. Meanwhile the United States didn't create any legal tender paper money from the Revolution until Lincoln's Greenbacks, but this over-reaction exacted a heavy toll.

The years immediately following the War for Independence were not happy ones for the people of the United States. The collapse of the monetary system, and the absence of sufficient gold and silver to facilitate trade, caused the country to experience its first great depression. Debtors who had been able to pay creditors with cheap money during the inflationary period now had to pay with money that was scarce and therefore dear. Thus, as Richard B. Morris explains, "each one of the thirteen states found creditors arrayed against debtors."[19] The depression constituted the second half of the lesson in monetary theory. Whereas too much money leads to inflation, too little leads to economic paralysis. Unfortunately these inalienable truths proved to be an insufficient guide for future policy makers.

For almost a century following the War for Independence arguments about "money questions" and the role of banks raged on. The number of banks in the U.S. increased from thirty, in 1800, to seven hundred and thirteen by 1836. By then they had created $306 million in banknotes, plus deposits, but had only about $40 million in gold in their vaults. The ratio for the banks total liabilities – bank notes plus deposits – to metallic reserves was just about seven and a half to one.[20]

It was the Civil War, however, which had the biggest impact on the system. Once again gold was in short supply so the banks suspended payment, making the issue of United States Notes [greenbacks] unavoidable. Although the need was to meet the exigencies of war, there had long been a need for a "universal" or national currency to replace the hodgepodge existing at the time. One historian estimated that in 1860 there were "7,000 kinds of paper notes in circulation, not to mention 5,000 counterfeit issues."[21]

VICTORY OF THE BANKERS

From the time greenbacks first came into circulation in 1862 they carried the words: "The United States of America will pay to the bearer five dollars ... payable at the United States Treasury." In fact, however, they were government-created inconvertible money until 1879 when they first became convertible into gold at face value. Convertibility was introduced by Hugh McCulloch, a former banker and gold monometallist who became secretary of the treasury in 1865. He agreed with his old buddies in the banking fraternity that steps should be taken to make greenbacks convertible into gold as soon as possible.

Since there were hundreds of millions of dollars in paper outstanding at the time, and little gold in the treasury with which to redeem it, McCulloch concluded that it would be easier to reduce the number of greenbacks than to increase the gold in the treasury. So he sold bonds in exchange for greenbacks and then destroyed the greenbacks. In other words he exchanged interest-bearing bonds for non-interest-bearing cash.[22] It is interesting to speculate what might have happened had McCulloch been a farmer or a businessman. In any event, he decided to emulate England by putting the country in debt. There is little doubt that it was the bankers and moneylenders who won that round.

THE GOLD STANDARD — ANOTHER STRAIT-JACKET

In retrospect one wonders why support for the gold standard was so deeply entrenched. It was obvious that every time gold went out of the country to pay for imports the money supply contracted and this had a negative effect on the domestic economy. On the other hand when gold came into the country, or new gold discoveries occurred, the money supply increased rapidly and inflation took hold. This uncritical attachment to the gold standard must have had something to do with mysticism or its long romantic history as a prize worthy of kings and buccaneers. As an economic regulator, however, it was a continual nightmare.

It is difficult for me to credit that such an absurd system would last until August 15, 1971, when President Richard Nixon announced that the United States would no longer redeem U.S. currency held by foreign central banks for gold. This action was the last gasp of the gold standard. It is even more difficult to believe, as Michael D. Bordo says in his essay on the Gold Standard in the *Encyclopedia of Economics*: "Widespread dissatisfaction with high inflation in the late seventies and early eighties brought renewed interest in the gold standard."[23] If true, it only reinforces my case that some economists are incapable of learning.

To put the issue in perspective, just imagine that a group of visiting little green men and women from some other planet came to earth with a special laser gun which attacked only gold and caused it to disintegrate. In the course of their invasion they destroyed the entire gold supply on and in the earth. The effect on the real economy would be minimal. Jewellers would have to find substitutes for their brilliant wares and dentists would have to find something else to fill the gaping holes created in so many teeth. But apart from a few special cases, little would be affected. Our ability to grow food, in infinite variety, would not be changed. The potential for the production of bicycles, cars, ships and planes would not be affected. In other words we could cope quite nicely thank you. To say that without gold we would shut down the entire economy, or even slow it down dramatically, is too absurd for serious consideration. It should never have been the regulator of economic activity in industrialized economies.

It makes little difference to most of us how much gold our income will buy. What concerns us is the kind of "basket" of goods and services that Yale economist Irving Fisher wrote about and which is now the basis for a consumer price index. How much food, clothing, and shelter will our pay-check buy and will there be anything left over for dinner out and family vacations? Also, will it buy as much next year as it does now? And what about a few years from now, after we retire? It is the prices of the things we need and do that we hope will remain more or less constant over the years, and not how many gold or silver wafers we can buy with our dollars, euros, pounds or yen. It is the package of goods and services that these currencies can be exchanged for which determine their value.

BANK LEVERAGE

When most of the world was on the gold standard, i.e. that its money could be exchanged for gold, on demand, the system was already a confidence game because there was always more "money" than there was gold to back it up. Gold was the "high-powered money" which banks could use as the base for the creation of several times as much "credit" money. So it is not surprising, as countries abandoned the gold standard one by one, that they would substitute cash (legal tender) for gold. Cash became the new "high-powered" money which banks were allowed to use as their "fractional reserve" for the creation of many times more "credit money".

This ratcheting of a little bit of real money into a lot of credit money is what the economists call leverage. It probably won't surprise you that over the years, due to the greed of the banks and the complicity of politicians, the ratio has become much more generous. In the late nineteenth century, when the gold standard was still in effect, federally chartered U.S. banks were required to maintain reserves of twenty-five percent. In other words they could lend the same money four times. This reserve requirement was reduced about the time the Fed was established in 1913 and the slide has continued, periodically, ever since. On December 31, 1992, the Fed reserve requirement for net transaction accounts (deposits against which you can make withdrawals or transfers) was 3 percent for the first 46.8 million, and 10 percent for deposits in excess of that amount; 0 reserve was required against non-personal time deposits (savings); and 0 reserve against Eurocurrency liabilities.[24] The regulations are very complicated but what they say to me is that the Fed and the banking industry have jiggered definitions in a way that permits excessive leverage.

Whereas in 1963 there was one real dollar in bank vaults for every ten dollars that you had on deposit, that is no longer the case. Today your bank may have as little as one dollar in cash for very 50 or 100 dollars you have on deposit. This is obscene. Greed knows no bounds!

I don't think it is necessary to go through the actual mechanism of how a million dollars cash can be translated into $20 or $30 million bank credit. For anyone who is sufficiently interested it can be found in any good textbook or in *Fortune's Encyclopedia of Economics*. But, basically, when the Fed or any other central bank wants to increase the money supply by $20 to $30 million it prints $1 million in cash and buys government bonds in that amount. When the $1 million is deposited and works its way through the system from bank to bank the loans granted and deposits created finally add up to the $20 to $30 million total.

Bank credit can be used either to create real wealth or to finance speculation and it is critically important which it is. If you have ever borrowed money for creative purposes you will know how the system works. You want to borrow $20,000 to expand your bakery due to increased demand for your special brand of bagels. A visit to your friendly banker will set the ground rules. You will have to provide collateral — stocks, bonds or a mortgage on your house — to an amount double the value, or more, of the loan required. Failing that, a personal guarantee from a rich relative might suffice.

Once satisfactory collateral has been provided you will be asked to sign a note for the principal amount plus interest. Minutes later a computer will deposit the $20,000 in your account. The important point is that just minutes earlier the $20,000 didn't exist. It was created out of thin air based on nothing more than a small fractional reserve held by the bank.

An even more striking illustration of how the system works is to consider someone in the building business who borrows $150,000 to build a house. This money is used to pay the people who dig clay from a pit and make bricks, the bricklayers who lay the bricks, the woodsmen who cut trees to make lumber, the carpenters who use it to build the frame, the miners who extract the metals for the hardware and the manufacturers who turn out the plumbing, wiring and fixtures. But when they are all finished it is the bank which owns the house. The bank did little more than create the "money" which acted as the intermediary to facilitate construction. Nevertheless, because it was created as debt, all of the money used to pay for the new house had a lien on it. Consequently the builder has to sell the house at a price that will allow him to repay the bank and, if he is lucky, leave a little over to reward him for the work he has done and the risk he has taken. If he can't, and there is a shortfall, he will have to make up the difference to prevent the bank from liquidating part or all of the collateral pledged to get the loan.

In reality, then, the banks have turned the world into one humongous pawn shop. You hock your stocks, bonds, house, business, rich mother-in-law or country and the bank(s) will give you a loan based on the value of the collateral. Still there is an element of uncertainty in dealing with the banks that doesn't apply with legitimate pawn shops. The latter don't phone you and ask for their money back if the price of gold or silver goes down after they have given you cash for your gold watch or silver candlesticks. The banks, on the other hand, often change the terms of the deal with little warning. If the market value of your collateral goes down, they phone and insist that you either provide additional collateral, which you may not have, or give them their "money" back which isn't always easy. Especially if too many banks are simultaneously insisting on the repayment of too much "money" (in cash) which doesn't really exist. In the case of loans to countries, of course, the banks can't really foreclose so they just begin to act like owners and tell the political managers, or have the IMF and World Bank tell them, how they want the country run.

NEGATIVE TRENDS IN BANKING

When banks finance small business to expand and create jobs they are at least contributing to economic growth. Some of their other activities, however, are highly questionable and in need of review. When they finance takeovers, for example, they are creating money for the benefit of the privileged minority of company officials and shareholders. The takeover binge of the late 1990s eclipsed that of the 1980s which would have been difficult to forecast.

The winners, of course, include the banks themselves with their big up-front fees and mega loans. They are so much easier to administer than the pesky small business loans. Why bother with a thousand small entrepreneurs when you can lend the same amount of money to one or two mega-corporations? This is a matter of concern because monetary dilution affects everybody from the poorest beggar with a cupful of change through to the multi-billionaire.

In the real world some are treated much more generously than others and to a very large extent the banks decide who the winners and losers will be. Giving them a virtual monopoly on the creation of money, and then allowing them almost unrestricted liberty as to what they can do with it, can best be described as double jeopardy. The banks may not have invented the maxim "the rich get richer and the poor get poorer" but they certainly do their best to prove its validity by giving the lion's share of the increase to their friends and close associates.

They create money to lend to the rich to buy stocks on margin. This is pure inflation of stock values and doesn't create any new real wealth to make the money "good". Banks are even more reckless in lending money to buy bonds on margin. This is doubly questionable when the loans are made to hedge funds like Long-Term Capital. It is financing speculation for the benefit, or hoped for benefit, of people at the top of the economic scale while contributing further to the irreconcilable divorce of the financial and real economies.

ZERO PERCENT BANK RESERVES

Allowing banks to operate with zero cash reserves is, in my opinion one of the most worrisome developments of the last quarter century. It is a product of bad theory and lax or no regulations. The bad theory got its validation from Milton Friedman who concluded that if 100 percent cash reserves was not politically feasible he would opt for zero percent because either extreme would "get the government out of the business of having anything to do with the lending and investing activities of private financial entities."[25]   I don't think his conclusion is necessarily true but the philosophical implications are profound and will be discussed in the next chapter. For now I will just deal with the practical effects.

Friedman was right when he suggested that zero percent reserves would be more likely to gain political acceptance than would the ideal 100 percent.[26] When the Canadian Bank Act was amended in 1991, the government of Brian Mulroney foolishly eliminated the requirement for reserves over a two-year period. In doing so he gave up one of the most powerful economic levers — the right to raise or lower cash reserve requirements as economic circumstances might demand. Now Canadian banks only keep enough cash to meet the immediate demands of their customers which is about a cent to a cent and a half for each dollar of deposits.

A point of interest is that depositors don't actually own the "money" they have on deposit in the bank. The banks do. Depositors are merely creditors of the banks so should the banks fail they have to take their chances along with other creditors. Deposit insurance, allegedly to protect depositors, is really a "soother" to prevent nervous clients from creating a run on the bank by attempting to withdraw cash that doesn't exist. If, at any time, confidence should be lost the confidence game collapses.

Canadian banks now operate under a new set of rules designed by the Bank for International Settlements (BIS), known as the Gnomes of Zurich, even though BIS headquarters is actually located in Basle, Switzerland. It is a system known as "capital adequacy" which rates the risks of various kinds of bank investments and the amount of capital required in each case. For example business loans are regarded as somewhat risky whereas government bonds of any OECD country are considered risk free — a somewhat dubious assumption.

This risk-weighting system tips the scales against entrepreneurship in favor of financing government deficits and coupon clipping. Why would banks bother to risk making loans to new ventures when they can create money to finance government debt and then just sit back and let the government levy the taxes to repay principal and interest?

Once of my favourite examples is this. If you were lucky enough to win a million dollars in a lottery and you decided to buy long-term government bonds paying, say, 5.5 percent you would earn $55,000 interest each year. But if a bank increases its capital by $1 million it can buy $20,000,000 in government bonds by creating a deposit for the government. Assuming the same term of bonds and the same interest rate it would earn $1,100,000 in interest, each year, on its original investment of $1 million. And guess who pays that interest? The taxpayers of course!

EURODOLLARS — THE WORLD'S ACHILLES HEEL

This is another case of a profoundly important economic development that was never designed for the role it came to fill. It just began as an expedient. In 1949 when Chairman Mao's forces took control of China they inherited the banks. The communists feared that America would freeze their U.S. accounts so they transferred these assets to a Paris bank on the understanding that they not be converted into francs but remain in U.S. dollars. It was an ingenious manoeuvre later copied by the Russians.

In addition to maintaining access to the principal currency of international trade, deposits outside the U.S. were not subject to American banking laws so these incentives soon drew other deposits including large blocks of petrodollars which flowed to the Middle East at the time when the Organization of Petroleum Exporting Countries (OPEC) cartel exercised its most rigorous control over the market. There were few places in the world where such large amounts of money could be accommodated so much of it wound up in developing countries which soaked up tens of billions.

As these Eurodollars began to be accepted as an unofficial international currency, American and other banks scrambled to gain equal advantage. In 1960 only eight American banks had branches abroad but by 1972, there were 107. Meanwhile, as competition heated up, the banks were taking unjustifiable risks and were granting loans to second and third rate borrowers. Soon, encouraged by MacNamara and the World Bank, developing countries were loaded up with more debt than they can ever repay.

The seeds of a world financial crisis of unprecedented proportion had been sown and these would raise their ugly heads when a storm of high interest rates rained down upon them in the early 1980s. The debt was too great to be serviced, let alone repaid. It was the beginning of the great re-cycling scam that is still going on. More and more money is lent to pay more and more interest on a debt that was unsustainable twenty years ago and is doubly so today.

From all around the globe taxpayers' money that should have been spent on health, education and the environment is being siphoned off to reward the irresponsible. And the drain will never end until taxpayers revolt and the whole house of mirrors comes crashing down with earth-shattering consequences. That could be the reason that the game is still in play. There is a premonition that, like the blind Sampson, bringing down the roof of the temple might provide the satisfaction of seeing the Philistines crushed in the ruble but at the cost of his life, too.

SUMMARY

That is the essence of the crisis. We have an inter-national banking system that can create as much credit money as it wants. It does just that and saddles the world with a debt load that cannot be repaid. In the absence of strict governmental control the invisible hand of unregulated capital becomes an invisible monster bent on destruction.

George Soros has suggested an international agency to allocate credit on a worldwide basis. But who would do the allocation? How would the pie be divided up? And would the super rich still get the lion's share?

I think there are better solutions that would allow people in each nation state to regain some semblance of control over their own lives and destiny. That might necessitate the end of highly-leveraged international banking as we now know it. If so, so be it.

CHAPTER 9

THE DEATH OF DEMOCRACY

*"Democracy is on trial in the world, on a more
colossal scale than ever before. "*

Charles Fletcher Dole

Government of, by and for the people is a noble ideal
but is there any country where it is being practised? Is a
country really democratic where any candidate for high elected
office who does not have the financial backing of the rich has
little chance of success? Then, once elected, is it really
democratic for legislators to pass laws that benefit their
benefactors to a greater extent than their electors? Finally, is
it democratic for both the executive and the legislature to
abdicate their responsibility for the most powerful economic tool
of all? Especially when their electors suffer undue hardship as
a result? Let's take a quick peek at each question in turn
beginning with that most powerful of economic levers, money.

When America accepted Alexander Hamilton's
preference for the British banking system and rejected Thomas
Jefferson's dire warnings about the effective slavery of the
privately-owned banking system it started down the path of
much unnecessary grief. Several disastrous depressions and
innumerable recessions were a high price to pay for Hamilton's
obsession. If he were alive today it would be interesting to see
if he would recant his prediction that "a little debt might be a
national blessing. " Five and a half trillion dollars? Some debt!
Some blessing!

The volatility and unpredictability of the private banking

system led to demands for reform and central banks appeared to be part of the answer. They were expected to regulate the excesses of highly-leveraged, panic prone private institutions. In the United States the Federal Reserve System was established in 1913, no doubt with high expectations. That these expectations were not met is readily apparent to anyone who will take the time to read the record. Even some of the Fed's sponsors were soon disillusioned.

William Jennings Bryan, who acted as Democrat whip and is credited with a major effort in getting the Federal Reserve Act of 1913 passed, later said: "In my long political career, the one thing I genuinely regret is my part in getting the banking and currency legislation (FR Act) enacted into law."[1] Senator Carter Glass, one of the original sponsors of the Act of 1913, said on June 17, 1938: "I never thought the Federal Bank System would prove such a failure. The country is in a state of irretrievable bankruptcy."[2] An early view from the Oval Office sounds the same note. President Woodrow Wilson, just three years after passage of the Act wrote: "A great industrial nation is controlled by its system of credit. Our system of credit is concentrated (in the Federal Reserve System). The growth of the nation, therefore, and all our activities are in the hands of a few men.... We have come to be one of the worst ruled, one of the most completely controlled and dominated governments in the civilized world."[3]

These observations were justified by the Fed's role in the Great Depression. When the Federal Reserve Banks closed their doors on March 4, 1933, "The central banking system, set up primarily to render impossible the restriction of payments by commercial banks, itself joined the commercial banks in a more widespread, complete, and economically disturbing restriction of payments than had ever been experienced in the history of the country. One can certainly sympathize with [Herbert] Hoover's comment about that episode: 'I concluded [the Reserve Board] was indeed a weak reed for a nation to lean on in time of trouble.'"[4] Not only has there been little change in attitude since the 1930s, it appears that little has been learned from the experience. Americans still put their trust in a system regulated by a Fed which gives the interests of the banks and the money-lenders a higher priority than the interests of the country. A legitimate question is why, when the system has been such a disaster for so long, that nothing has been done about it.

The only time that central bankers really came through with the goods was to help save "democracy" when it was threatened by Adolf Hitler in World War II. Then they came through with some creative financing. First, they kept interest rates very low by buying and offering to buy government securities in the open market. Second, they increased their portfolios of government securities quite dramatically which was the equivalent of creating money for the government interest free, or virtually interest free. The interest paid to central banks on these securities was returned to government as profit so the net cost was close to zero. This kind of interest-free accommodation by central banks should not be confused with government-created debt-free money like Lincoln's greenbacks. One is included in the total debt that has to be repaid and the other is not.

The change of heart was to be short-lived, however. Almost as soon as the war was over and "democracy" guaranteed for bankers and others, the Fed began to tip the balance of its priorities more in the direction desired by financial markets. At first privately and then publicly the Fed asked to be relieved of its wartime commitment to support the price of long-term Treasury bonds at a level that would keep the yield from rising above 2.5 percent.

The Treasury, of course, had a vested interest in a guaranteed market for its new issues. There was also political concern about the effect on the price of 2.9% savings bonds that millions of Americans had bought for patriotic reasons. This was a sensitive subject with President Harry Truman who recalled his experience with World War I bonds he had bought during his service in the army. So he was most reluctant to see another generation submitted to the pain that he had felt.

In an effort to hold the line he summoned the Board of Governors to the White House but was unable to convince them.

A committee of Treasury and Fed officials was created to break the impasse and it finally recommended what became known as the Treasury-Federal Reserve Accord of 1951 which gave the Treasury a little time to adapt after which the Fed would once again reign supreme.

There is little doubt that long-term rates could not be held at 2.5% very long in the face of the inflationary pressures generated by the Korean War. But had that been the only issue it could have been resolved in other ways. The real issue, in my opinion, was who would have the final authority for setting interest rates and controlling the money supply — the Fed or the duly elected representatives of the people. That is still the central issue today. Should the world be run by unelected, unaccountable — in practice, if not in theory - central bankers or by politicians who can be turfed out if they err. Is it to be dictatorship or democracy?

It is a moot point whether the mild recession of 1960 was a factor in Richard Nixon's narrow loss to J.F. Kennedy in the presidential election of that year. There is no doubt that Fed Chairman Paul Volcker's resolute determination to crush inflation by monetary means was a principal factor in Jimmy Carter's defeat in 1980.

I had just been a member of Louis S. St. Laurent's government for a few weeks before it was defeated by the Bank of Canada in 1957. The Bank had refused to allow the Minister of Finance, Walter Harris, to increase the universal Old Age Pension by $10 a month. The compromise of $6 a month, to compensate for inflation to that date, was considered an outrage by pensioners and the final straw for electors who considered the government arrogant and out of touch. Since then, three additional Canadian governments have been defeated on the basis of economic conditions determined by the central bank, rather than over-rule it on behalf of electors.

More frightening than the political carnage already caused by central banks is twenty-five years of neo-classical brainwashing to the effect that they should be above and exempt from any control by either the executive or legislative branches of government. That is the central message of Milton

Friedman's theology. In order to confirm my understanding I wrote Professor Friedman to ask him why he opted for one extreme of 100% cash reserves or the other extreme of zero cash reserves rather than settling for some intermediate position like 50% or perhaps 25% as had been the case for U.S. federal banks in the early part of the century.

He replied: "The answer to your question is very simple: the objective is to get the government out of the business of having anything to do with lending and investing activities of private financial entities. Either 100 percent reserves, i.e. a narrow banking system, which is what I would prefer, or zero percent reserves so government has no supervisory power over banks has that result. That is why I prefer that extreme to anything in between."[5]

To me the naiveté of this position is mindboggling. The whole notion of absolute independence for a banking system which is a creation of the Congress I consider to be preposterous. In an earlier book I raised a rhetorical question. I asked readers if they could imagine any congressman introducing a motion to this effect: "Be it resolved that the Congress of the United States hereby issues exclusive licences to chartered banks to manufacture all or nearly all of the new money put into circulation each year and to direct and divide it in accordance with their own best interests and those of their friends and close associates."[6] Doesn't that strike you as silly? Yet that, in reality, is exactly what the Banking Act of 1935 did. It gave privately-owned chartered banks, regulated only by a federal reserve system owned by some of them, an exclusive mandate to manufacture or create money – apart from the small amount of treasury notes still in existence. Monetary sovereignty for the United States of America has been delegated to private banks.

The system is so silly that I really have difficulty knowing how to describe it. In the Fall of 1998 the world financial system was coming apart at the seams so the President of the United States, allegedly the most powerful man on earth, suggested a general interest rate cut might help stabilize the situation. But Fed Chairman Alan Greenspan, who only a few weeks earlier had confirmed that inflation was his principal fear,[7] sat on his hands, as did Hans Tietmeyer, President of the German Bundesbank.

Days later, after demonstrating who the most powerful man in America really was, Greenspan acted. A second unexpected interest rate cut stabilized financial markets worldwide and the bull market reappeared. The mere thought of so much autocratic and unaccountable power should be highly offensive to all true democrats. Personally, the fact that the trend to absolute, monetary monarchy is spreading like the plague fills me with horror.

I was dismayed when the first act of the newly elected British Prime Minister Tony Blair was to abdicate to the Bank of England the ultimate authority to set interest rates. If that action had been taken by a Conservative prime minister I would have understood. But a Labour prime minister? Incredible! It is just a mark of how pervasive the neo-classical religion has become. The members of the European Union are putting their fate in the hands of an institution modelled on the Bundesbank. Japan was conned into going down the same dead end road. And Third World countries are systematically abandoning political control of their central banks at the insistence of the IMF and the World Bank.

Where are the champions of democracy? Have the British locked up the Magna Carta in the archives beyond the reach of inquiring minds? And what about the Americans? Where are the sons and daughters of those early patriots who fought a War for Independence to free the colonies from taxation without representation and the tyranny of British monetary control? (Any bank which is allowed to create money to buy government bonds or T-Bills is imposing a tax on the people.)

Can you think of anything more ironic than for a country that fought a War for Independence to free itself from the evils of the British banking system to now be imposing that same system on "colonies" all over the world? They are no longer allowed to print their own money but are forced, instead, to borrow from international banks, many of them American.

This chapter is being written in the days leading up to November 11, 1998, the anniversary of the end of World War I and the day several countries observe to pay tribute to all those who fought and died to preserve democracy for us. By abdicating our hard won freedoms and permitting a return to monarchial absolutism we have broken faith with those who died.

RESPONSIBLE GOVERNMENT

Not only have politicians delegated their monetary power to unaccountable autocrats they are increasingly passing laws favorable to a tiny minority of their electors — the richest and most powerful. This is a travesty of responsible government where elected representatives are supposed to represent the best interests of all the people without fear or favor.

When I studied political science at university one of my most colorful and entertaining professors, McGregor Dawson, lauded the principle of responsible government. Voters elect representatives to serve a term of office and for that time, which varies from one country or legislature to another, they are given complete freedom to exercise their best judgement on behalf of their electors. If they are true to their mandate they are likely to be re-elected. If not their fate is to be replaced by someone else.

It is a convincing theory and Dawson certainly sold it to me and for many years I was a stout defender. Many of the issues facing electors are so complex that only someone in the thick of debate would possess sufficient knowledge to intelligently vote yea or nay. That was the party line that I would pass along to constituents or students who might question the wisdom of some particular piece of legislation.

Eventually I began to recognize a slightly hollow ring to the argument. Indeed the legislation was complex and the volume so great that I found myself voting for bills I hadn't even read. Worse, I recognized that I invariably voted with the party even when my conscience would have led me to a different conclusion. This is a far greater problem in the parliamentary system than it is in the congressional system but still there are times, as we saw during the tense impeachment proceedings of 1998-1999, when most of the allegedly reasonable Republicans were of one view and most of the allegedly reasonable Democrats were of an opposite view. This is not the coincidence of identical conclusions reached as a result of exercising independent judgement.

Much more worrisome is the ongoing bias of legislators. Tax cuts for the rich are proposed as an economic stimulus to create jobs and alleviate poverty. That may have been the effect in the era of John F. Kennedy, before the income gap was so great as to be a threat to both the economy and democracy. In early 1998 the journal *Smart Money* advised that the top 1 percent of Americans — fewer than 3 million individuals — now have incomes equal to the total of the incomes of the bottom third of all Americans, 88 million people. The top income earners, on balance, already have all the homes, cars, yachts, clothes, food and drink that they can reasonably use so a tax cut for them is more likely to be used to acquire more stocks and bonds rather than products of the real economy which would create employment and income for people at the bottom end of the scale.

Many of the most important measures of recent years have been tilted in favor of the rich and powerful. The North American Free Trade Agreement, for example, was designed to be of principal benefit to banks and big corporations on the acquisition trail. It was sold, of course, on the basis of the general benefit. But this is largely myth and public relations hype. I have not yet seen any conclusive evidence of significant benefit to American, Canadian and Mexican workers. On the contrary, there has been a strong downward pressure on wages in the U.S. and Canada and only a small minority of Mexican workers have been blessed while the majority have been ravaged by the dollarization of their domestic prices.

The Multilateral Agreement on Investment is an even more powerful and diabolical plot to line the pockets of the rich at the expense of the poor.   Not one of the governments of the United Kingdom, the United States, Australia, Canada and New Zealand told the people the truth about the treaty and the loss of sovereignty that was involved. I am informed that other OECD countries were equally secretive. This is representative democracy at its darkest and most sinister level. Now that ordinary people are catching on and organizing protests there is an effort to stifle dissent as when the Swiss police arrested MAI protesters without cause and without warrant.[8]

Why is the deck being stacked in favor of big corporations and against main streeters? One can only suspect that it has something to do with the way politics is financed. The cost of getting elected is so great that few individuals can afford it on their own. With rare exceptions it requires corporate support by one means or another — lots of it.

I am not saying that money is everything. I know it isn't. My textbook of personal experience includes two examples of very wealthy men who ran for office, spent a lot of their own money, and lost. And the fact that the Republicans spent $110 million more than the Democrats in the 1998 U.S. mid-term election didn't tip the balance in their direction. Instead, many of the millions spent on attack ads backfired. Still, in every election there are many routine expenditures essential for a winning campaign and in the majority of cases money does count.

A report in the *New York Times* tells the story. "Over the last decade, victory has increasingly gone to the richest candidate. In 1992, 89 percent of the House candidates with the most money won, as did 86 percent of the richest Senate candidates. ... By 1996, those candidates with the most money won 92 percent of House races and 88 percent of Senate races.

"When the final accounting is done, the 1998 midterm elections will raise the financial bar and break fund-raising records. More than $1 billion was spent to elect a House and a Senate that changed only slightly. A total of $387.3 million was raised by the 775 House candidates, and $243.2 million by the 68 Senate candidates. On top of this was the money raised by the parties: $284.6 million by Republican committees and $173.8 million by Democratic committees."[9]

Incumbents have a built-in advantage, as I know well from experience. Contributors know that statistically the odds favor incumbents so they place their bets accordingly — which helps perpetuate the system. Referring again to the U.S. 1998 midterm election: "In more than 60 House districts, for instance, incumbents had a 10-to-1 cash advantage. More incumbents were re-elected — 98 percent — than at any time in the past decade, one of the highest rates in this century."[10]

The astronomical cost of modern elections, which virtually guarantees that anyone who has not been given the seal of approval by the corporate elite has little chance of success, lends credence to the allegation that Congresses and parliaments are just gigantic stage plays sponsored by corporations at regular intervals to give the impression that democracy is alive and well. In reality, however, it doesn't matter which actors are hired to stage the play. The script is written for them by what is increasingly known and recognized as the permanent government.

THE PERMANENT GOVERNMENT

It has been described in various ways at various times by various people but I thought Lewis Lapham, editor of *Harper's* magazine, summed it up well in one sentence as part of his 'On Politics, Culture and the Media' keynote address to the Canadian Institute of International Affairs national foreign policy conference in October, 1996. His definition: "The permanent government is the secular oligarchy that comprises the Fortune 500 companies and all their attendant lobbyists, the big media and entertainment syndicates, the civil and military services, the larger research universities and law firms."[11]

That pretty well sums it all up in a way that conforms with my sense of the real politic. The big supranational corporations with their lobbyists, public relations firms and lawyers, the international banks with their close ties to both the Fed and the Treasury Department, not to mention the IMF and World Bank, the close, almost incestuous relationship between Bretton Wood institutions and the State Department, the information conglomerates that blur the lines between the manufacture of news and culture and its dissemination, these are all parts of the permanent government that hold the reigns of real power. It is a power camouflaged by the diversions created by the antics of the politicians comprising the parallel provisional government.

"Just as the Catholic church was the predominant institution in medieval Europe, and the Roman legion the most efficient manifestation of organized force in the 1st and 2nd centuries BC, so also the transnational corporation arranges the affairs of the late 20th century. The American congress and the American president serve at the pleasure of their commercial overlords, all of whom hold firmly to the belief that all government regulation is wicked (that is, the work of the Devil) and that any impulse that runs counter to the manly interests of business is, by definition, soft, effeminate, and liberal. On behalf of the corporations that pay the campaign money, the politicians collect taxes in the form of handsome subsidies and congenial interest rates. The president performs the duties of a mendicant friar — sympathetic to the sufferings of the peasantry but alert to the concerns of the lords and nobles. Fortunately for the domestic tranquillity of the United States, the American political system allows for the parallel sovereignty of two governments, one permanent and the other provisional.

"The permanent government ... hires the country's politicians and sets the terms and conditions under which the citizenry can exercise its right — God-given but increasingly expensive — to life, liberty, and the pursuit of happiness. Obedient to the rule of men, not laws, the permanent government oversees the production of wealth, builds cities, manufactures goods, raises capital, fixes prices, shapes the landscape, and reserves the right to speak to the customers in the language of low motive and base emotion.

"The provisional government is the spiritual democracy that comes and goes on the trend of a political season and oversees the production of pageants. It exemplifies the nation's moral aspirations, protects the citizenry from unworthy or unholy desires, and devotes itself to the mending of the

American soul. Positing a rule of laws instead of men, the provisional government must live within the cage of high-minded principle, addressing its remarks to the imaginary figure known as the thinking man, a superior being who detests superficial reasoning and quack remedies, never looks at *Playboy*, trusts Bill Moyers, worries about political repression in Liberia, reads (and knows himself improved by) the op-ed page of the *Wall Street Journal.*"[12]

About a year before I began to write this book I saw the title of one called *Arrogant Capital*, by Kevin Phillips,[13] and asked my wife to get me a copy. I assumed that it was arrogant money and, as I planned to do something on that subject, I wanted to have it available as one of the dozen or so new books I read each time before I set pen to paper in order to have an up-to-date snapshot of what others are thinking and saying.

When I finally got around to reading it in the summer of 1998 I found, to my amusement, that the arrogant capital was Washington and the principal theme of the book was the parallel between the declining years of succeeding empires — the Dutch, the Spanish, the British, and now the American. In each case the expansion of domestic industry had given way to foreign investment and financial speculation and this had always been the beginning of the end and could be for the U.S. if it doesn't quickly learn the lessons of history.

Phillips also outlined some of the factors involved in the evolution of the permanent government in Washington and the impact this is having on the political process. He cites James Thurber, a professor of government at American University, who estimated that the number of lobbyists and people associated with lobbying activity in and around Washington at ninety-one thousand, including 69,000 people working for trade and membership associations, in 1993. "The number of U.S. corporations with offices in Washington grew from under a hundred in 1950 to more than five thousand in 1990, at which time they probably employed from 5,000 to 7,500 people. Foreign corporate giants were just as interested in Washington outposts as the U.S. megafirms. Of the fifty largest foreign multinationals, two thirds have offices in Washington, including giants like Siemens, British Petroleum, Rhone-Poulenc, and Toyota. Close to four hundred foreign corporations have some kind of representative on hand. We should also count the foreign embassies, about 150 of them with perhaps 10,000 employees. Many have been nerve centers for lobbying campaigns using hired government-relations consultants, lawyers, lobbyists, and trade experts."[14]

Even more interesting to an old pol like me was who was doing the lobbying. Scores of ex-Congressmen were lobbying their former colleagues. Dozens of ex-staff directors of permanent committees were capitalizing on the knowledge gained and connections made while on the public payroll. One senses that the pay and perks associated with lobbying were viewed as dividends earned.

"Nineteen ninety-three, however, pushed Washington interest-groupism to a new plane. Not only did the new president bargain with key lobbies almost from the start, but two congressmen actually resigned their offices — without waiting to serve out their terms — in order to take up well-paid and influential lobbying posts. Representative Willis Gradison, Republican of Ohio, resigned to head up the Health Insurance Association of America, while Representative Glenn English, Democrat of Oklahoma, left Congress to run the National Rural Electric Cooperative Association. Nobody could remember anything like it. But senior White House officials were doing the same thing. The White House legislative director left to become the chairman of Hill and Knowlton Worldwide, while the deputy chief of staff left to take over the U.S. Telephone Association. Neither had served a full year in his job, and their departures mocked the president's earlier campaign promises. The exodus from both the legislative and executive branches was unprecedented, and doubly revealing of where Washington's real power had migrated."[15]

THE FREE (?) PRESS

A free press has long been touted as the guardian of democracy. It has been regarded as the unofficial guardian of truth keeping arrogant and arbitrary governments in line. That role, however, is subject to serious question on several fronts. Many of the largest, most powerful news outlets are either part of, or under the direct control of the permanent government. Others have adopted the neo-classical, globalization agenda as their own and sell it with the zeal of a religious convert.

In Lewis Lapham's words: "The *Wall Street Journal*, probably the most widely read newspaper in the country, heavily favours the conservative side on all questions of public policy; both the *Washington Post* and the *New York Times* fortify their op-ed pages with columnists who strongly defend the established order, and during the debate in congress about the North American Free Trade Agreement and the General Agreement on Tariffs and Trade all three papers omitted any references to the testimony of Ralph Nader, Jimmy Goldsmith, and anybody else who might have had something unpleasant to say about the social and political side-effects of international trade agreements subverting the will of a nominally sovereign people."[16]

This is a critically important issue. National governments have given up huge chunks of sovereignty under NAFTA and GATT and propose to give up even more under the MAI, the Free Trade Agreement of the Americas and other trade (read investment) treaties currently under negotiation. While governments and press try desperately to keep the consequences under a veil of secrecy, debate about the balance of benefit, who wins and who loses, is taboo.

The Canadian press is so heavily loaded on the neo-conservative side that it is almost impossible for dissenting voices to be heard. Neither of the two nationally distributed financial papers, the *Globe and Mail* and the *Financial Post*, now part of the *National Post*, will print articles critical of the banking system or globalized financial services. On rare occasions one slips through as a token of fairness but the balance is so loaded that it's like a platoon fighting a brigade. The public are not exposed to alternative ideas and consequently tend to accept the ones they read as ultimate truth.

Reflecting back over the years I recall that newspapers

have almost always displayed a bias and often a very strong one. But in many cities there were competing papers trumpeting diametrically opposed views. Today, it seems to me, there is much more of a sameness, the conventional neo-liberal ideology is almost universal. Only fringe papers, usually one or two person enterprises, speak in genuine opposition. The mainstream press has, in effect, almost opted out of its role as one of the major checks and balances in the system.

There are many examples that set off alarm bells but two or three are illustrative. In a lawsuit filed against Fox Television's Tampa Florida affiliate, WTVT, in April 1988 two former employees, Jane Akre and Steve Wilson, alleged that they were fired for refusing to broadcast lies about Monsanto's controversial bovine growth hormone, rBGH, [also known as rBST, recombinant bovine somatotropin] now being used by many of the nation's dairy farmers. The journalists say they were fired after completing a four-part series on BGH in the Florida milk supply.

The series alleged, among other things, that supermarkets in Florida had been selling milk from cows injected with BGH despite promises from those supermarkets that they would not buy milk from treated cows until the hormone gained widespread public acceptance. The hormone had been approved by the U.S. Food and Drug Administration (FDA) in 1993 over the objections of independent scientists who contend that its use poses health risks to milk drinkers. Such concerns have led the European Union, Australia and New Zealand to prohibit the use of BGH in cows.

Wilson says that just prior to the first scheduled air date, February 24, 1997, Monsanto's outside libel attorney sent a threatening letter to Roger Ailes, president of Fox Network News. As a result of the letter the series was postponed and Wilson and Akre agreed to go back to Monsanto to give the company another chance to respond to the allegations in the story which only drew another letter from Monsanto's lawyer. It soured relations between the reporters and their bosses and, according to Wilson, the letters were the beginning of a successful campaign by Monsanto to kill the story.

A meeting was held at the station March 5, 1997, to discuss the issue, but Wilson and Akre were not invited. "After that, the script was reworked," Wilson says: "Changes were ordered in the script. We were essentially presented with an order to run the script in the altered fashion that Fox lawyers suddenly thought was the way to tell the story." When the reporters refused to air what they considered to be false and misleading information, WTVT's vice president and general manager, David Baglan, according to Wilson, told them "you will either broadcast this story the way we are telling you to broadcast it, or we will fire you in 48 hours."

Refusing to be cowed, Wilson and Akre stood up to the corporate bosses. Wilson told Baglan, "If you fire us for refusing to broadcast this information that we have already documented to you is false and misleading, if you do that, we will go directly to the Federal Communications Commission (FCC) and file a complaint. You cannot knowingly broadcast news which you know to be false and misleading."

After threatening to go to the FCC, the station responded by offering about $200,000 to the reporters if they would agree to a gag order. Wilson and Akre refused and were then assigned to re-write the story 73 times over the course of the remaining nine months on their contract. At least six air dates were set and cancelled by the station. The reporters were fired on December 2, 1997.

In the lawsuit filed against the station, Wilson and Akre allege that the station violated the state's whistle-blower statute by firing them after they threatened to report wrongdoing to federal authorities. In a two-page statement, WTVT said that it "ended the employment of the Wilson/Akre team when it became apparent that their journalistic differences could not be resolved despite the station's extraordinary efforts to complete this story." The station also denied offering a "hush money" payment to the two reporters.

Wilson was having none of the station's explanation. "We set out to tell Florida consumers the truth a giant chemical company and a powerful dairy lobby clearly doesn't want them to know," Wilson said: "That used to be something investtigative reporters won awards for. Sadly, as we've learned the hard way, it's something you can be fired for these days whenever a news organization places more value on its bottom line than on delivering the news to its viewers honestly."[17]

Another case that demonstrates the pervasive influence of Monsanto involves England's leading environmental magazine, *The Ecologist*. Its September/October 1998 issue carried a special article on Monsanto and genetic engineering. Penwell, a small Cornwall-based company that has printed *The Ecologist* for 26 years decided to shred all 14,000 copies because England's stringent libel laws apply to printers as well as publishers.

"After the pulping of the Monsanto issue, the editors of *The Ecologist* then found another printer who printed a second run of 16,000 copies."[18] But then the U.K.'s two major retailers refused to carry the magazine on their newsstands.

One wonders where governments are in all of this. I was both surprised and disappointed to learn that the U.S. Department of Agriculture had been involved in the development of terminator seeds — seeds from which plants grow that cannot themselves produce fertile seed. How does that square with the needs of a world in which, according to a top official of the State Department, nearly one billion people go to bed hungry or severely malnourished every night.[19]

Surely public debates on these controversial issues should be encouraged rather than discouraged. In the Fall of 1998 Canadians witnessed a shameful attempt by their government to gag six Health Canada scientists who had reservations about the safety of the bovine growth hormone. When the government finally agreed, under pressure, to let three of them appear before a Senate committee it still attempted unsuccessfully to send their superior with them to "lead" them and "intervene as required."[20]

Again Monsanto was in the background pressuring the government not to release information it brands as confidential. "Monsanto lawyers in St. Louis and its Government Relations representatives in Ottawa have expressed concern that, in responding to senate committee and others, we may choose to disclose protected information ... They also have commented on leaks of confidential information, apparently by Health Protection Branch employees." The government memo continued: 'this concern could become industry-wide' and have implications for other applications for drug approvals."[21]

So who is looking out for the interests of ordinary people? It should be the special ones they elect to represent them but that is no longer the case. The permanent government has become so all pervasive that the provisional governments of elected representatives are little more than puppets whose moves are directed by the strings of big business. Politicians know that they should reduce their reliance on corporate financing but when push comes to shove they don't because they have become too dependent.

The press, too, is fast abdicating its role as the champion of the underdog. Its ownership is so concentrated and its ideology so fixed that it no longer does justice to its role as the "loyal opposition". There are a few exceptions, of course, and we thank God for those. But they are rare and have about as much impact on mainstream thinking as flies on the elephant's back.

So there really is no one except a clutch of mavericks, skeptics and concerned individuals banded together in non-governmental organizations, fighting valiantly against incalculable odds yet they fight on, knowing that they must. They are in mortal combat with a system out of control.

Former Harvard professor David Korten sums it up succinctly. "Contrary to its claims, capitalism is showing itself to be the mortal enemy of democracy and the market. Its relationship to democracy and the market economy is now much the same as the relationship of a cancer to the body whose life energy it expropriates.

"Cancer is a pathology that occurs when an otherwise healthy cell forgets that it is part of the body and begins to pursue its own unlimited growth without regard to the consequences for the whole. The growth of the cancerous cell deprives the healthy cells of nourishment and ultimately kills both the body and itself. Capitalism does much the same to the societies it infests."[22]   It is really unfettered capitalism that is destroying the system that gave it life.

In his book *Global Public Policy: Governing without Government?*[23]   World Bank economist Wolfgang H. Reinicke describes the transfer of decision-making authority from national governments to international bodies such as the World Trade Organization and the Bank for International Settlements as a "democracy deficit". This is a masterpiece of understatement. His highly esoteric apologia for globalization is based on the assumption that it is good for humanity. If the premise is false, which is becoming increasingly obvious, then the trend to plutocracy must be challenged. The real choice is between a system governed by big banks and supranational corporations for their benefit, or government of, by and for the people on behalf of the common good.   Globalized capitalism, unrestrained by nation states, is incompatible with democracy.

CHAPTER 10

WORLD WAR III —
THE BANKS vs THE PEOPLE

"The old pro-slaver serpent, beaten in the South, crawled up North and put on anti-slavery clothes and established his headquarters in Wall Street."

Congressman Alexander Campbell[1]

The above quote was prophetic. One brand of slavery was abolished on the basis of high and noble principles, no man or woman should be forced to live as a mere chattel of some other person. The emancipation was less than complete, however, because one form of bondage was replaced by another. Debt became the new and merciless slavemaster that deprived millions of people of their right to liberty and the pursuit of happiness.

The war of liberation and emancipation from the tyranny of the fractional reserve system is not new. It could be called the 200 year war because its grievous consequences have spanned more than two centuries. Still the central issue has not yet been resolved. The issue is who is going to run the world and for whose benefit will it be run? Will it be run by the big international banks and their offspring the supranational corporations primarily for their own benefit, the privileged few? Or will the world be governed by its citizens in pursuit of the greatest benefit for the greatest number?

This is far from an academic question. In fact, it is pivotal. Let your mind's eye scan the world's financial trouble spots and almost invariably the word "bank" will appear in the

141

context of the chaos. In the midst of the credit crunch of the early 1980s Federal Reserve Board chairman Paul Volcker had to jawbone banks into making new loans to Latin American countries so they could pay the interest on old loans until he could get the IMF to ride to the rescue with taxpayers' money. Without the ruse, word would soon have leaked out that several of America's largest and most powerful banks were technically insolvent.[2]

While world leaders were patting themselves on the back for rescuing Mexico's financial system little was said about the Mexican government's proposal to convert $62 billion in bad bank loans bought by the Mexican deposit insurance corporation, Fobaproa, into public debt. The debate centered around the fact that the move could increase the public debt from 26 to 42 percent of GDP and, equally contentious, the list of 310 top creditors included some of Mexico's best known and richest businessmen. It was one more case of taxpayers' money being used to bail out the banks and the rich in spite of the fact that outlays for social spending in Mexico had dropped by 40 percent since the peso crisis of 1994.[3]

Japan's troubled banks will wind up taking taxpayers for the biggest ride in history. They are saddled with more than 77 trillion yen ($879 U.S.) billion in problem loans. An agency is being set up to buy those loans and it is inevitable that the net losses will become part of the national debt.[4] The Japanese experience is the largest and most striking example of what has been happening to banks in many countries.

Even in those countries where the banks are not in trouble there is considerable disenchantment due to practices that put profits before people. In Canada the big banks have been cutting back on service in a deliberate attempt to force customers to use automated tellers. They have also been closing branches, especially in rural areas, and forcing people to travel many miles to meet their banking needs.

Similar complaints are heard from Australia where the country's big four banks closed one-sixth of their branches in four years. This, plus growing resentment against rising fees for services, profits and executive salaries has led to revolt in the outback. When the last of the big banks pulled out of the railway town of Henty, New South Wales, the population fought back. A retired farmer, Milton Taylor, led a movement to establish a Henty Community Branch of the Bendigo Bank, a bank inspired by Mohammed Yunus, founder of the Grameen Bank in Bangladesh, who was named winner of the Sydney Peace Prize in November, 1998.[5] Populist solutions of this nature are reminiscent of the 1930s.

DISSENT AND POPULISM

Dissatisfaction with the banking system ebbs and flows more or less in proportion to the economic circumstances existing at the time or the personal experience of the skeptic. One man who understood the financial process was Alexander Campbell, a mining engineer and entrepreneur elected to Congress from Illinois in 1874 for a single term on a Democrat-Independent ticket. In *The True Greenback* he wrote: "The war has resulted in the complete overthrow and utter extinction of chattel slavery on this continent, but it has not destroyed the principle of oppression and wrong. The old pro-slaver serpent, beaten in the South, crawled up North and put on anti-slavery clothes and established his headquarters in Wall Street where ... he now, through bank monopolies and non-taxed bonds, rules the nation more despotically than under the old regime. ... I assert ... that an investment of a million dollars under the National Banking Law, or in non-taxed government securities, will yield a larger net income to its owner than a like amount invested in land and slaves employed in raising cotton and sugar did in the South in the palmiest days of the oligarchy."[6]

In the late 19th century a combination of high interest rates on the part of the banks and government largesse toward the railroads led to acute unhappiness especially on the part of the farmers. From this developed a kind of populism which embraced both the nationalization of money-creation and of the railroads. The platform of the People's Party of America in 1892, for example, called for "a national currency, safe, sound, and flexible, issued by the General Government only, a full legal tender for all debts, public and private, and this without the use of banking corporations. ..."[7]

Their presidential candidate, Brigadier General James Baird Weaver, received more than a million votes in the 1892 election and probably would have done even better if the banks had not asked many of their industrial customers to assemble their employees and warn them of the danger inherent in voting for the People's Party of America. The populist movement eventually petered out as gold was discovered in Alaska and good times returned.

THE GREAT DEPRESSION

Although there were four recessions between the turn of the century and the crash of 1929, there was little interest in monetary reform until disaster struck. Then the original backers of the federal reserve system became disenchanted with their creation and I often wondered what had gone wrong.

So, for "light" reading on a holiday in March, 1994, I took along *A Monetary History of the United States 1867-1960* the 800 plus page opus by Milton Friedman and Anna Jacobson Schwartz.[8] Reading it is enough to make one cry – or to get very, very angry, depending on the mood of the moment. It chronicles the failure of the system to provide consistent and measured monetary growth proportionate to the potential for increased goods and services; the inability of the Fed to prevent widescale bank failures; and the near-total paralysis of the system when it came to addressing the needs of the real economy, especially during the Great Depression.

As someone who had long believed that the Great Depression was the ultimate in economic folly I was fascinated to learn that the term depression was applied to create the impression that the disaster which began in 1929 was in some way less severe than a "panic", the word previously associated in the public's mind with severe economic downturns. In retrospect it was just another ruse to mitigate the potential backlash from one more overdose of human misery when the banking system failed.

Will Rogers, the great American humorist and folk hero reported general agreement as to who was responsible for the monetary mess. On February 24, 1932, he warned that: "you can't get a room in Washington ... Every hotel is jammed to the doors with bankers from all over America to get their 'hand out' from the Reconstruction Finance Corporation ... And I have asked the following prominent men in America this question, 'What group have been more responsible for this financial mess, the farmers? ... Labor? ... Manufacturers? ... Tradesmen, or Who?' ... And every man – Henry Ford, Garner, Newt Baker, Borah, Curtis, and a real financier, Barney Baruch – without a moment's hesitation said, 'Why, the big bankers.' ... *Yet they have the honor of being the first group to go on the 'dole' in America!* "[9]

There may have been consensus as to who was responsible for the crisis but there was certainly no agreement on what to do about it. The contrasting attitudes of politicians, elected to serve the people, and the economic elite strikes a familiar chord.

"In Congress, however, there was growing support for increased government expenditures and for monetary expansion, proposals widely castigated by the business and financial community as 'greenbackism' and 'inflationary'. On its part, the business and financial community, and many outside it, regarded federal deficits as a major source of difficulty. Pressure to balance the budget finally resulted in the enactment of a substantial tax rise in June 1932. The strength of that sentiment, which, in light of present-day views seems hard to credit, is demonstrated by the fact that in the Presidential campaign of 1932, both candidates ran on platforms of financial orthodoxy, promising to balance the federal budget."[10] Doesn't that sound like déjà vu?

As always in times of trouble the Great Depression of the 1930s renewed the intellectual ferment both in academic and political circles. In the face of a banking system in crisis, in 1933, a number of economists at the University of Chicago produced what later became known as the Chicago Plan. It called for outright public ownership of the Federal Reserve

Banks and the establishment of new institutions that accepted only demand deposits subject to a 100 percent reserve requirement in lawful money and/or deposits with the Reserve's Banks.[11]

One of the eight signatories of the six page memorandum authorizing the plan was Professor H.C. Simons. Three years later, in March 1936, he summed up succinctly the essence of his concern. "Given release from a preposterous financial structure, capitalism might endure indefinitely its other afflictions; but, assuming continuance of our financial follies..., it becomes academic to consider how the system might be saved."[12]

President Franklin D. Roosevelt must have considered the enlightened, though radical, views of professors Lloyd Mints, and Henry Simons and their colleagues at the University of Chicago — views similar to those of Yale's Irving Fisher. In the end, however, it was the bankers' interests that prevailed when they persuaded the Congress to entrench the fractional reserve system.

Not only have private banks managed to hang on to their near monopoly to create money they have also managed to persuade regulators to allow them to increase their leverage, i.e. the number of times they can lend the same money. Remember that when the Bank of England was established just over 300 years ago, the initial leverage was 2 to 1. In effect they were allowed to lend their capital twice. Over the years, as we have already seen, the ratio has steadily increased. As the end of the twentieth century approaches leverages of 20 to 1 are routine and 25 or 30 to 1 not uncommon.

Unfortunately, as we have seen too often, the higher the leverage the greater the risk. A bank with a large portfolio of bonds, for example, could see its equity wiped out by a sharp rise in interest rates which send the market value of the bonds in its portfolio plummeting. In layman's terms, the higher the leverage the bigger the credit bubble. One sharp pinprick is enough to deflate it.

A HOPELESS SYSTEM

A problem of global proportion is the mountain of debt for which there is no practical mechanism for repayment. It is easy — too easy — for big banks to create credit money. All it requires is a book — a computer — entry to cross with the bonds or notes they accept as collateral. But once they have created the money they have to get it back. Failure to do so has to be booked as a loss and taken off their bottom line. A portfolio that includes more than 5 percent of non-performing loans is enough to wipe them out — if the truth were known.

But there is no way they can get all their credit money back. The money doesn't exist to pay it all back. The total, which includes billions in interest, is far, far too great to ever be repaid. Not only is it impossible to repay the principal, the world is unable to pay the current interest without going further into debt because the tab for interest is greater than the growth rate of the world economy.

A WORLDWIDE CONFIDENCE GAME

As we discussed, when Third World debt became too great to service at interest rates imposed by the First World, the IMF was jaw-boned into making loans with which the interest could be paid. In layman's terms, the IMF acted as a portable compressor putting fresh air into one flat tire after another. If it hadn't, and the true state of Third World debt had been allowed to surface, the big banks would have been as flat broke as the punctured tires constantly in need of reflating.

This action didn't solve the problem, however. It just created the illusion that the Third World vehicles were really mobile. Actually the IMF action only exacerbated the problem because they charged for the air-fill and that increased the burden on the overloaded vehicles even more. Additional refills were required and when the IMF couldn't move from one soft tire to the next fast enough it asked the World Bank to bring in its compressor because the illusion of stability had to be maintained at all costs.

When financial markets finally sensed that what they were seeing was some kind of legerdemain, a rocky ride of financial volatility followed. This lasted until the Fed and the G7 fire brigade came up with a combination of interest rate cuts and standby credits to calm frazzled nerves. Their particular black magic amounted to more of the same. The IMF would be given access to additional taxpayers money and government guarantees to keep the compressor going for a while. It was one of the most naive packages imaginable but about what you would expect from government leaders advised by officials reading from the Washington consensus of neo-classical nonsense. Their basic assumption is that the system is self-correcting and that time will solve the problem. Any national or world economy based on a highly-leveraged banking system to create nearly all of its money has never been self-correcting and never will be. It is basically flawed! It is a boom-bust system.

CAPITALISM's BLIND SPOT

When talking about capitalism it is important to be a little bit precise. The Soviet system, which we call communism, was also a capitalist system in the sense that large accumulations of capital were in play. But the ownership and administration of the capital was in government hands so we labelled it communism. What we loosely call capitalism is a system where most of the capital is privately owned and administered. It is not this decentralized, and consequently more efficient, system that is at fault. It is the banking and monetary system that supports it. That is where the problem lies.

Keith Helmuth has a novel way of explaining the debt problem caused by compound interest. "At this point there are two obvious questions: (1) Isn't the money that exists needed for circulation in the productive economy until such time as it goes to pay back the loans which created it, and (2) if a part of the money which is in circulation in the productive economy is used to satisfy compound interest charges, (for which no corresponding money has been created) won't there be a short-fall in the ability of the productive economy to repay the debt it had previously contracted? The answer to both questions is, "yes". Under this arrangement the financial system captures back more money that it created. Capital accumulates in the financial sector and is depleted in the productive sector. The working capital of the productive economy is like a flock of chickens in the farmyard of society. Compound interest is like a chicken hawk which periodically swoops in, nabs a hen, and takes it out of production.[13] Eventually we run out of hens.

There are two very different ways of describing the consequences of this phenomenon. The most common one is to say that capitalism tends to overproduce. Look at the situation existing today. There are too many car manufacturers so it is feared that cars will soon be a glut on the market. There are too many steel producers so many are being accused of dumping their products on other countries. There is a surplus of nickel, copper and aluminum so production is being cut back and new developments delayed. North American farmers face disaster because they have far more grain than they can sell at break-even prices. The list of surpluses could go on and on.

The opposite way of looking at the world situation is this. Millions of people are undernourished or starving because they don't have enough food. Millions are sick because they don't have clean water to drink or health care available. Millions are homeless because they can't afford shelter. My own city of Toronto passed a resolution in November 1998 declaring homelessness to be a "National Disaster". Why is this so? In part, at least, because both federal and provincial levels of government stopped building affordable housing. Why did they do this? To balance their budgets, of course. They had bought into the Washington consensus.

So you have a world of stark contrasts. There is a surplus of food in some countries while people are starving in others. There are unemployed health care workers when people are dying from lack of attention. There are unemployed con-struction workers and homeless people freezing on the street.

There are unemployed needleworkers and millions of people dressed in rags. There is infrastructure in need of replacement and city cores in need of renewal while thousands of able-bodied men and women languish in jail. The broad picture is totally irrational. It is the basic problem we experienced in the 1930s and many times before. There are people willing to provide goods and services and people in need of goods and services but no money to close the circuit.

MONEY IS THE MISSING LINK

Let's start with something nearly all economists agree with. Nominal GDP grows in almost direct proportion to nominal increases in the money supply. So, if too much money is created the economy will operate at capacity but prices will rise. If, on the other hand, too little money is created the economy will operate at less than capacity and unemployment will rise. Many economists believe that it has to be one or the other — either inflation or unemployment. But a strong case can be made that this conclusion, too, is largely myth. But I digress.

If an economy only grows in proportion to the growth in the money supply, and any increase in the money supply has to be created by private banks, then it is axiomatic that the economy can only grow when someone is willing and able to take on additional debt. It can be government, business or individuals – and, historically, it has been a combination of the three — but somebody has to go deeper into debt in order that the economy can grow in a system where nearly all new money is created as debt.

So when the bubble burst in 1929, and the economy ground to a violent halt, the criteria for economic growth vanished. Banks, those that survived, became reluctant lenders while government, business and individuals became reluctant borrowers. So the money supply contracted instead of expanding and economic growth collapsed with it.

I was reminded of this fact in November, 1998, when I heard President Clinton lecturing the Japanese on the evils of protectionism. There are still people who blame the Great Depression on the Smoot-Hawley bill. It may have contributed marginally to the length and depth of the debacle but only marginally. The principal source of the Great Depression, as of earlier depressions and crises, was the collapse of the monetary system. Any economy with the size and diversity of the U.S. economy is capable of financing full employment and maximum utilization internally. All it needs to do is free itself from the slavery of monetary mythology.

THE MAGIC OF LOW INTEREST RATES

It is widely recognized that lower interest rates act as an economic stimulus. Interest sensitive industries like housing, for example, usually respond positively to cuts in interest and output increases. This triggers a ripple effect that reinforces activity in other sectors of the economy.

This is all taken for granted but you seldom hear a discussion of the actual mechanics behind the increase in growth. The explanation is something like this. A cut in interest rates reduces the cost of servicing debt. This increases the capacity of individuals and businesses to assume additional debt. There may also be a psychological impetus as they study the merits of taking on a mortgage or issuing bonds before rates rise again. A decision to act, if the banks are involved in any way, will result in an increase in the money supply and, by extension, higher economic growth.

It is now becoming clear that there are finite limits to this time-tested device. It worked well in the post-World War II era because the total debt to GDP ratio was more or less constant and there was room to manoeuvre. With the advent of monetarism, and an era of higher real interest rates, however, debt to GDP ratios have risen alarmingly, worldwide. There is a limit to the burden of debt that governments, businesses and individuals can carry and there are increasing numbers of countries approaching, reaching or exceeding that limit.

In effect, one of the most powerful engines of economic

growth is being restricted. For lower interest rates to work their magic requires both lenders and borrowers willing and able to make the deal. If one balks there can be no deal, no monetary expansion, no economic growth. It is certainly not original but nevertheless true; you can lead a horse to water but you can't make it drink.

Japan provides the best example to date of the limitations of interest rate policy in a time of financial crisis. Its interest rates are as low as they can go but without effect. The essential conditions for this policy no longer exist in the Japanese economy. Banks are reeling from bad loans and struggling to survive so there is a reluctance to lend. At the same time, business is not in a mood to borrow and expand in the face of huge, unsold inventories and recession conditions. Consumers are concerned about their jobs and future prospects so they, too, are reluctant to take on additional debt load, even if they could. The economy, in the latter part of 1998, faced a no-win situation.

One thing the Japanese were not short of was foreign advice. They were urged to stimulate their economy — presumably for their own sake but mostly for the spin-off benefit to the world economy. They were told to let some of their weaker banks go down the tube. And Madeline Albright, U.S. Secretary of State, wanted Japanese banks to sell their bad loans at firesale prices presumably for the benefits of U.S. vulture funds.

Market economists blame the whole Japanese fiasco on government interference. It had long been held up to the world as a shining example of what can be achieved by a close working relationship between the private and public sectors. When trouble struck the miracle was ignored and attention focused on the problems resulting from the cross holdings of financial and industrial institutions.

Indeed they did cause a problem and it was exacerbated by the large Japanese banks' holdings of industrial stocks which they classified as capital under a special exemption under the Bank for International Settlement rules. But this was a symptom of a deeper problem which was Japanese acceptance of Western-style, highly-leveraged banks. They used their own production planning arrangements which served them well until, like capitalists everywhere, they produced more than they could sell. Then, like capitalists everywhere, they cut back production in a desperate effort to regain an equilibrium between supply and demand. That meant a serious recession with the usual and all too typical consequences of plummeting profits and soaring bankruptcies. The pin was stuck in the credit bubble which translates into hardship all around.

THE CAPITALIST SOLUTION

The tragedy of the Japanese situation in the late '90s is the same one that has plagued capitalism for 200 years. A meltdown in the financial economy precipitates a contraction in the real economy. Business slows and jobs are lost. Government revenues fall and uncertainty reigns as bankruptcies and devaluation of asset values — the prices of factories, farms, stocks and real estate — determine who the winners and losers will be. Historically the losers outnumber the winners by a very high multiple.

The real culprit, of course, is overproduction or, more precisely, as I stated earlier, under-consumption. It is another classic case of insufficient aggregate demand — the phenomenon which is visible to the naked eye but apparently invisible to economists blinded by the pedagogues who taught them. The Japanese economy is capable of producing at a much higher level than it has been in the late '90s. It should be producing at a higher level. It could be with a massive increase in aggregate demand resulting from tax cuts and increased government spending made possible with GCM — as opposed to additional borrowing.

This brings us back to the way money is created and the reason that the money supply is not growing fast enough to support optimum production. In a recent article Professor Paul Krugman, one of a handful of economists that I find worth reading, alleged that central banks had been so pre-occupied with the pursuit of zero inflation that interest rates had fallen to a point where it limited the scope of further reductions to act as an economic stimulus. His point has validity, as we saw in the case of Japan, but it does not address the core issue. At best lower interest rates would only stimulate economic growth to the extent that someone assumed more debt. The core issue is that the level of debt, worldwide, is already unsustainable. Any addition will only increase the magnitude of the inevitable meltdown.

In his excellent book *Arrogant Capital* Kevin Phillips describes this kind of boom-bust capitalism in its most positive light. "For over a century, this had been the genius of American political finance. The legacy of these cycles, of the buoyant capitalist expansion that comes first, followed by a speculative excess, a crash of some degree, and then a populist-progressive countertide, is simply this: they have managed to give America the world's most successful example of self-correcting capitalism. Or at least that has been true until now."[14]

I really think genius is a much too generous word for such a system. I would have been much more favorably impressed if Roosevelt had listened to Simons, Mints and Fisher and ended the Depression in 1933. It was not genius that left millions of people in America and elsewhere in abject poverty for years until they were "rescued" by a terrible war. I will tip my hat to America if it prevents the next great crash from happening by reversing the bankrupting policies of Alexander Hamilton and adopting those of Thomas Jefferson who could see what the bankers would do to us if left to their own devices.

THE JEFFERSON SOLUTION

Thomas Jefferson was the first U.S. president to understand the power and influence of money. Many of the most telling quotations on the subject have been attributed to him. For example he said: "The issuing power of money should be taken from the banks and restored to the government and the people to whom it belongs." Indeed it should, and there are many who believe that banks should not be entitled to create any money whatsoever, as the Jeffersonians claimed.

Certainly they have no entitlement. The patents for money creation belong to the people. Their governments, for reasons that are obscure, have given private banks licenses to act on their behalf, usually without payment of any royalty. The result has been a bonanza for the banks who even charge the patent-holders for the money created for them, for the public good.

A question and answer exchange in the U.S. House Banking Committee with Marriner Eccles, a former governor of the U.S. Federal Reserve, is illustrative.

> *Question*: Mr. Eccles, how did your [private] bank get the money to buy those two billions of government securities?
> *Answer*: We created it.
> *Question*: Out of what?
> *Answer*: Out of the right to issue credit money.

It is not a right, as Mr. Eccles claimed, it is a privilege granted by Congress. It is also a privilege that is greatly abused. Not only do private banks create money for the patent owners when they buy government bonds or T-Bills, they charge interest on it. The patent owners are obliged to repay both principal and interest from taxes they levy. *In effect the bank-created credit money is itself a tax and the government a tax collector for the banks*. Little wonder that Jefferson said: "The bankers and credit dealers of this age have placed the citizens in a prison house."

It is a prison house from which there is no escape as long as private banks maintain their virtual monopoly on money creation. If you consider the mountain of government debt in the U.S., Australia, Canada, France, Germany, New Zealand and the United Kingdom, for example, it is not primarily due to successive generations of profligate politicians, as some neo-classicists suggest. It is primarily due to the way that money is created and the eternal burden of compound interest.

FREEDOM FOR THE SLAVES

There is no great hope for the world's masses of hungry, sick and unemployed people as long as their countries are burdened by a crushing load of debt. There will be precious little hope for the people displaced by automation in developed countries if governments continue to cut back the level of services, reduce employment and put a higher priority on debt reduction than on health care and education. Everywhere I go, except when I talk to my well-to-do-friends, especially in the financial service industries, there is growing despair about the future. Young people are warned that they should not expect to be as well off as their parents.

To replace despair with hope it will be necessary to reverse the system of debtizing the money which has predominated for most of the last two hundred years. First, a big chunk of the existing debt will have to be monetized to reduce the debt burden to manageable proportions, and then the money creation function will have to be democratized so that the cycle will not start all over again.

As I am a pragmatist rather than a purist in monetary matters I will not recommend that the bank licenses be revoked completely. Instead, I will suggest that the money creation function be split 50/50 between the banks and government — at least long enough to find out if that will produce a stable, sustainable recession-free system.

Even that much will pit the banks against the people to an extent that hasn't been seen for generations. It will be a worldwide war of independence. World War III will be the war to restore Jeffersonian democracy and end the plutocracy of the Friedmanites.

CHAPTER 11

Y2K — YEAR OF THE JUBILEE

"I repeat ... that all power is a trust - that we are accountable for its exercise - that, from the people, and for the people, all springs, and all must exist."

Benjamin Disraeli

As the year 2000 approaches one has a sense of awe and wonder at the golden opportunity for a fresh start. Of course there are going to be some world-class headaches as myriad computers pretend they were born a hundred years ago when even the thought of such a machine would have been considered a sure sign of advanced dementia. The discoveries that have been made during the course of the twentieth century have been astonishing and one gets the sense that we are just scratching the surface of total knowledge.

Incredible knowledge does not automatically translate into notable wisdom, however, and it is how we use the information we have available to us that marks our success or failure as a civilization. A computer is of little use to children who cannot afford to go to school. Remarkable techniques for pre-natal surgery offer small comfort to accident victims without access to sterile bandages and tylenol. Risk assessment for derivative traders is far from the minds of millions of people who are malnourished or starving from hunger.

We live in a world where the top two percent of innovators will continue to invent new toys and technologies for their own enjoyment and that of their well-to-do friends. They can afford the benefits of an accelerating pace of scientific and technological experiment.   At the other end of the satisfaction scale you find the vast majority of the world's population who have little to look forward to. The debt burden they carry is like a noose tied around their individual and collective necks.   They are little more than slaves to circumstances which were not of their own making and which are now beyond their control. For them the excitement of participating in a fabulous future will only be possible if they are first freed from the bondage of a crushing burden of oppressive debt.

The problem has been widely recognized by people who care about these things and who are now promoting the Jubilee 2000 campaign.   It started in Britain in 1997 and has since spread around the world.   It aims to collect 22 million signatures calling international lenders to offer significant debt relief to the world's 45 poorest countries by the year 2000. Its petition, intended to be the largest in history, is slated for presentation to leaders of the G7 world's largest economies at their annual meeting in Cologne, Germany, in June 1999.

The year of the Jubilee, which is supported by the Vatican, the Anglican Communion, the World Methodist Council, the World Council of Churches, and others, is based on a biblical precedent to be found in Leviticus 25. Every 50 years was designated the year of the Jubilee, a year of rest, renewal and the beginning of a fresh start. It is a concept the world can use to great advantage in the year 2000.

It is the idea which is relevant today. The world system is now far too complicated for a general and total debt forgiveness which would create as many problems as it would solve. But in a world suffocating from debt we need, and must have, sufficient debt reduction to restore financial stability and preclude another worldwide depression on the one hand, as well as restoring hope to the millions of our fellow earthlings who otherwise face a dead-end of despair.

What is needed, indeed essential, is debt reduction on a scale far more massive than that envisaged by the originators and promoters of the year of the Jubilee. It should not be limited to the world's 45 poorest countries. All the heavily indebted countries are in need of relief. So, too, are most of the rich countries. I doubt that there is a country in the world which is not in need of debt relief in order to provide the level of services expected. The only exceptions might be the islands of Jersey and Guernsey that have no debt because they adopted sensible monetary reform policies generations ago.

I am in no way criticizing the backers of the year of the Jubilee for "thinking small". I can only applaud them for an initiative that I heartily endorse. Few of them would have been exposed to the intricacies of monetary theory and practice and consequently they are unlikely to know just how much is possible without undue hardship to anyone. In my opinion it is quite feasible to pay off the entire $2 trillion or more of Third World debt, as well as reduce the debt of donor countries, without imposing a single additional cent in taxes. On the contrary, reductions in donor country debt would allow significant tax cuts or enhanced services or some combination of the two.

OPERATION FRESH START

What I am proposing, that I hope the year of the Jubilee committees will consider and endorse, is the elimination of all Third World external debt, and most of the foreign debt of those European countries still struggling to effect the transition from state-capitalism to a privately-administered capitalist system. The write-off would include all of the money owed to the International Monetary Fund, the World Bank, Regional Development Banks, individual country loans and private bank loans to debtor governments. To the extent that this would require reimbursement to third parties, including the redemption of World Bank bonds, for example, it would be paid for by the world's richest countries in an amount proportional to each country's 1998 GDP in U.S. dollars as a percentage of the total GDP, in U.S. dollar equivalent, for that list of countries. The United States would be the largest contributor followed by Japan, Germany, France, Italy, the U.K., and Canada. The Scandinavian countries, and some of the smaller European countries including Switzerland, as well as Australia and New Zealand, would also want to be included on the list as a matter of principle.

The whole operation would be paid for by the simple expedient of increasing the cash reserve requirements of private banks and other deposit taking institutions by 1% a month until they reach 50 percent. In the United States, for example, total deposits are roughly of the same order of magnitude as the federal debt at about $5.5 trillion. So raising reserve requirements over a period of 5 years would allow the creation of approximately $2.75 trillion. The first trillion or so would pay the U.S. share of world debt reduction and the balance would be enough to reduce the U.S. internal debt by about $1.75 trillion. That amount of debt relief would save taxpayers $75 to $85 billion in annual interest charges which could then be used to lower taxes and increase government expenditures for the common good. The figures for other countries are roughly proportionate.

As I suggested in the previous chapter the mass monetization would be phased over a period of approximately five years. Money required to extinguish Third World debt would have first claim so that it could be dealt with expeditiously. Once that part of the operation was complete the balance would all accrue to First World taxpayers.

IS DEBT FORGIVENESS JUST?

It all depends on your point of view. There are naysayers who insist that all debts must be repaid. But does that mean that individuals are to be forever shackled by debts incurred on their behalf by others? Especially if it is beyond their financial capability to repay?

The World Bank cannot escape part of the responsibility. It actively sought projects to finance and encouraged large scale borrowing. It was like taking kids to the candy store and telling them they could have anything they liked. The rub comes later when they realized that they were obliged to repay the candy store owner out of their meager allowance. The tragedy is compounded by the fact that many of the projects were not self-liquidating. The money was spent but the debt remained.

Nor can the monetarists and neo-classical economists escape responsibility. It was the implementation of their views that pushed interest rates to intolerable heights which resulted in debt compounding several times as fast as any reasonable borrower might have expected. This was a complete reversal of the trickle down economics of the post-war period and the substitution of trickle up economics. Every increase in interest rates was the equivalent of an extra tax on the poorest members of society for the benefit of their rich creditors.

Western governments have a responsibility for allowing this to happen. They also have a responsibility for allowing the establishment of Eurodollar bank lending without any limits or constraints. They allowed Third World countries to be inundated with debt and then insisted the IMF exacerbate the problem when the solvency of European and American banks was threatened.

So a good case can be made that Third World debt was the product of misdirected altruism, very bad economics, greed and subterfuge on the part of the First World. It is quite justifiable in the circumstance to invoke force majeure. Let the people and the institutions responsible for the disaster accept the consequences and set the situation right.

The United States itself set a precedent in respect of Odious Debt when it repudiated Cuba's debts after Spain "lost" Cuba in the Spanish American War. As Patricia Adams, author of *Odious Debts*, put it in an interview with Julliette Majot: "The repudiation was based on the grounds that Spain had borrowed the money without the consent of the Cuban people and had used the money to suppress the Cubans' legitimate rebellion against Spain's colonial rule. The legal scholar who coined the phrase "the doctrine of odious debts," Alexander Sack, also said that debts incurred to subjugate a people or to colonize them should also be considered odious to the indigenous people."[1]

IS DEBT FORGIVENESS JUSTICE OR SELF-INTEREST

As often happens in such cases it is both. There is no doubt that extinguishing Third World debt is the moral thing to do. It is akin to admitting paternity and accepting financial responsibility for the consequences. The other major consideration is that the world will benefit as a result, both politically and economically.

Financial markets have been so volatile in the latter half of 1998 that it is impossible to predict what they will be like by the time this book hits the market. But if they continue to be as bullish as they appeared in late November it is only because investors are living in a fools' paradise. World debt is rising at an unsustainable pace and a meltdown is inevitable whether it is imminent or not.

The G7 leaders package of reforms enlarging the role of the IMF is nothing more than a perpetuation of the confidence game.[2] It merely papers over the cracks of a system coming apart at the seams. No doubt unintended, it is, nevertheless, deceit. The saddest aspect of the whole plan is the misuse of the word "transparency". Every one of those leaders has been demanding greater transparency on the part of banks, financial institutions and Third World governments. The IMF, one of the most secretive of organizations, has used the word so often that I want to throw up every time I hear it. The whole official reaction to the world financial crisis is one of cover-up rather than transparency.

So G7 leaders are faced with two choices. They can continue in denial, and pretend that the obvious symptoms were an aberration until the cancer breaks through in full force. Or they can adopt a wonder cure and let it work its magic of ridding the world body politic of its crippling disease.

The status quo offers few attractions. An economic meltdown will hurt the rich as well as the poor. Rich people should re-read the history of the 1929-1931 period to be reminded just how many of their kindred spirits of that era committed suicide when the value of their assets collapsed overnight and they were unable to adjust to the reality of being poor. They should also refresh their memories as to how government-created money ended the Great Depression — but only years later when war broke out and necessity became the mother of invention. We can learn from that experience and avoid a repetition. The 64 trillion dollar question is will we?

A TAX ON THE BANKS?

A few years ago I watched a television debate on the subject of money-creation and the role of the banks. It was suggested that governments should play a more significant role and that, as a consequence, the banks would be obliged to keep more cash in their vaults. A spokesman for Canada's largest bank, the Royal, insisted that would be a tax on the banks. He looked hurt that anyone would suggest it.

I look at the situation quite differently. Raising cash reserve requirements in order to neutralize the effect of monetizing government debt should not be regarded as a tax on the banks. It would simply be restitution. And not full restitution by any means. It would only be partial restitution for 200 years of gross injustice. Banks have no inherent right to own assets equal to twenty or thirty times their capital and collect interest on all of it. This is usury gone wild. And while there is no way that banks can make amends for all the hardship they have created over the centuries they can now, collectively, provide the world with the debt relief essential to absolve them of present and future crimes against humanity.

ALL BANKS MUST CONFORM

It will be argued that it would be unfair to impose cash reserve requirements on some banks if the so-called offshore or tax-haven banks are immune. That is true. The new rules must apply to all banks, everywhere. The OECD countries have the power to make sure this happens. They can pass legislation which would make it a criminal offense for their citizens or landed immigrants to own shares in, deposit money in, borrow money from or otherwise do business with any bank, anywhere in the world, which fails to comply.

To be eligible for international transactions each bank would have to have its books audited by two internationally recognized accounting firms and one of them would have to be changed every two years to reduce the risk of creative accounting practices creeping in and becoming entrenched. It would also be necessary to end bank secrecy rules to make the criminal law effective. This is the perfect, if belated, opportunity to end the practice of banks operating as handmaidens to crooks and rogues.

TIGHTER BANKING REGULATIONS

Stricter rules would appear to be going against the trend but it should be obvious by now that too much deregulation can give birth to massive problems. As we have already seen, unregulated credit creation was a major contributor to the Third World debt crisis; it has been assisting in the elimination of competition and the creation of globalized market power, or oligopoly; it has financed the elimination of jobs through acquisitions and takeovers; it has contributed to global financial instability by financing hedge funds and other speculation. We don't allow arsonists to go around starting one fire after another so there is no reason why banks should be allowed to do the financial equivalent.

So as the world moves to a system with a much fairer and more secure balance between cash (legal tender) money and bank-created credit money it would seem both wise and reasonable to restrict the purposes for which banks can create their half of the annual increase. It would be a good time to eliminate money-creation for the purchase of stocks and bonds on margin. The change could be phased in over a five year period to ease the adjustment.

The day this section was being written I saw a story about an American medical student who wanted to sue his broker because he had lost $40,000 buying on margin through the internet and this sum represented his tuition fees for the coming year.[3] There will be many more cases as people learn to take advantage of the internet and a lot of hardship and heartache can be eliminated by removing the gambling component from the transaction.

It is my opinion that banks should only be allowed to create money to lend to producers or consumers. They are the two sides of the real economy. Financing both will encourage balanced growth of goods and services as opposed to merely financing an increase in the market value of existing financial assets. After all, money created by the banks dilutes the money supply for everyone and the value of that money can only be maintained if the new money encourages real economic growth and not just another puff into the stock market balloon.

Derivatives

Banks should also be required to get out of the gambling business. Chart No. 2 shows the dramatic growth in derivative trading.

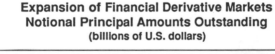

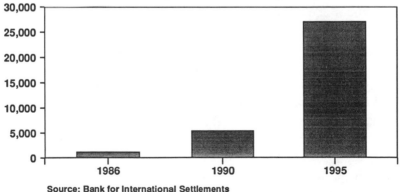

Source: Bank for International Settlements

Chart No. 2

Their involvement with derivatives in general and exotic derivatives in particular constitutes a worrisome trend. The first is a further estrangement between the paper and the real economies. Instead of concentrating on the growth of the real economy, banks devote their energy and ingenuity to playing the paper game. When they encourage their industrial customers to gamble, rather than promoting their core businesses, they compound the felony.

Derivatives were originally sold as a means of risk management. Over time, however, they have become a source of risk creation to an extent that is impossible to evaluate. The practice is a source of volatility that has to be curbed. One suggestion has been to tax the practice out of existence. A more acceptable solution would be to subject banks to fairly strict regulations as to the derivatives they can write. Otherwise they may yield to the temptation to try to increase their profits from derivatives as those from traditional banking begin to decline.

THE 50 PERCENT SOLUTION

I have often been asked why I am recommending that cash reserve requirements be set at 50 percent of deposits instead of 100 percent as suggested by many monetary reformers including the original Chicago school of Simon, Mints and colleagues, Irving Fisher and others including Milton Friedman, who still claims it is his preferred solution. In reply I freely admit that the choice is an arbitrary one. It is the compromise that I believe is most likely to produce the fairest and most advantageous balance of benefit — just another way of saying the greatest good for the greatest number.

I can't say for certain if 40 percent would do, or if it should be 60 or 70 percent. Nor can anyone else because the system is far too complicated and it may take 10 or 20 years of experience to know if a 50/50 split will be sufficient to put a permanent cap on the total debt to GDP ratio once the proposed monetization has reduced it to a more manageable proportion. I strongly suspect that anything less than 50 percent might prove to be inadequate.

In any event, the 50 percent solution is much easier to

defend than either the 100 percent solution or the zero percent solution, the two extremes Milton Friedman prefers. In the first case of 100 percent, you would be removing from the banks a very large proportion of their interest-bearing assets. In my opinion it would be too disruptive. I don't mind seeing them scratch for a living, the way everyone else must, but I don't want to put them out of business altogether.

I am also convinced that they have, in times past, and can in the future play a useful role in the allocation of new money to productive enterprise. I suspect that there has been as much cronyism as there would be if governments were involved but much of that should disappear if they are forbidden to lend money for buyouts, takeovers and mergers on the industrial side, and financing margins on the financial side. In any event I am not willing to encourage government involvement in the direct allocation of credit — one point on which Milton Friedman and I agree.

Where we disagree totally is in respect of the zero percent option. The trend in that direction is primarily if not totally responsible for the financial mess in which the world finds itself. It is a system which, for 200 years, hasn't worked, is not working now and never will work to the general satisfaction. You cannot allow the banks to create all new money as debt without some means of paying the interest on that debt. It just keeps compounding until the next crash occurs. So governments must create the money with which to pay the interest. There is another fundamentally important reason for governments re-entering the money creation business which is becoming more urgent all the time. They cannot raise enough tax money to do all of the things they must do in future years without it.

GOVERNMENT-CREATED MONEY (GCM)

At this point it may be useful to review the money-creation process. Bank credit money is created by computers — which explains much of the concern about what might happen at the stroke of midnight, December 31st, 1999. You give your bank a note, or it decides to buy a stack of government bonds, a clerk taps the computer keys and, presto, a deposit appears in the account. The note or bonds appear as an asset on the bank's books and the deposit as a liability, so the books balance. The deposit, however, is not backed by either gold or cash — at least not more than a couple of cents on the dollar. The deposit is only as good as the liquidity (saleability) of the note or bonds acting as collateral.

Government-created money is fundamentally different in two ways. First, it is cash money which is legal tender for the payment of all bills and taxes. Second, it does not have to be repaid with interest and that makes a world of difference. If a government builds a bridge with money it creates it only has to pay the cost once. If it builds a bridge with money borrowed from a bank it may still be paying for the bridge a hundred years later with a total payout equal to several times the original cost of the bridge.

There are various mechanics by which governments can create money. They can just print it and spend it into circulation as President Lincoln did with his greenbacks. It was his good fortune, at the time, not to be encumbered by the Federal Reserve System.

Operating through central banks has involved a different approach. To escape the Great Depression and help finance World War II, central banks, including the Fed in the U.S., printed money with which to buy government bonds. The cash it printed was deposited in the government account to help finance its operations. Governments paid interest on the bonds but this was returned by central banks by way of dividends, in the case of government-owned banks, or as part of an operating surplus by the Fed in the U.S. In either case the real cost to the government was close to zero, so it was a kind of de facto interest-free accommodation.

The process was limited by what it does to the banking system. Cash is high-powered money. So in a fractional reserve system that allows banks to collectively create 20 to 30 dollars credit for every dollar of cash in their vaults, governments' hands are tied by their own regulations. The remedy is to increase the cash reserve requirements of banks (just the opposite of what central banks have been doing) and reduce their leverage to the extent necessary to neutralize the excess cash and limit total monetary expansion to the desired level. This will vary from country to country depending on the rate of unemployment and the amount of slack in the economy.

There is another problem with this system which may be largely cosmetic but still vitally important. Government bonds acquired by central banks as collateral for new cash still show on government books as debt. In taxpayers' minds debt is debt whether it is held by central banks or the general public. They don't differentiate one from the other and this plays into the hands of conservative newspapers and think tanks with their debt clocks intended to reinforce a public image of gross government incompetence.

As the object of the year of the Jubilee exercise is to diminish both the perception and the reality of overwhelming debt, any mechanics which fails to address both problems is unacceptable to my mind. Consequently, I am going to propose a system that meets that test. I have suggested it on earlier occasions in the context of new money creation, i.e. splitting the function 50/50 between government and private banks. This is the first time it has been put forward in the context of a mass monetization. Fortunately, it is a procedure which would work equally well in the implementation of both objectives.

MASS MONETIZATION

I am assuming that most countries will want to delegate the day-to-day operation of their monetary system to a central bank. There are a number of advantages including continuity. The disadvantages, to date, have been an absolutely dismal performance (they have been about 80 percent responsible for the world's financial chaos, in my view) and lack of accountability. They were established for the alleged purpose of serving the public but somehow that responsibility has been overtaken by their allegiance to the private banks. Witness the number of times and the extent to which they have reduced the banks' cash reserve requirements and allowed them to increase their leverage.

While this unsatisfactory record is cast in stone, central banks can, in theory at least, be reformed and required to act responsibly. The adoption of uniform cash reserve requirements and bank leverage will eliminate much of their capacity for mischief-making. If, in addition, they are made directly responsible to governments and/or legislatures for interest rate and anti-inflationary policies the dictatorship of the monetary authorities will end.

That said, it has to be recognized that central banks are very conservative and set in their ways. It would be difficult to persuade them that the money they print does not have to -be forever carried on their books as a liability, even when the only real liability is to replace one worn out bill with another, on demand. Consequently, it is the course of wisdom to play their game. If they must have collateral for the notes they print then by all means give them collateral. But instead of giving them government bonds to show as assets against the liability of their notes, it is expedient to find a substitute which is not debt.

The answer that comes to mind is common shares. Let each country sell its central bank common shares with a nominal value of its choice. For major economies one share might represent one billions dollars, euros or pounds. It would be the country's choice. The central bank would create cash in an equivalent amount to be spent by the government, or on its behalf. It must be clearly understood that the shares are neither transferable or redeemable. They are simply an accounting device and ownership rests with the government and people.

In the early days and throughout the approximately five years of the monetization the bulk of the money would be used to buy government and World Bank bonds and other debt instruments to be retired and extinguished as part of the year of the Jubilee emancipation. As soon as this part of the operation was complete stage two would begin. An amount equal to approximately one-half of the desired increase in the money supply for the year would be deposited to a separate government account to be spent by it to provide enhanced services, reduce taxes, balance budgets or whatever its government and legislators decide is most appropriate to that country's particular circumstances. The central bank would, of course, maintain the 50% reserve requirements of the private banks to ensure that the whole operation was non-inflationary.

The institutional framework is important. There is, in theory at least, no reason why the Federal Reserve System couldn't be the custodian and operator of the new system in the U.S. provided its jurisdiction was extended to all banks as it is essential that all deposit-taking institutions be subject to the same reserve requirements. It has the advantage of being in existence and having offices (Federal Reserve Banks) in all geographical regions. An off- setting disadvantage would be the necessity of replacing those Governors and senior staff who refused to accept the new system. Some attitudes and utterances have been so pro-bank that they might be psychologically incapable of adapting. Another disadvantage is that the Federal Reserve System is an expensive system!

A much better alternative would be to scrap the Fed completely and create a new Bank of the United States wholly owned by the people and staffed by committed reformers. A re-incarnated BUS would have the advantage of starting with a clean slate unencumbered by the Fed's dismal record beginning almost from the time it was created. But that is a decision only the Congress in its wisdom can make. The most important criterion is clear lines of authority and a regulatory framework that will permit fast and sensitive action.

THE INFLATION BUGBEAR

Whenever government-created money is mentioned in polite circles you can expect the knee-jerk reaction "It would be inflationary." This is a substitute for thinking on the part of monetarists and neo-classical economists and I have often heard and read it put forward in all seriousness as a defense. At *The Public Good: Lessons for the 3rd Millennium*, a conference organized to honor Hon. Allan J. MacEachen, a retiring colleague, on his home territory at St. Francis Xavier

University in Antigonish, Nova Scotia, I became discouraged after listening to Canada's "best and brightest" for several hours as they forecast that the high unemployment, then over 9%, and slow growth would continue well into the next century.[4]

When I couldn't take it any longer I took advantage of the opportunity provided by a floor microphone to suggest that we learn from the experience of the 1939-45 era and use government-created money to stimulate the economy and help finance the essential services being cut back due to budgetary restraint. The best that the Deputy-Minister of Finance, David Dodge, could say in reply was: "Mr. Hellyer's solution would be inflationary". Canada's top dog in finance merely echoed the conventional wisdom of the Washington consensus which he and his colleagues had bought without dissent or reservation. I have seen the same view expressed in letters written by the U.S. Congressional Budget Office — equally dogmatic.

Yet any undergraduate student of economics would or at least should know that it is the quantity of money which is created that determines prices and not who creates it. The "M" in Irving Fisher's money equation means money — not bank-created money or government-created money — just money.

One of America's genius inventors, Thomas Edison, put the whole question of bonds, bills and national credit in perspective. "If the nation can issue a dollar bond it can issue a dollar bill. The element that makes the bond good makes the bill good. The difference between the bond and the bill is that the bond lets money brokers collect twice the amount of the bond and an additional 20%. Whereas the currency, the honest sort provided by the Constitution, pays nobody but those who contribute in some useful way. It is absurd to say our country can issue bonds and cannot issue currency. Both are promises to pay, but one fattens the usurers and the other helps the people. If the currency issued by the people were no good, then the bonds would be no good, either."

That is true. Duly elected legislatures are the successors to kings and monarchs who held a monopoly on money creation. Legislatures may delegate part of their power over money but if they delegate all or most of it, sovereignty passes to the "money monarchs" who are fortunate enough to be the recipients of rich benevolence. Any country that doesn't control its own money supply is neither sovereign nor democratic.

A CONSTITUTIONAL AMENDMENT

If there is nervousness about the possibility of monetary inflation under the new system, although there is no particular reason why there should be, there is a remedy of last resort. Objectors might be placated by a constitutional safeguard to come into effect once the monetization was complete, requiring that the increase in government-created money in any one year could not, under any circumstances, be more than proportional to the increase in real output for the preceding year, adjusted for the velocity of circulation and forecast changes in the size of the labor force.

The provision could only be set aside by a seventy-five percent vote in both the Senate and the house of Representatives in the U.S., or comparable majorities in the parliament or legislatures of other countries. The escape clause would never be used with the possible exception of a wartime emergency. Meanwhile there are other aspects of inflation in need of more urgent attention. In view of the fact that there have been few cases of too much money chasing too few goods in Western economies in the last thirty years a more diversified arsenal is required to remove the necessity of imposing tight money and high interest rates when that action is not appropriate.

AN INCOMES POLICY

It is only a few years ago, in October 1995, when Fed Chairman Alan Greenspan told the Economic Club of Chicago: "We have to be careful not to lull ourselves into the presumption that somehow the institutional structure of the American economy and its increasing globalization is permanently suppressing inflation."[5]

At the time he must have been concerned about the possibility of renewed wage inflation and that appears to have been the underlying determinant of the policies he followed in subsequent years. The sudden switch in policy in the Fall of 1998 was based more on the fear of deflation rather than inflation. But just because a problem is temporarily out of sight doesn't mean it should be removed from mind altogether.

Two strikes in Canada in 1998 were sharp and unhappy reminders of the kind of thinking which activates wage-push inflation. Air Canada pilots struck, not because they were underpaid compared to other occupations, but because they wanted wage parity with U.S. pilots. Apart from the unnecessary disruption for the travelling public and financial disaster for the company, the pilots line of reasoning was exactly the same as that of the Seaway workers who helped initiate the serious inflation which began more than thirty years earlier.

A second strike by employees at Pearson International Airport in Toronto invoked a similar principle. They wanted parity with airport workers in Vancouver. The problem is that not everyone can have parity with the highest paid anywhere. The arithmetic won't sustain it. And while these two strikes are unlikely to lead to a general round of demands in a slack economy they are a clear warning of what is likely to happen when prosperity ultimately returns.

Consequently it is absolutely essential to have an incomes policy in place. The reason, in terms of economics, is this. If the new money created each year is distributed vertically, through higher wages for the already employed and consequently higher prices for existing output, it will not be available to finance additional employment and increased output. If there is any one concept which must be learned in order to understand the failure of monetarism it is this. To the extent that the increase in money stock – translated into income – is distributed vertically, in excess of increases in productivity, it contributes to higher wages and prices rather than increased output. Unless wage increases to the already employed are limited to the average increase in real output, inflation will continue. If that occurs interest rates will be higher than necessary because lenders will continue to demand a premium as a hedge against the anticipated inflation. This has negative implications for governments and for the economy as a whole. It is the people who must bear the extra burden.

The other great advantage of continuous low inflation is that it permits a significantly higher level of employment. If there is one benefit which tops the list from a humanitarian point of view it is the availability of jobs for people who want to work. This has been the over-riding motive in my life-long obsession with economics because I think the need to contribute to the common well-being is fundamental to one's feeling of self worth. Finally, it should be noted, negligible inflation protects the value of savings for everyone.

The incomes policy I have been promoting for thirty years avoids all of the pitfalls of earlier experiments. It applies exclusively to monopoly and market power. It would limit the total financial package that unions could negotiate to the average annual increase in real output per member of the labor force for the previous year; and where the employer enjoyed monopoly or market power, and did not engage in genuine price competition, profit guidelines would apply that would ensure that the benefits of stable labor unit costs would be passed on to the consuming public.

I have written on this subject several times so I will not repeat all of the discussion about problems of hardship, catch-up, allocation of labor and other questions here.[5] But I can assure skeptics that there would be no significant problems for either labor or investors. No additional bureaucracy would be required and the application of rules to monopoly power would produce a fairer, more efficient and productive system that would allow most economies to grow at a rate about one percent above current levels with no increase in inflation.

In fact, computer simulations from a model developed by Laurence H. Meyer, a Clinton appointee to the Federal Reserve Board, demonstrate that for both Canada and the United States a combination of GCM and the incomes policy I propose would result in both higher output and less inflation, a win-win situation.[6]

Other tools to fight inflation include increasing margin

requirements. I have already suggested that they be increased to 100%, over a period of five years, for stocks and bonds. In addition, someone, either the central bank or the Treasury, should be given standby power to increase minimum monthly payments on credit card balances in the event that consumer purchases began to overheat the economy; and to require higher equity to debt ratios for either residential or non-residential real estate, or both, in case the construction industry started to bid up prices.

Non-residential construction is one of the few exceptional cases where there has been demand inflation in a few cities where the banking system went berserk with its lending practices. This is a perfect example of where the brakes could have been applied in one industry, in relevant locations, without the necessity of carpet-bombing the whole economy.

A TAX ON FOREIGN EXCHANGE TRANSACTIONS

While the monetization of a large slice of world debt, the introduction of government-created money on a continuing basis and the adoption of an incomes policy to limit monopoly and market power are the three most important reforms on the world agenda, a tax on currency transactions is another top priority. There is no part of the financial economy in greater need of being slowed down than the currency traders. Clipping the wings of these high-flyers is the fourth essential economic reform. It has been estimated that the volume of currency transactions is now between $1 and $2 trillion a day – a sum so large that it is greater than the annual gross domestic product of many countries. Exchange transactions on that scale accomplish no earthly good. Most of it is speculation, pure and simple, and totally disruptive of the domestic economies which become its targets of convenience.

Reformers were hoping that the leaders of the G7 group of nations would take advantage of their meeting in Halifax, in the summer of 1995, to recommend the universal imposition of a tax along the lines of the one first proposed by Nobel Prize-winning U.S. economist James Tobin, in 1978.[7] The rate proposed was 0.5 percent and it has been estimated that if the tax were imposed on a global basis it could increase government revenues by \$300 to \$400 billion per annum.[8]

Unfortunately, the leaders of the industrial world blew their golden opportunity. Their cool response was stated in the G7 communiqué as follows: "Internal and external balances, together with unhelpful fluctuations in financial and currency markets, could jeopardize achievement of sustained non-inflationary growth as well as the continued expansion of international trade."[9] The astronomical increase in cross-border transactions in bonds and equities shown in Chart No. 3 is merely a symptom of the problem.

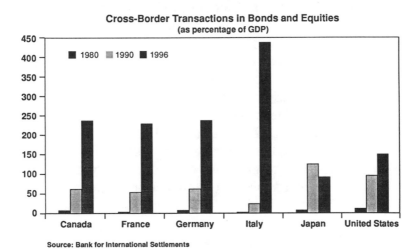

Cross-Border Transactions in Bonds and Equities
(as percentage of GDP)

Source: Bank for International Settlements

Chart No. 3

The world leaders' detachment from reality can be understood, though not necessarily condoned, by anyone familiar with the fact that they don't write their own communiqués. This one, obviously, was written by economic fundamentalists who fail to comprehend that unbridled self-interest has no saving grace. It is simply savagery – the law of the jungle. There is no invisible hand guiding currency traders except the one they slip into the pockets of taxpayers worldwide.

THE EURO

The creation of the Euro, combining 11 European currencies, is a historic milestone both politically and economically. Its promoters hope that it will be a significant step in the direction of European political union, strengthen the collective economy and give Europe more clout in a world that has been dominated by the U.S. dollar.

The design is consistent with a world market economy and both the new currency and the erosion of borders will benefit large companies and conglomerates in their scramble to compete on the world stage. This was reflected in an immediate rise in stock market prices. The Euro, too, showed strength and it is fair to say that members of the financial community were the first winners.

It is the future of the real economy that is less certain. Industrial production has declined in Germany and the double-digit jobless rate has begun to rise. In France and Italy the outlook is equally bleak and all this comes after the first year of strong growth since 1994 for all 11 Euro nations. Growth had been slow as countries struggled to reduce their spending in order to conform to the terms of the Maastricht treaty.

The current slowdown is putting pressure on the new European Central Bank to reduce interest rates and stimulate growth; but here is the problem. Each country has surrendered its sovereignty over monetary policy and they are now completely in the hands of one man. And even if he wanted to oblige, which is not certain, it will be difficult to follow a monetary policy that is appropriate to all regions. Some may be in far greater need of stimulation than others. It will be interesting to see how the new system operates and whether or not it will be politically acceptable. One possible dissenter is French Prime Minister Lionel Jospin who appears to be one of the first important politicians to question the conventional wisdom. In a much discussed magazine essay in the Fall of 1998 he wrote: "These [financial] crises carry with them, in my eyes, three lessons: capitalism remains unstable; economics is political; and globalization calls for regulation."

He also noted that: "The globalization of economic activity demands ... an equivalent globalization of politics." It certainly would, if that were the best route for all humanity. But it isn't. Not now, or in the foreseeable future. Either globalized economics or globalized politics would be managed by the people responsible for the present mess and the needs of the vast majority of humanity would continue to be ignored. European countries can abdicate their individual sovereignty to a monetary dictator if they wish but most other parts of the world will be better off and better served by paddling their own canoe.

A WORLD BANK AND A WORLD DOLLAR

I have often wondered if the time were not ripe to replace the U.S. dollar with a world dollar. It could be called "The Universal" or "Uni", for short. It would be the currency of travellers cheques that would be accepted around the globe. The coincidence of the world financial crisis, that threatens world economic stability, and the adoption of the Euro as a common currency for the European Union has convinced me that there would be no better time than when the global financial system must be almost totally revamped. No national currency should enjoy the benefits that have accrued to the U.S. dollar in time of crisis. No single currency, or even two or three regional currencies, should achieve the exalted position of temple money. All should be allowed to fluctuate in terms of each other and in terms of a world currency which is the property of all and the privilege of none.

To effect the changeover would require a new world bank empowered to issue the universal world currency backed by reserves of currencies of all nation states. It would be the bank of international settlements and money-changer for the world. Its doors would never close.

I do not think the present Bank for International Settlements is suitable for this role. It is subject to much distrust in all circles except central banks. It has not yet escaped the stigma of its Nazi association and collaboration in

World War II, and its post-war role in helping establish a banking system increasingly unaccountable to democratic control. This makes it suspect with all true democrats.

The BIS has been a party to the myth that the South-East Asian meltdown was a result of the lack of transparency and cronyism. This from the heart of a banking system which has been the epitome of both. The BIS is one of the least transparent reservoirs of autocratic power on earth. It doesn't even allow secretaries of the treasury or ministers of finance to attend its meetings.

At the Bretton Woods Conference of 1944, Resolution Five was adopted calling for the earliest possible liquidation of the BIS. For reasons that have never been properly explained the resolution was not acted on. If it is still on the books it should be acted on when the new World Bank is established. Even if it has lapsed the major powers can effect the changeover by requiring their national banks to clear through the World Bank and ordering the central banks to cease and desist from any further contact with the BIS.

With democracy must come complete transparency!

A WORLD OF ADVANTAGE

The advantages of the reforms suggested in this chapter are so broad and so extensive that they defy synopsis. I will elaborate on a few specifics in chapter 12 so the following is just a summary of the highlights.

- The less developed countries would be relieved of the bulk of their debt burden and given the opportunity for a fresh start.
- They would have their independence restored by the removal of all conditions, restrictions and limitations imposed by the World Bank, IMF, and creditor nations.
- They would be free to use their own central banks in the interests of their own citizens.
- Developed countries would have their national debt substantially reduced which would give them much more fiscal flexibility.

- Developed countries would be able to use government-created money to supplement the tax revenues needed to provide essential services.
- All countries would have the fiscal flexibility to balance their budgets.
- All countries would have the ability to create jobs.
- All countries would have the ability to maintain price stability.
- All countries should be able to keep interest rates low enough to prevent their total   debt to GDP ratios from rising again.

ARE THERE ANY LOSERS?

Very few. Certainly the banks would be less profitable but not as much as might be expected at first blush. A banker friend said that what I am proposing would mean that the banks would have to call loans and sell securities. That is true. Certainly their balance sheets would look different than they do now. But the transition would be gradual. They would, over a period of five years, have to call the loans of the brokers, including those to the houses that they own; they would have to call the loans made to hedge funds; they would have to call loans to individuals who had bought stocks and bonds on margin, as the margins on these purchases were gradually eliminated; they would have to call their loans to governments who wouldn't need them any more anyway because they would have enough cash to finance their operations; and they would have to sell their government bonds which is the purpose of the exercise. They should never have been allowed to create money to buy them in the first place.

Before you shed too many tears, however, you should remember that there are big changes taking place in the banking industry. As a shareholder I read several of their annual reports and note their boasts that they are becoming less dependent on traditional banking all the time. They are earning fees for underwriting and for money management. They are entering other lines of business such as insurance and leasing. They charge significant transaction fees and their revenue from all those sources is gaining in importance.

The banks, too, are winners when it comes to fundamentals. The reduced leverage will almost eliminate the risk of bank failures. Shareholder interests will be far more secure and taxpayers will be off the hook for banks "too big to fail".

The final consideration is justice. Robbery is illegal for most people — certainly it is for any one who tries to rob a bank. It should be illegal for banks to rob the owners of the patents from which their licenses derive. Justice demands a levelling of the playing field.

CHAPTER 12

DEMOCRACY
AND HOPE RESTORED

"The world is a fine place and worth fighting for."

Ernest Hemingway

In order to achieve the twin objectives of restoring hope for those untold millions of people who either have lost hope or who are fast losing it, and of restoring the kind of democracy which puts people first, it will be necessary to do an "about turn" before marching into the chasm of another worldwide depression. It will be necessary to reverse many trends that are presently considered irreversible.

The concept of "free trade" will have to be limited to the extent necessary to allow nation states to encourage and protect the indigenous industrial base essential to provide a rapid rise in standard of living for their citizens. They cannot be expected to remain hewers of wood and drawers of water forever, which is just another way of describing eternal impoverishment. This is the first pillar in the cathedral of hope.

The second is that nation states must be allowed to restrict capital flows when required in their own interests and to determine the terms and conditions on which direct foreign capital investment is welcome. Allowing foreign investors to buy both your most promising and your most profitable industries is not progress. It is just the fast track to a serious balance of payments problem when those profits begin to flow out of your country.

The third pillar in the cathedral of hope comprises

banking and financial services. The whole system must be brought under democratic control. Banks must serve people instead of keeping them in bondage. And the banks must learn that their primary responsibility is to the people from whom they get their charters, and whose money they dilute. Even when their leverage is reduced from an insane twenty or thirty to one, to something closer to that of other businesses, they will not be corporations like other corporations. They will still have licenses to "print" money which is a sacred trust that they hold, not solely on behalf of their shareholders, but also for the benefit of the patent holders of the money — all the people.

The fourth pillar comprises the central banks. Increasingly, over the last two decades, they have boasted that they are not influenced by politics and they have thumbed their autocratic noses at governments on numerous occasions to prove it. Already it is the trademark of the new European Central Bank as Wim Duisenberg, its Dutch president, made clear when the bank's initial interest rate policy was announced in December 1998.[1]

They are not influenced by politics even though politics is about people — their lives, their jobs, their hopes, their aspirations. Yet central banks have had a profound effect on all of these, and often negatively. They were set up to help people by easing the peaks and valleys of the boom-bust cycle. But, like the IMF, their original mission has changed to the point that it no longer bears any relevance to the original. By allowing the private banks to increase their leverage, and simultaneously abdicating their responsibility to provide governments with low cost money, central banks have not only precipitated serious cutbacks in essential services, they have guaranteed the perpetuation of the boom-bust cycle.

Each and every one of us, as voters and concerned citizens, must insist that central banks be subject to political control of some kind. In theory I have no objection to the Canadian system under which the Bank of Canada is responsible for the day-to-day operation of monetary policy, *as long as the government has the final say*. In the event that differences cannot be resolved amicably in private, which they usually are, the Minister of Finance can send the Governor a letter directing him to alter course.

The safeguard is that the letter has to be made public so that the press and informed voters know who is calling the shots and who should be held accountable. I know that had I been Canadian Minister of Finance in 1990-91, when Bank of Canada Governor John Crow led the parade of central bankers by raising interest rates and inducing a recession, I would have dispatched a letter instantly ordering him to cease and desist and to lower interest rates to more reasonable levels.

Of course he might have refused, and chosen to "walk the plank" instead. That would have been a great blessing for Canada which has suffered unconscionable levels of unemployment, and which has been underproducing by $60-65 billion a year ever since.[2]

Unfortunately the minister of the day was "sold" on Mr. Crow's reading of the Washington consensus, which he had learned as an employee of the IMF, and tens of thousands of innocent Canadians have been caught up in a whirlwind of misery and discontentment as a result.

CREATIVE GOVERNMENT

When governments are relieved of part of their debt they will save a lot of money in interest payments. When this saving is added to their 50% share of the new money created each year, they will have a lot of surplus cash at their disposal. At that point there will be no shortage of advice as to what to do with it. The majority of the rich will demand debt and tax reductions while the majority of the poor will expect improved government services.

There will be no compelling reason to reduce the debt further because it will have shrunk substantially with the bank reorganization; and even if it remains constant in absolute terms it will continue to shrink as a proportion of GDP which is the most important yardstick. Still, a case can be made for long-range thinking to provide future generations with a broader range of options. My suggestion is to pay down 1/2 to 1% of the outstanding principal each year with a 100 to 200 year time frame for total elimination.

A case can be made for modest tax cuts, especially for those people most likely to spend the savings back into circulation. An equally compelling case can be made for a major overhaul of the entire taxation system to adjust to the new realities. Tax avoidance has become big business and new approaches are required to minimize the advantages to both business and individuals from playing the tax avoidance game.

A GROWTH DIVIDEND

Every once in a while people have said to me that government-created money is really just another tax. That is technically true, although I prefer to call it a growth dividend. The people finance the growth (increased output) through their government — in the role of financial intermediary — and in turn they get the benefits from the kind of services governments provide. In effect GCM allows a higher growth rate, and a higher level of government services, without the imposition of higher explicit taxes.

The positive role for government is to contribute to an improved quality of life for all its citizens. This can cover a wide spectrum of activity but I will just emphasize a few of the most obvious and most important areas where I think government has a positive role to play. These are the areas that put flesh on the dry bones of political rhetoric which correctly assumes that the future of any country lies in a healthy, well-educated and highly motivated population, living in a healthy and congenial environment. It is a tall order because the chasm between rhetoric and reality in most countries rivals that of the Grand Canyon.

HEALTH CARE

I put health care at the top of the list because a healthy person is a productive person, and more likely to be a happy person. There is simply no substitute for good health and no satisfactory alternative to fast, easy access to medical advice and follow-up treatment.   Consequently, health is not any better suited to strictly market-oriented solutions than it is to bureaucratic bungling.

Canadians once thought they had the Shangri-la of medical care, and with very good reason.   Access was universal, service was almost invariably fast, courteous and efficient and the cost was not unreasonably high.   Then came the problems I have attributed to the monetarist counter-revolution with its deep recessions, big deficits and soaring debt.   The federal government cut back its transfer payments to the provinces by billions of dollars.   The provinces closed hospitals, reduced budgets and shifted responsibility down the line to less qualified staff, including family-supported home care.   A once great system is coming apart at the seams.

As Canadians, we have been reluctant to face the issue because our health care system has been one of the most visible defining differences between us and Americans.   The bad old days of losing one's life savings, or house or farm, due to protracted illness, is gone.   That is still true, but now there can be frustrating delays in getting service and only a lingering hope that some magic wand will set the situation right.   Still, there is a growing realization that it is not about to happen.   A survey, conducted by the Harvard University School of Public Health, documents the trend in public thinking.   Ten years ago only 5 percent of Canadians thought the system needed rebuilding and 37 percent thought fundamental changes were needed.   In a 1998 survey, using the same questions, 23 percent said the system needs to be rebuilt while 56 percent, after acknowledging the good aspects of the system, thought that fundamental changes are needed.[3]

Attitudes are changing, although more slowly in Canada than in some other jurisdictions.   When Canadian economist Monique Jerôme-Forget, who heads the Institute for Research on Public Policy, a Montréal think tank, travelled through Europe in the mid-1990s, she was struck by the fact that every country with a public health-care system was embroiled in a vigorous debate about how to overhaul it.

As Carol Goar reported in the *Toronto Star*: "The British, Dutch, Swedes, Germans and French had gone beyond asking whether change was needed. They were devising — and in some cases implementing — radical reforms: putting doctors on salary, forcing hospitals to compete for patients, shifting decision making from governments to community health boards."[4]

The provision of health care has also become a topic for vigorous debate in the United States. Some of the largest health maintenance organizations (HMOs) are quitting managed care programs for the poor and the elderly. This retreat is most pronounced in Medicaid programs where several companies have shut down Medicaid services in at least 12 states. While many companies remain in the business the tensions that are now appearing are inevitable in a for-profit system where some funding depends on fee schedules set by government. In order to maximize profits, high risk patients have to be excluded, and doctor-patient relationships interfered with.

In a feature article entitled: "Rx for the Health Care System"[5], in October 1998, the *Wall Street Journal* quoted the views of several prominent Americans as to what should be done to repair a health care system rife with leaks and fissures. Most of the prescriptions appeared to me like symptom-treating — apply a few band-aids here and there and hope that the problem will go away. Two, however, struck me as fundamental in their approach.

The pioneering heart surgeon Michael DeBakey, M.D., director of the DeBakey Heart Centre at the Baylor College of Medicine in Houston, Texas, provides the following advice: "First, do no harm. That is the overriding precept of medical practice. The paramount objective of managed care — profit — is diametrically opposed to this precept. Under the pretext of containing costs, managed care has introduced strictures inimical to the physician's best judgment and the patient's best interest. This poses a grave obstacle to competent health care. Intrusive government and the interposition of corporate managed care have imposed regulations that not only are burdensome and costly (more than 20% of health care expenditures), but are subverting the crucial physician-patient relationship.

"The utilization-review process used by some HMOs is a good example of a malign cost-cutting strategy. Physicians should not be penalized for seeking more time and greater discretion with patients. And patients should not be denied the freedom to choose their physicians or seek specialized attention. Doing so degrades the health care system and places the patient in genuine peril."[6]

Dr. DeBakey goes on to suggest the need for an authoritative, independent and objective body, such as a National Council on Medical Care, to establish uniform national guidelines for the health care industry. It is a proposal which makes sense regardless of whether the system is a "for-profit" system, or one that is altered to be primarily "not-for-profit." Let's call that the first principle.

The second was stated by Howard Dean, M.D., the Democratic governor of Vermont. Dr. Dean argued that universal health insurance is the key to improving health care in the U.S. Cutting edge technology and first-rate facilities mean little to families who cannot afford it. This would include the 40 million Americans who do not have health insurance.[7]

This is not a new problem, and not one that is likely to go away with a system that is primarily profit-oriented. Private insurers are happy to write policies for young, healthy individuals. They are less enthusiastic about insuring the elderly, the sick and the accident- prone. In addition, there are always people whose personal circumstances prevent them from affording insurance premiums of any kind. So the difficulty legislators face is how to get a system that works for everyone, without having it subject to widespread abuse.

I well remember the debates which led to the intro-duction of Medicare in Canada. The original motive was to prevent individuals and households from being wiped out financially as a result of serious illness. I personally knew people who had lost all of their financial assets, and others who lost their homes and farms as a result of a protracted illness by a family member. It was this tragic, random unfairness that was the original motivation for reform, and not free attention for the first cough or sore throat of the season.

In the end, we opted for a system based on the European model rather than risking innovation. The result was a system that worked extraordinarily well for a number of years notwithstanding a significant element of abuse. Some people see their doctor at every hint of a scratchy throat because it is free, or so it seems. An extreme case was an elderly next door neighbour who booked into a hospital for a week of tests each Christmas because he had no relatives to celebrate with, and he liked being with the cheery nurses and listening to the carollers who visited.

Personally, I still prefer the system that I recommended as an alternative. The criteria included equal access to the best medical care for rich and poor alike; minimum red tape; and the least incentive for people who can well afford their own routine "throat check" to take advantage of the system and demand services just because they are "free". I believed this latter consideration to be important after checking the Swedish and United Kingdom systems and noting considerable abuse.

My formula to satisfy all three requirements was this. Every person or family would go to the doctor and/or hospital of choice and be responsible for their own medical bills up to a limit of two percent of their gross income. They would be one hundred percent insured for expenditures in excess of that amount. Those with an annual income of $100,000 would pay their own bills up to $2,000. Those earning $30,000 would pay up to $600, while people with no income would pay nothing. No one would be subjected to financial hardship as a result of medical expenses because the burden would be proportionate to their ability to pay. At the same time, the fact that the majority would pay most of their own medical expenses in a normal year would relieve governments of the responsibility of collecting and then disbursing billions in routine transactions and would eliminate much of the abuse of state administered systems.

To ensure that a temporary lack of cash would not deter anyone from seeking needed medical attention, and also to guarantee that doctors and hospitals would be reimbursed for services provided, patients could send their bills to the Government Insurance Agency for immediate payment and subsequent adjustment in their following years's Income Tax calculations. Expenses might be averaged over two or three years to discourage people from "storing" medical problems for the specific purpose of incurring major expenses in one taxation period, but apart from technical details like the range of procedures to be covered and agreed schedules of fees for service, there was no fine print to detract from the simplicity and efficacy of the plan.

When I finished presenting this option to the Canadian cabinet on July 16, 1965, every minister who spoke — and most of them did — said it was a better, more efficient proposal than the one before them (Medicare). There were no exceptions. Walter Gordon, who had proposed the Medicare plan, was the last to speak. He, too, said it was a better plan. "But", he added, "it wouldn't be politic." With those five words rational debate ended; the discussion of alternatives was over.

A universal insurance plan offers three great advantages. Assuming that genuine competition exists in the provision of hospital, laboratory and other services, the profit motive ceases to be an impediment to the sick. Government involvement is minimal, and all citizens have universal access to the best care available. It is easy for Milton Friedman to say that: "Medical care should be financed out of after-tax income, just as food, clothing and other items are."[8] But that is small comfort to people who have no after tax income or whose income is inadequate to cope with major medical emergencies. Governments have to be involved in ensuring a healthy population. That is what governments are for.

EDUCATION

If health care heads the list of human needs, education is a close second. Young people are constantly being lectured on the necessity of post-secondary education in order to compete in a world of incredible complexity. Cars are becoming more complicated, computers are more complex and a whole panoply of technological gadgets require the ability to read and understand minute step-by-step instructions to ensure that they are operated safely and efficiently.

It would be difficult to find a politician who doesn't cite the advantages of a good education, and the subject is almost always mentioned in the election platforms of political parties. Well-educated people can more easily adapt to the demands of new technology, their range of employment opportunities is much broader and their pay is significantly higher than that of their contemporaries with less to offer. It would seem, therefore, that one of the top priorities for the next millennium would be universal access to increasingly high standards of learning.

If that is the desired course, then it is deplorable to note that public policy, almost worldwide, is leading in the opposite direction. Children and young people are no longer classified as students; they have been redesignated as consumers of education. But many of them come from families with insufficient disposable income to pay the increasing cost. They cannot consume what they cannot afford. Education, of necessity, is taking a back seat to essential food, clothing and shelter. Consequently universality of access to education is giving way to exclusivity.

Tuition fees in some First World countries have been rising. In Canada, for example, about 60 percent of all full-time students need to borrow in order to attend college and university. The average debt load for these hundreds of thousands of students at graduation has grown from $8,700 in 1990, to $22,000 in 1997. This burden is expected to reach $25,000 by the end of the millennium.[9] As a result, some students are no longer willing or able to assume such a heavy burden. As I was about to begin this chapter, a friend told me that his daughter needed another year of university in order to qualify for the only jobs available in her field. She had reluctantly decided to abandon the idea because she couldn't afford the tuition fee.

If the situation in First World countries ranges from worrisome to alarming, it is closer to desperation for most

Third World countries. Access to schooling is becoming more difficult and any hope of liberation from poverty through education is fast fading for millions of children, thanks to the restrictions imposed by market driven economics.

A whole book could be written on this subject, but for my purposes one example from Michel Chossudovsky's *The Globalisation of Poverty* is illustrative of Third World trends. He is reporting the experience in Vietnam.

"The reforms have deliberately and consciously destroyed the educational system by massively compressing the educational budget, depressing teachers' salaries and 'commercialising' secondary, vocational and higher education through the exaction of tuition fees. The movement is towards the transformation of education into a commodity. In the official jargon of the UN agencies, this requires: ' ... consumers of [educational] services to pay increased amounts, encouraging institutions to become self-financing, and by using incentives to privatise delivery of education and training where appropriate.'

"Virtually repealing all previous achievements, including the struggle against illiteracy carried out since 1945, the reforms have engineered an unprecedented collapse in school enrolment with a high drop-out rate observed in the final years of primary school. The obligation to pay tuition fees is now entrenched in the constitution which was carefully redrafted in 1992. According to official data, the proportion of graduates from primary education who entered the four-year, lower-secondary education programme declined from 92 per cent in 1986/87 (prior to the inauguration of the tuition fees) to 72 per cent in 1989/90, a drop of more than half a million students. Similarly, some 231,000 students, out of a total of 922,000, dropped out of the upper-secondary education programme. In other words, *a total of nearly three quarters of a million children were pushed out of the secondary school system during the first three years of the reforms* (despite an increase of more than 7 per cent in the population of school age). While recent enrolment data is unavailable, there is no evidence that this trend has been reversed."[10]

If the experience in Vietnam, which is typical of that in dozens of other countries, is supposed to be progress it makes you wonder if a number of well known words have lost their meaning. Instead of moving forward, the word "reform" is increasingly associated with moving backward — to regress, rather than to progress. Just think of all the political rhetoric and the plethora of programs associated with getting people off welfare and breaking the cycle of poverty. Education is often cited as a key element, yet here is a world system that will perpetuate mass poverty and the need for international welfare. Market-driven education will never break the cycle. Governments must.

THE ENVIRONMENT

Another area of universal concern is protecting the global environment for the enjoyment of generations to come. Here again, Darwinian economics is a major part of the problem and offers no hope that self-regulation will provide an adequate solution. Higher environmental standards, better enforcement and a much higher level of public spending is required if homo sapiens are to escape indictment as the only species guilty of fouling their own nest.

There are so many environmental concerns in need of attention that it is difficult to know where to start. Certainly there are numerous sites where the soil has been contaminated by toxic waste that should be cleaned up. And while in theory the persons or corporations responsible for the pollution should be required to do the clean-up that is not always practicable. If it isn't, governments must step in and do it because the job must be done.

Mining

In some cases there is procrastination when governments themselves are culprits. There are tailings from Eldorado Mining Corporation, as it was known when the Canadian government owned it, which refined uranium for U.S. atomic bombs, that still pose a threat to the health and peace of mind of people living in affected sub-divisions. A problem of greater magnitude, for all countries that have built atomic reactors to produce electricity, is what to do with the spent fuel that will remain highly radioactive for centuries.   The cost of implementing socially and environmentally acceptable solutions will be enormous.

Air quality poses another gigantic challenge. People in my city of Toronto used to thank their lucky stars that they didn't have to breathe the air in Los Angeles, let alone Mexico City. That smugness is now giving way to the reality that no large city is immune.   Certainly not one where traffic increasingly sits in gridlock, while exhaust fumes and profanity pollute the air. No doubt there are solutions, but the dollar tags attached to some of them are truly staggering.

Industrial Waste

When it comes to industrial pollution, my home province of Ontario ranks third in North America after the states of Texas and Louisiana.[11] Toxic chemical waste in Canada is on the rise, however, while similar pollution in the United States is dropping. The 155 million kilograms of Canadian industrial pollution produced in 1995 was a 4 percent increase compared with the 1.15 billion kilograms in the U.S., a 2 percent decline.[12] A realist might conclude that the record in both countries leaves much room for improvement. Consequently, it is heart-warming to learn that after years of delay the U.S. Environmental Protection Agency (EPA) has finally moved decisively to deal with windblown pollution that originates mainly in the Midwest and drifts eastward to poison the air over New York and other Northeastern states, as well as areas north of the border in Southern Ontario and Québec.[13]

This action, by EPA administrator Carol Browner, is a clear victory for public health. It is a common sense ruling in opposition to sustained lobbying by the Mideastern Governors and the coal-fired electric utilities that will bear most of the cost. Yet it is a small price to pay for a big step in the direction that the world must march if the legacy of the present generation to the next is to be a worthy one. Leadership has to be given by those countries that can well afford to show the way. Then they must go the second mile by helping those countries where basic needs have yet to be met.

Clean Water

In terms of public health concerns, the twin of clean air is clean water. A looming crisis in the distribution of potable water is being exacerbated by too much industrial pollution and too many accidents, many attributable to the mining industry. One of the worst in recent years involved a Canadian company, Boliden Ltd. Its mine near Seville, in the South of Spain, spilled about 4 million cubic meters of acidic water, as well as mine tailings containing sulphur, zinc, copper, iron and lead, into the nearby Rio Agro river after a mine reservoir ruptured in April, 1998, sending a torrent of toxic material flowing downstream. The company subsequently undertook a study to determine the extent of the damage and agreed to foot the bill.[14] Accidents are inevitable, but some of them are avoidable with just a little more care and initial expense. My files include several examples of spills that might have been due to cutting corners — a decision that proved to be the most costly in the longer run.

No discussion of water quality would be complete without reference to the Great Lakes basin, one of the world's largest reservoirs of fresh water straddling the border between Canada and the United States. The two countries established an International Joint Commission (IJC) to resolve disputes under the 1909 Boundary Waters Treaty and to assist in the protection of the trans-boundary environment, including the implementation of the Great Lakes Quality agreement. Anyone living on one of the Great Lakes, as I do, will know that significant progress has been made in cleaning them up. Anyone who drinks the water, as millions of people do, will agree with the cover statement on the Ninth Biennial Report of the IJC that says: "There is much work to be done ..." The issue, as the report states, is "toxic and persistent toxic substances."[15]

"Despite years of effort to stop inputs, clean up contamination and eliminate the use of chemicals that have long been known to cause injury, all remain widespread in the ecosystem and many continue to be used. Through its consultation process, the Commission has heard the question, 'Why are we unable to effectively deal with these persistent toxic substances?' The question becomes more critical as evidence continues to build regarding subtle, insidious effects of these and other chemicals on key body processes, including the endocrine system. Moreover, society now realizes that not only fish and wildlife are affected, but humans as well."[16] If two of the richest countries on earth are having problems coming to grips with these genetic concerns think of the magnitude of the global challenge.

A challenge of equal scope is learning to respect and protect our oceans. They are the foundation of the biosphere that sustains us, yet for far too long we have just taken them for granted. They are our principal highways of commerce and our most varied and attractive playgrounds. They are one of our most plentiful sources of food; but we forgot that the supply was not inexhaustible, and has to be replenished by nature's natural cycle. So we have been harvesting some species of fish and marine life at an unsustainable rate, and for the first time see the results of our careless stewardship. Now we are feeling the pain of the disruption that results in people's lives when there are no fish remaining to be caught.

Protecting our oceans is an area where international cooperation is essential. Conservation is impossible in the face of incessant poaching. Reducing the incidence of oil spills requires that ships operating under "flags of convenience" must also obey the rules. Ceasing to use the oceans as a world-scale garbage dump requires the understanding and cooperation of all peoples and all nations. The oceans are our common treasure and must be protected for our common good.

Forests

Forests, too, are part of nature's life-preserving

apparatus and have to be treated in that context. There are too many examples in history where excessive destruction of the forests in order to clear land for agriculture has resulted in soil erosion, dust storms and changes in climate. The fact that we haven't learned from this experience, and that the practice is continuing, is less than reassuring — especially when some of the over-cutting is a result of IMF imposed policies.

The practice of the forest industry in some countries to clear-cut large areas of prime or virgin forest has been very controversial and nowhere more so than in Canada.   Vast hillsides have been completely denuded. On the industry side of the argument there are economic advantages and safety considerations.   It is cheaper to clear-cut, and there is less chance of branches falling on workmen's heads.   Environmentalists, on the other hand, are outraged. They see the huge, ugly scars on the mountainside and resent the near-total obliteration of the ecosystem including the habitat for birds and animals.

There are alternatives. Many European countries have banned clear-cutting. And the environmentalists have scored a major victory in Canada. The forest giant MacMillan Bloedel Ltd. has decided to phase out clear-cut logging over five years beginning in 1998. The company's new American president, Tom Stephens, denied caving in to pressure but he told a news conference "evidence everywhere tells us that some of society's values are shifting."[17] Indeed they are. It might be considered as "total accounting", as opposed to the narrow "bottom line" of a single company brand of accounting. What companies do has an impact far beyond that disclosed in their annual reports.

This lesson was etched on my mind in a conversation with Paul Carrick, a friend who had just returned to Canada from Honduras where he had been working with the Canadian Armed Forces in distributing aid to remote villages devastated by tropical hurricane Mitch. He said that where the hillsides had been clear-cut, there was nothing to prevent the mudslides that destroyed everything in their path. He then told of houses that had been saved by a few trees around the periphery — in one case, by a single tree. The environmentalists rest their case. Sustainable forests contribute more to human well-being than merely logs.

Global Warming

Preserving, protecting and, indeed, enhancing our forests is a natural launching-pad for a brief look at the problem of global warming. Of the many interesting and noteworthy large and small events of 1998 — and what a year it was — few were as full of wonderment as reports of birds laying eggs, and the sight of spring flowers in bloom along the boardwalk in front of our condominium in December. In December? In Canada? Readers should know that in my more than three score and ten years this has never, ever happened before. What is happening to our planet! Toronto residents might point out that an early January 1999 snow storm, one of the worst in decades, redressed the balance. But that doesn't detract from the fact that 1998 was the warmest on record.

For years there have been scientists warning us of the effects of greenhouse gases that would result in global warming. These gases, mostly water vapour, carbon dioxide, methane and nitrous oxide, trap the heat from the sun and prevent it from being radiated back into space. Without this thermal blanket scientists believe that average temperatures would drop to the point that the oceans would freeze and life, as we know it, would be impossible.

There can be too much of a good thing, however. By burning coal and oil the concentration of carbon dioxide increases. Cutting too many trees, which absorb carbon monoxide, contributes further to the concentration which has increased 30 percent since pre-industrial times. Using sophisticated computer models, scientists have predicted that global temperatures might rise by two degrees over the next century due to the increase in global gases.

There are skeptical scientists, of course, who claim that it is difficult to distinguish between normal climate fluctuation and the impact of human activity. These are the ones referred to by the oil and auto lobbies wishing to downplay the urgency of reducing emissions. It was the dominant view at the 1998 World Economic Forum in Davos, Switzerland, where Cor Herstroter, the chairman of Royal Dutch/Shell, one of the world's energy giants, stated his position as follows: "The issue of climate change is still fraught with complexity and uncertainty. Personally, I welcome the implicit message from Kyoto that there are no easy answers or rapid solutions. A prudent, precautionary approach is, in our view, the right one."[18] The oil industry argument is that there is no conclusive evidence of global warming due to the burning of fossil fuels. So don't panic until there is. It is reminiscent of the position taken by the tobacco industry when it claimed, for decades, that there was no conclusive evidence that smoking was injurious to the health.

When it is a question of life and death I prefer to err on the side of caution. Some years ago I was bitten by a bat that I had stunned but not killed when I hit it with a badminton racquet. The bat revived and got away so it couldn't be tested for rabies. My doctor agreed that the probability of the furry creature being rabid was low but he added that it was not impossible that it could be. I asked him how many humans had survived rabies. "None, so far", he replied. I decided to take the shots.

I do not want to give the impression that the probability of global warming is low. Far from it. I accept the cautious endorsement of the United Nations Intergovernmental Panel on Climate Change, an international group of experts studying global warming, which by 1995 considered the mounting evidence sufficiently compelling that it issued a statement saying: "The balance of evidence suggests a discernible human influence on global climate."[19] The point of my story is that we had better act now because by the time the evidence is "absolutely conclusive" it will be too late.

ECONOMIC GROWTH AND THE ENVIRONMENT

On several occasions in the course of my travels I have been accosted by environmentalists who berate me for talking about increased economic growth. In their view, the opposite should occur. Economic growth should be slowed or stopped altogether in order to end environmental degradation and preserve the planet. I have noted that the suggestion usually comes from people who are quite well educated, well clothed and, apparently, well fed.

When time permits I try to make three points that I consider relevant. The first is that it would be unfair for those of us whose basic needs have been met to say to the rest of the world that they are not entitled to strive for similar benefits. It is reasonable to hope that they will avoid some of the conspicuous consumption and planned obsolescence that has been built into our system; but they have an inalienable right to try to free themselves from the miserable conditions under which many of them live, and to improve their lot.

The second point is strictly economic. If the rate of growth of the world economy is less than the average interest rate on its debt, the latter will grow until it becomes unsustainable and the whole system will collapse. That has been the history of the last quarter of the twentieth century, and the reason the world economy is teetering on a knife's edge. The principal thrust of this book is the suggestion that we can escape the impending disaster by eliminating some of the debt, and adopting policies that keep interest rates low so that the cycle will not repeat. But there will still be plenty of debt remaining, and interest to be paid, so economic growth will be required to carry that cost.

The third point is the good news. Economic growth can be environmentally-friendly, or environmentally-positive. It doesn't have to follow the pattern of most of the twentieth century which, incidentally, is ending with some encouraging signs. New cars consume less fuel and emit less pollution than the old ones, but there are still millions of the latter waiting to be replaced when economic circumstances permit (this is especially true in some less developed countries.) Pollution from electricity generation is being sharply curtailed and fortunes are being spent on the development of new forms of energy to make us less dependent on fossil fuels. All of this activity is included in Gross Domestic Product, but it translates into environmental improvement.

One further example from the myriad available — one of major, and perhaps critical, importance. Whereas excessive deforestation has contributed significantly to the problem of greenhouse gases, a major program of reforestation would have the opposite effect. Both show up in GDP but one is negative and one is extremely positive to the environment. Our goal, therefore, should not be to slow economic growth but rather to harness it positively for the benefit of both present and future generations.

GOVERNMENT AS EMPLOYER OF LAST RESORT

If there is one area above all others where classical or neo-classical economics has been a total failure it is in creating jobs for everyone willing and able to work. For two hundred years we have gone through cycles of full employment and then unacceptably high levels of unemployment. This has been a major fault in the capitalist system — one that only governments can cure.

Although full employment has been a long-term problem, it is likely to become more acute in the years to come. In his book *The End of Work*, Jeremy Rifkin forecasts that increasingly large numbers of marginalized workers will be unemployed as they are replaced by machines. A meeting of top CEOs held in San Francisco not long ago came up with an even more dire prediction. The chief executives concluded that some time in the not too distant future 20% of the workforce could produce all of the goods and services required.

In each case, what they are really saying is that an exclusively market-oriented economy can only usefully employ a limited fraction of the available workforce. This is not a statement that all of societies needs will be met through the efforts of the smaller numbers employed. They won't be. The powerful, the inventive and the lucky will fare well while everyone who doesn't fall into one of those categories will be dependent on welfare. Unless, of course, governments use the tools available to them to allow everyone to contribute something worthwhile.

The future lies in governments becoming, in effect, the employers of last resort. This does not mean that vast numbers of people must be on the public payroll! Far from it. It just means that governments must show leadership and use the financial resources available to them under a reformed monetary system to maximize the common good. Examples include universal access to health care, more and better educational opportunities, and massive expenditures for environmental protection and enhancement. It should also include very large expenditures for the repair and replacement of old infrastructure including roads, bridges, sewerage systems and so on.

The list is very long. There are city cores to be rebuilt and revitalized. It would be economically and socially profitable to let some of the able bodied men and women out of jail and involve them in creative activity. They could build public parks and recreational facilities for people who can't afford membership in golf or fitness clubs.

The bottom line is that there is no shortage of work to be done if the quality of life and the common good are key to the equation. More money can be spent on pure and applied science and the results made available for the benefit of all, and not just the privileged few. In many countries governments could provide greater support for the visual and performing arts. This may not be important to the U.S. where there are substantial private funds available, but in countries less well endowed, like Canada, increased funding is urgently needed. The end result, of course, would be a massive increase in domestic economic activity that would offset reductions in trade and exports.

All of this is possible and, from the perspective of the vast majority, highly desirable. It is just wishful thinking, however, if the "permanent government" of big vested interests tells the "provisional government" of elected politicians that they must reject monetary reform, reject debt forgiveness for the Third World, reject the concept of full employment and maintain the status quo. In this highly probable scenario, new checks and balances will be required — made possible through a revolution of the ballot box.

REVOLUTION BY BALLOT BOX

Is it possible, as we are about to embark on a new millennium, that the greatest single impediment to progress and justice both nationally and internationally is the kind of representative democracy we have been taught to revere? The question ceases to be hypothetical when nearly all of the major political parties, in many countries, have emerged from the pressure-cooker of the Washington consensus as dull, gray, blah. It requires either a very sophisticated or a prejudiced palate to distinguish between them.

This is the kind of observation that I resented when I was in active politics — probably because I knew there was an element of truth to the charge. People would say that it didn't matter which one of the two major parties was elected, nothing would change because they were so much alike. In part, this was because a party in opposition would espouse brave new alternatives but, once elected, they would drop their radical and often attractive ideas because, after submitting them to bureaucratic review, they were said to be impractical. So the new government would follow most of the policies of its predecessor and the new opposition would inherit the mantle of innovation.

I saw this process in action. Public servants could give you a dozen good reasons why any change from existing policy would be folly. I also learned that they wouldn't hesitate to share that view with the press, "off the record", if you persisted and demanded change. After I left the government, the top public servant, Gordon Robertson, Clerk of the Privy Council, told students at Carleton University in Ottawa that my problem was that I thought politicians were elected to go to Ottawa to set policy. He was right about that. I was naive enough to think that was the essence of democracy. Robertson, who exercised more power than any cabinet minister other than the Prime Minister, set the students straight on that score.

My fear now is that the parties are even more alike than they were twenty or thirty years ago. President Bill Clinton has shifted the Democratic Party away from the influence of the lobby groups that represented seniors, minorities and labor into the arms of a centre-right group representing transnational corporations, international banks, bond dealers, investment firms and trade interests. In effect the Clinton Administration is indistinguishable from what one might expect from a moderate Republican one. So it is fair to ask, as some Americans are now doing, what happened to Democratic liberals?

I can remember when there were really significant differences between the major parties in the United Kingdom. As in many countries, Labor insisted on a social safety net while this idea was stoutly resisted by the Tories. Today they are side-by-side on the political spectrum. Prime Minister Tony Blair's initial act of giving the Bank of England total control over interest rates was pure Washington consensus. The U.K. seems to be quite content to act as America's junior partner in foreign and trade policy, and any difference between the Labor government and the Conservative and Unionist Party opposition led by William Hague, appears to be primarily cosmetic.

Until recently, Canada could boast three major parties that were about as similar as triplets. Prime Minister Jean Chrétien's Liberal government, the official opposition Reform Party, led by Preston Manning, and the Progressive Conservative Party, which was a force in national politics until it suffered a humiliating defeat in the 1993 election — now led by former prime minister Joe Clark — are all small "c" conservative parties based on the U.S. Republican model. Canada's traditional liberalism died under the withering blast of the Washington consensus.

Late in 1998 Alexa McDonough, leader of the New Democratic Party which has traditionally hovered between socialist and social democratic, announced that she would follow in the footsteps of Tony Blair and lead her party, too, into the globalist camp. The only remaining vestige of social-democracy is found in the Bloc Québecois, the party which was formed to promote the break-up of Canada.

In Australia both the Liberal/National Party coalition government of John Howard, and the Labor Party opposition, have accepted the monetarist, neo-classical consensus with its emphasis on free trade and globalized markets. The result has been cut-backs in many essential services in the name of fiscal probity and international competitiveness.

As already pointed out, New Zealand has been trumpeted as the "Exhibit A" success story for open borders and globalized capital. Miraculously, all the major parties got on the bandwagon so the debate became woefully lopsided. Thoughtful New Zealanders are wondering aloud if there is not some mid-way point between a closed economy and one that is almost totally dependent on the whims and uncertainties of transnational corporations and global finance.

I will not continue the catalogue of national politics except to wonder how much difference the election of some left-wing governments in Europe is likely to make. To what extent will the new German government of Gerhard Schroeder push policies that are radically different from that of his predecessor, Helmut Kohl? The answer may provide some clue as to the degree of manoeuvring room open to any government that has totally surrendered its monetary sovereignty. To what extent can you steer a ship of state when someone else is at the helm?

I must admit genuine doubt that any of the major parties, anywhere, possess the fortitude to command the about-turn necessary to move away from the abyss. One can always hope that an avalanche of sustained popular pressure might effect the miraculous transformation required, but the odds against it happening are formidable. A more likely remedy would be the formation of new populist parties with platforms so appealing that they prove to be irresistible to disenchanted voters — parties that are not prisoners of the "permanent government" and subject to its strait-jacket.

The idea would be pure fantasy if it were not for the internet. Electoral revolutionaries would be fighting a disciplined army with immense resources at its command. But this same army, with virtually unlimited resources, was backing the 29 governments supporting the secretive MAI negotiations at OECD headquarters in Paris. Still it was dealt a humiliating defeat by Non-Governmental Organizations (NGO) freedom fighters all around the globe. The war against globalization has not yet been won but victory in such a major battle should provide comfort and courage to the combatants.

DIRECT DEMOCRACY

One of the goals of the freedom fighters should be the adoption of contemporary forms of direct democracy. It is becoming increasingly obvious that the form of democracy that has evolved in the 19th and 20th centuries is an unfinished creation, and must evolve further to reach its full potential. Representative democracy was an essential stage in the process, but it is no longer acceptable to elect people once every few years and then have no further say in public affairs until the next time. Voices are allegedly equal on election day but then they are very unequal from that day on.

Initiative and Referendum

The remedy appears to be some form of direct democracy which allows voters to decide those matters of greatest concern. A national referendum is the modern version of the ancient Greek practice of getting everyone together in the city square to debate and decide public issues. The idea has been copied in several jurisdictions with some success. Australia has held almost 50 nationwide referendums and its component states almost as many again. The Italian referendums of 1991 and 1993 are credited with breaking up the corrupt Italian party system.

More than half the American states have such laws although the practice has never been elevated to the federal level. In Canada the idea is still considered foreign to the parliamentary system although in 1992 proposed constitutional amendments were submitted to the people at popular insistence and the proposal was defeated despite the favorable recommendation of all the major parties. It is my belief that had a system of national referenda been in place for the last twenty years, Canada would have been spared almost all of the bad legislation some of us find so irritating.

It is the Swiss, however, who have pioneered and proven the system over 130 years. Several hundred questions have been submitted to the population at large and each time citizens were invited to read meticulously impartial documents before they made up their minds. A certain number of signatures on a petition is sufficient to require that any new law be submitted to popular vote. Twice as many signatures are required to have new ideas that may lack parliamentary approval submitted to voters for a decision. This is called citizen's initiative — a procedure which empowers ordinary voters who have become totally frustrated by the lack of interest from their electoral representatives.

Citizens initiative is important if you want a level playing field. If the wording of a referendum is left exclusively to government the dice may be loaded in advance. Canadians are acutely aware of this from experience with two referendums on the subject of the separation of Québec from the rest of Canada. The questions were deliberately loaded to obtain the votes of some people who wanted to remain in Canada but at the same time negotiate a better deal. In the Québec government's mind, however, it intended to interpret a majority vote as a mandate to separate. Citizen's initiative, it if were in operation, might require a clarification of the question or a separate unequivocal question.

Skeptics suggest that the Swiss model is not applicable to larger countries. There is not a shred of evidence to support the contention. If Switzerland with its linguistic diversity can make the system work, any country should be able to.

Recall

One further possibility would be provision for citizen recall of an elected representative for misdemeanor or for blatantly ignoring voters' wishes and concerns. In a sense it helps perform the same function as citizen's initiative and referendums. Politicians would no longer be able to ignore voters wishes in-between elections in the hope that they would have short memories, and be willing to sell their votes for a few bon-bons when the next vote is held. Politicians would have to be acutely aware of voter approval or disapproval of every new law being proposed, because failure to do so might result in voters taking the law into their own hands.

There is only one major problem with these proposals. In many countries it may not be possible to put them into effect soon enough to permit citizens to force the fundamental changes, including bank reform and debt forgiveness, necessary to start the new millennium with a joyful fanfare.

I HAVE A DREAM

"America is great because America is GOOD.
If America ever ceases to be good it will cease to be great. "

Alexis de Toqueville

The postscript is dedicated to men and women of goodwill like the late Martin Luther King, whose dream of justice was an inspiration to millions; to Nelson Mandela whose policy of reconciliation rather than retribution became a model for the world; and to mother Theresa who dedicated her life to the poorest of the poor. These three, and thousands more, suggest by the priorities of their lives that there can be no economic solution in the absence of a moral and spiritual renaissance. All of us must try to recognize one another's worth, to understand the differing points of view and to care about each other.

Inevitably this leads us to a review of what life is all about. Is the purpose of economic organization to enhance the human existence, to provide us with comfort and security and to enrich our experience? Or are we simply economic units to be bought, sold, traded and ultimately consigned to the junk heap of humanity when we become redundant or obsolescent? These are the basic questions to be addressed before we decide which route to take.

My bias must be clear by now. I believe that people are more important than corporations or governments, than banks or bullies. That is why I think that for the final quarter of the twentieth century we got our priorities all wrong. True believers in the monetarist, neo-classical brand of fundamentalist economics led us to believe that if we just let the lions out of their cages the world would inevitably become a safer, happier habitat for the rabbits and deer. Two hundred years of economic history demonstrates that is not so and common sense guarantees it never will be so.

For twenty five years, increasingly, the rewards have gone to the financial economy, the people who play with money, at the expense of the real economy, the people who grow food, sew dresses and build houses. There has been a vast increase in interest income at the expense of earned income. There have been more people out of work and the distribution of income has lost all relevance to real worth.

The Evil Empire

Money has replaced people as the governing body. As far back as September 24, 1995, Mansoor Ijaz, an American ex-nuclear physicist running an investment firm in New York, alleged that economic forecasts are an anachronism because people like him run our economies now. "There is no central bank in the world that can take on the top three or four speculators", he said, "they just don't have enough money."[1] In his view politicians are now irrelevant because hedge funds and speculators call the shots. "I think, in fact, we are more like a supra-national government of the world", he concluded.[2] It is an evil system which allows financial predators to determine the health of the body politic worldwide. For hundreds of millions, perhaps billions, of people it has led to impoverishment as a result of disruption in subsistence farming, reduced access to health care and education and the crushing burden of unbearable debt. For millions of unfortunates unfettered capitalism has actually meant the difference between life and death.

For millions of people in the more advanced economies it has taken the fun out of work and raised stress levels to unprecedented heights. Ever since the streamlining and downsizing rampage hit its full stride in the 1990s I have talked to one unhappy person after another. In September, '96, I attended Transport Canada's 60th anniversary celebration. I chatted with senior officials who had been in the department years earlier when I was minister and their final words were: "It's not fun any more." In the years since, I have heard the same story from nurses at understaffed hospitals, from teachers who have had their workloads increased to the point where they can no longer help students with extracurricular activity and from bank employees expected to do the work formerly performed by two people.

Unhappily these people are often afraid to complain for fear of being fired. It is a cruel system which creates a climate where nobody is happy — the unemployed because they have no jobs, and many who have jobs but are stretched to the breaking point. This is certainly the case in Canada. In a Southam News Compass poll in late October, 1998, a whopping 92% of people surveyed said family stress was greater than it was a half-century ago. "In an age when Canadians are physically healthier and more robust than ever before, the Southam-Compass poll paints a picture of a society suffering from chronic emotional ill-health because of pressure on families."[3] Friends in other countries paint a similar picture.

The alternative, of course, is a world with greater national control and less international competition with its inevitable race to the bottom in wages and benefits. It would be the kind of system I have described in this book where demand management at the national level would permit maximum participation and maximum output without draining the emotional life-blood from most participants in the insatiable quest to maximize shareholder values. The concept of shareholder value has to be broadened to include all stake-holders, including employees and the host community.

PERSONAL AND NATIONAL SECURITY

The word community is, of course, foreign to neo-classical economics. If each person cares only about him or her self they can expect minimum compassion from the victims of their self-indulgence.   A world of fenced and guarded compounds may look like a solution, but that is a delusion. Real security is impossible in an economic system lacking in moral resonance.

Hungry, unemployed people are tempted to rock the boat because they have little to lose.   There are already signs of unrest in countries as disparate as Germany, Zimbabwe, and Malaysia and the potential for trouble exists in many more. People with long memories will recall that it was mass unemployment and political unrest which set the stage for World War II, and there is no reason to believe that it couldn't happen again.

Unfortunately the leaders of the G7 countries appear to be blind to the reality.   They are so consumed with the explosive potential of the world financial economy that they have become immunized to the equally explosive potential of millions of people who are sick-to-death of having foreign systems, foreign culture, foreign values and foreign debt rammed down their throats.   They are seeking freedom and justice, and they are not finding it.

Ironically, it was the United States which insisted that the European countries grant independence to their colonial empires in the years following World War II.   Today those countries have been re-colonized to an extent that would have been considered inconceivable.   Their economies are managed for the near-total benefit of the globalized financial economy with devastating consequences to the people being governed.

In November '98 I asked Kent Hotaling, one of my long-time American friends who is personally familiar with the distress and hardship caused by IMF and World Bank policies in several African countries, if he thought many of his compatriots had any idea of the extent of the damage that U.S. foreign policy, as enforced by these two agencies, had done to Third World countries.   He thought that the majority were unaware.

I had to admit that my fellow Canadians were also poorly informed.   I certainly had been until I began to consider these matters seriously.   In both Canada and the U.S. the tiny minority who do understand include people who work for non-governmental organizations active in these countries, some recent immigrants and a handful of researchers in North-South institutes. Some of the people I talk to actually believe we are too generous with our assistance to poor countries and resent paying taxes ear-marked for foreign aid.

Our lack of foresight and sensitivity toward the needs of our fellow man is bound to catch up with us. We were euphoric when communism collapsed in the Soviet Union. It was a capitalist rout and many people thought that the millennium had arrived ten years in advance. We were presented with a golden opportunity to assist in a gradual transformation from a centralized system to a more decentralized, market-oriented one. We botched it up unbelievably — worse than an opportunity missed. Neo-classical ideologues insisted on the instant transformation, as if that were possible, and offered nothing more tangible than advice, most of it bad. A January 1999 report from Moscow summarized the average Russian's perception of Boris Yeltsin's brand of capitalism as one of crime, greed and poverty. With all the rosy promises unkept it is little wonder that Stalinism has not yet been pronounced completely dead.

Russia, like much of the rest of the world, will require decades of economic experiment to achieve the right balance between markets and government-provided service. It would be a terrible mistake to re-nationalize everything as some disgruntled Russians now propose, just as it was a terrible mistake to attempt to privatize everything in one fell swoop. Gradualism is required to learn skills that take a generation to acquire. Meanwhile the West, and the U.S. in particular, has to abandon its expectation of a miracle on the cheap. Something grand, on the scale of a Marshall Plan, is required.

U.S. novelist Mark Helprin is not optimistic that this will happen. In an article in the *Wall Street Journal* entitled "A Marshall Plan for Russia", he wrote: "An initiative of this magnitude is a Hope diamond for an administration that thinks in sequins and may be remembered for its statesmanly regulation of hot-dog additives. This is not the age of American probity or sacrifice. Europe and Japan are burdened by the kind of economic problems that compromise foresight. It would take Churchill, Truman, and Marshall to clear the air. Of course, we do not have a Churchill, Truman, or Marshall, not, at least, in office, as our brief respite from the consequences of history begins to end."[4]

National Security

This is a shrewd assessment by Helprin and one that should be borne in mind when making strategic decisions. It encouraged me to wonder aloud what kind of advice I would give the President of the United States if I were his top national security adviser.

I would point out that there are two diametrically opposite strategies. The first is the sword and shield strategy — you might call it the "In Power and Technology we Trust" approach. This would include increased military preparedness including vast expenditures for the development and deployment of an anti-missile missile system to intercept unwelcome intruders launched by some mad renegade. Every time I read about anti-missile missiles, however, I think of the Maginot line and the false sense of security it gave the French between World Wars I and II. Little did they dream that the Germans would just go around it safe in the knowledge that the guns were all pointed in one direction and couldn't be swung around to fire in the opposite direction.

A comprehensive anti-missile missile system might be capable of intercepting an occasional missile fired in anger but it would provide the same false sense of security that the Maginot line did because there is no such thing as absolute security in the world in which we live. There are far too many "how to" books and manuals that describe in detail how to make atomic bombs, nerve gases and deadly bacteria. And any amateur strategist could devise ways of delivering them to vulnerable targets. So a policy of dropping a bomb on any basement suspected of being a laboratory is just not practical in guaranteeing security.

The other alternative is an all-out effort to reduce the number of people who would like to harm you — a sort of smother them with kindness approach. Again there are no absolute guarantees but the probability of success would be much greater. So I would advise the president to take the initiative with the G7 leaders when they meet in June '99 and present a plan that would fundamentally reform the banking system; require that cash reserves be increased to 50 percent over five years; use the opportunity this presents to eliminate virtually all Third World external debt, as well as that of other countries including Russia and struggling East European countries that were previously in the Soviet orbit; wind-up the International Monetary Fund, the World Bank, the World Trade Organization; and rescind all of the trade, capital flow and other conditions imposed by the IMF and World Bank.

With that revolution underway, to undertake a world-wide effort to help people to help themselves and to learn the skills necessary for economic as well as political emancipation. The world has the capacity to see that every one of its citizens has access to potable water and adequate food and shelter, as well as increased access to health care and education, within a decade. If these goals were our principal agenda the transformation would be unprecedented. And if it were a united effort, everyone would feel good about their participation whether direct or indirect. There would be a new sense of community — of working together for the common good.

I am convinced that this strategy has by far the greatest chance of creating a more secure and congenial environment for both individuals and nations. People who are busily — and one would hope happily — involved in creative pursuits are far less likely to indulge in mischief. This is the morally correct solution as well as the one most beneficial to the long-term interests of the sponsoring countries, the solution that would offer the greatest economic benefits as well as the most harmonious international relations. So it is my fond hope that the United States will seize the initiative and show the way by making the year of the Jubilee a turning point of modern history — the year of a new beginning for the world.

FIRE SALVO ONE

There is no absolute guarantee that the United States will recognize that the moral course is also the one that is in its own best long-term interests. I have no doubt that thousands of Americans will come to that conclusion but will that be enough to encourage the government and the Congress to act quickly and decisively? What if the permanent government of vested interests decides that it prefers the status quo and the unequal power that it enjoys? Will it not, in that circumstance, try to dampen political enthusiasm with its classic "wink and nod" techniques?

Fortunately, for themselves and for the world, the Third World countries have the power to bring the G7 leaders to their knees. All they have to do is to write individual letters to each of the leaders of the G7 countries and say something like this.

Sir:

We would like you to stop and think about the power you have over the lives of billions of people and the opportunity you now have to emancipate us from the tyranny of the Bretton Woods institutions and the oppression of our external debt, which can never be repaid and which condemns us to perpetual economic bondage. We therefore respectfully request that you act now to implement the package of reforms necessary to set us free and give us renewed hope as we begin a new millennium.

We consider these actions to be so important to the future of our people and the peace and security of the world that we wish to advise that in the event satisfactory action has not been taken by June 1, in the year 2000, that we will be obliged to suspend all interest and capital payments on our external debt.

With every best wish for a happy and prosperous new millennium.

Yours very truly,

It would be encouraging if all of the underdeveloped countries wrote letters to this effect quickly and spontaneously but even a few of the most heavily indebted could exert enough pressure to do the trick. It wouldn't take long after the suspension of loan repayments for the whole international financial system to come crashing down like the house of cards it really is. Only action along the lines suggested in this book could save it, so Third World countries have at their disposal the enormous power necessary to win a bloodless revolution.

There are lots of good ideas around which are routinely ignored because they clash with one powerful vested interest or another. The package of reforms I am suggesting will engage the all-out opposition of some of the most powerful vested interests in the world. They will not capitulate without a fight so I consider it prudent to suggest that some ammunition more powerful than wishful thinking should be available in reserve. That ammunition is the organization necessary to put contingency plans into effect quickly and successfully. A revolution is far more likely to succeed if it has been meticulously planned.

Nelson Mandela

A good leader would help to ensure concerted action and maximum participation of the less developed countries and I can't think of anyone better suited to the job than Nelson Mandela. The South African president plans to retire in the Spring of 1999 following the election in his country. Apart from his hope to grow old in Qunu, the village of his birth, Mandela has a dream for his native Africa and for the poor and oppressed people of the earth.

Addressing the United Nations General Assembly for the last time as South Africa's president he said: "I will continue to hope that Africa's Renaissance will strike deep roots and blossom forever, without regard to the changing seasons."[5]

On the subject of the world economy, Mr. Mandela said that poverty "has been and is the condition of the daily existence of even larger numbers of ordinary working people. Put

starkly, we have a situation in which the further accumulation
of wealth, rather than contributing to the improvement of the
quality of life of all humanity, is generating poverty at a
frighteningly accelerated pace."[6]

He then went right to the core of the issue and the
subject of this essay. "Fortunately, the matter is no longer in
dispute that serious work will also have to be done to
restructure the multilateral financial and economic institutions
so that they address the problems of the modern world economy
and become responsive to the urgent needs of the poor of the
world", he said.[7]

Hear, hear! And the best contribution that some of
those institutions can make is to forgive their outstanding loans
and die gracefully as part of the grander renaissance. For his
part Mr. Mandela, currently leader of the Non-Aligned
Movement, which includes all developing countries, is perfectly
positioned to rally these countries in one united front to seek
their economic and political liberation. One of Nelson
Mandela's dreams, the end of apartheid in South Africa, has
already come true and the fulfillment of his latest one is within
his grasp. "Were all these hopes to translate into a reasonable
dream and not a nightmare to torment the soul of the aged, then
will I, indeed, have peace and tranquillity. Then would history
and the billions throughout the world proclaim that it was right
that we dreamt and that we toiled to give life to a workable
dream."[8]

FIRE SALVO TWO

While the odds that a Mandela led Armada of Hope
would succeed in bringing the international financial system to
heel are about a hundred to one, there is still a one percent
chance of a successful counter-attack based on the old strategy
of divide and conquer. There is no doubt that the world's
wealthy and mighty elite will use every conceivable strong-arm
trick known to mankind. They will attempt to rally the support
of the wealthy elite in Third World countries by reminding them
of the benefits of their privileged position. Brazilian and

Malaysian millionaires may feel that they have more in common with American millionaires than they do with their own countrymen.

In addition, just as the old Soviet Empire planted agents in every country so, too, have the IMF and World Bank installed their moles in almost every government apparatus. They are called advisers, of course, but they can be counted on to fight a desperate rearguard action. They will proclaim, as neo-classical apologists have been saying for twenty years, that the fuss is premature. All that is required is a little more patience to give their "reforms" time to work through the system and deliver the great things that have been promised.

It would be another case of false hope. Apart from twenty years of broken promises and increasing distress on almost every front, all you have to do is look at the arithmetic. The system is fundamentally flawed and has to be fundamentally fixed. So I am suggesting that the trade unions of the world should make it clear that in the unlikely event that all else fails, that they will not. They would give notice that if action has not been taken by July 1, 2000, that they will shut the world economy down until governments realize that all people have rights. Labor could strangle the money-making machines of the rich until the squeals could be heard from one Pole to the other. Unlike the unsuccessful skirmishes of earlier generations, this has to be a fight to the finish and few groups have more at stake and more to protect than the organized workers of the world.

A united labor front, too, would require a leader and I have one or two excellent candidates in mind. A challenge of this magnitude would be an appropriate way to top off a career. Chances are that labor will never have to make good on its threat but being prepared is the best guarantee of that.

THE FINAL WORD

I would like to make it clear that I am not a Utopian. I know that there will always be ethnic and racial tensions; there will always be people who give greater allegiance to power than to principle; there will always be those willing to exploit the weaknesses of others; some people will always be poor and some will decide not to work even when there are jobs available, in which case they should not expect someone else to feed them; there will always be conflicts and there will sometimes be wars. No set of reforms, no matter how broad, will right every wrong. So the dream does not envisage a perfect world — if it did it would just be fantasy and not meet Mandela's test of "reasonable".

On the other hand, realizing the dream would offer a new beginning for billions. They could hope for a higher standard of living and an improved quality of life. They could reasonably expect, without undue delay, to have potable water to drink, food enough for a balanced diet, a roof over their head and a bed to sleep on. Health care and education would be more universally available. Millions of new jobs would be created and many of those would be directly tied to sustainable development and the preservation of the planet for future generations.

And most exciting of all, there would be a million ways to innovate and create for the common good. Each young person who wanted to could find a niche, great or small, that would give them the satisfaction of leaving the planet just a tiny bit better off than they found it. For, after all, isn't that what life is all about?

NOTES

Chapter 1: Something Has Gone Desperately Wrong

1. World Debt Tables, The World Bank, Volume II, 1999.
2. As reported in the *New York Times*, September 1, 1998.
3. As reported in the *Financial Post*, September 4, 1998.
4. As reported in the *Wall Street Journal*, September 14, 1998.
5. As reported in the *New York Times*, November 13, 1998.
6. As reported in the *New York Times*, September 3, 1998.
7. As reported in the *Wall Street Journal*, July 23, 1998.
8. Stiglitz, Joseph, as reported by the Canadian Broadcasting Corporation News Roundup.
9. As reported in the *Toronto Star*, October 23, 1998.
10. As reported in the *Toronto Star*, September 13, 1998.
11. Federal Reserve, as reported in the *Wall Street Journal*, December 31, 1998.
12. As reported in the *Financial Post*, January 31, 1998.
13. *Ibid*.
14. United Nations Development Report/Unicef 1997 and World Health Organization, 1998.
15. As reported in the *Toronto Star*, September 24, 1998.
16. As reported in the *New York Times*, September 1, 1998.
17. As reported in the *Wall Street Journal*, December 22, 1998.
18. Cohen, Stephen F., "Russia's new dark age", in *The Nation*, 1998. Reprinted by permission.

Chapter 2: The Washington Nonsensus

1. Hellyer, Paul, *Surviving the Global Financial Crisis: The Economics of Hope for Generation X*, Toronto: Chimo Media Limited, 1996, Table 2, p. 34.
2. Friedman, Milton, and Friedman, Rose D., *Free to Choose: A Personal Statement*, New York: Harcourt Brace Jovanovich, Inc. 1981, p. 251. Reprinted by permission.
3. Source: IMF - International Financial Statistics Yearbook, 1993 and 1995.
4. Annual Report of the Council of Economic Advisers, Washington, D.C., January 1981, p. 39.
5. O.E.C.D. Main Economic Indicators, 1965-70.
6. Hellyer, Paul, Several books including *Surviving the Global Financial Crisis: The Economics of Hope for Generation X*, op. cit.
7. Friedman, Milton, "A Monetary and Fiscal Framework for Economic Stability", *American Economic Review*, XXXVIII, June 1948.

8.   Friedman, Milton, *A Program for Monetary Stability*, New York: Fordham University Press, 1959, p. 65. Reprinted by permission.

9.   *Ibid*. Henry C. Simons, "A Positive Program for Laissez Faire: Some Proposals for a Liberal Economic Policy", in *Economic Policy for Free Society* (Chicago, 1948), pp. 62-5 (first published as Public Policy Pamphlet, No. 15, ed. Harry D. Gideonse (Chicago, 1934); Lloyd W. Mints, *Monetary Policy for a Competitive Society* (New York, 1950), pp. 186-87. Albert G. Hart, "The 'Chicago Plan' of Banking Reform", *Review of Economic Studies*, 2 (1935), pp. 104-16. Reprinted in Friedrich A. Lutz and Lloyd W. Mints (eds.), *Readings in Monetary Theory* (New York, 1951), pp. 437-56.

10.   Friedman, Milton, *A Program for Monetary Stability,* op.cit., pp. 65-66.

11.   *Ibid.*, p. 75.

12.   Friedman, Milton, in a footnote reply to a letter from William F. Hixson, November 9, 1983.

13.   Friedman, Milton, in a letter to Professor John H. Hotson, February 3, 1986.

14.   *Ibid.*

15.   Russell, Marcia, *Revolution: New Zealand from Fortress to Free Market*, Auckland: Hodder Moa Beckett Publishers Limited, 1996, p. 7. Reprinted by permission.

16.   Economic Report of the President, 1991, 1997.

17.   *Ibid.*

18.   *Ibid.*

19.   Budget of the United States Government, Fiscal Year 1999, Historical Tables.

20.   As reported in the *Wall Street Journal*, January 11, 1999.

Chapter 3: The IMF: 50 Plus Years Is Too Long

1.   Soloman, Steven, *The Confidence Game: How Unelected Central Bankers Are Governing the Changed Global Economy*, New York: Simon & Schuster, 1995.

2.   Stevenson, Merril, "A Game of Skill as Well: Survey of International Banking", *The Economist*, March 21, 1987, p. 18.

3.   Chossudovsky, Michel, *The Globalisation of Poverty: Impacts of IMF and World Bank Reforms*, Penang: Third World Network, 1997, professor of economics, University of Ottawa, Ottawa, Ontario, Canada.

4.   Danaher, Kevin (ed.), *50 Years is Enough: The Case Against the World Bank and the International Monetary Fund*, Boston: South End Press, 1994.

5.	Chossudovsky, Michel, op.cit., pp. 58-59.	Reprinted by permission.
6.	As reported in the *Toronto Star*, March 10, 1998.
7.	As reported in the *Financial Post*, May 6, 1998.
8.	*Ibid.*
9.	As reported in the *Globe & Mail*, January 13, 1998.
10.	Finlay, J. Richard, "Inner workings of IMF remain a mystery", in *The Financial Post*, January 31, 1998, p. 25.	Reprinted by permission.
11.	As reported in the *Globe and Mail*, May 6, 1998.
12.	As reported in the *Wall Street Journal*, October 13, 1998.
13.	*Ibid.*
14.	Kissinger, Henry, "Le FMI fait plus de mal que de bien", in *Le Monde*, as reported by Agence France Presse, Paris, and copied in *La Presse*, Montréal, October 15, 1998, p. E4.

Chapter 4: World Bank — World Disaster

1.	Kapur, Devesh, Lewis, John P., and Webb, Richard, *The World Bank: Its First Half Century*, Washington: Brookings Institution, 1997.
2.	Caufield, Catherine, *Masters of Illusion: The World Bank and the Poverty of Nations*, New York: Henry Holt and Company, Inc., 1996. Reprinted by permission.
3.	*Ibid.*, p. 78.
4.	*Ibid.*, p. 81.
5.	*Ibid.*, p. 83.
6.	Pearson, Lester B., "Partners in Development", 1969.
7.	Bello, Walden, "Global Economic Counterrevolution: How Northern Economic Warfare Devastates the South", in *50 Years is Enough: The Case Against the World Bank and the International Monetary Fund*, Kevin Danaher (ed.), Boston: South End Press, 1994, p. 16.
8.	*Ibid.*, p. 17.
9.	*Ibid.*, p. 18.
10.	Shiva, Vandana, "International Institutions Practicing Environmental Double Standards", in *50 Years is Enough: The Case Against the World Bank and the International Monetary Fund*, Kevin Danaher (ed.), Boston: South End Press, 1994, pp. 102-103.
11.	Arruda, Marcos, "Brazil: Drowning in Debt, Marcos Arruda, Interviewed by Multinational Monitor", in *50 Years is Enough: The Case Against the World Bank and the International Monetary Fund*, Kevin Danaher (ed.), Boston: South End Press, 1994, pp. 44-45.
12.	Caufield, Catherine, *Masters of Illusion: The World Bank and the Poverty of Nations*, op. cit., pp. 173-174.

13. George, Susan, "The Debt Boomerang", in *50 Years is Enough: The Case Against the World Bank and the International Monetary Fund*, Kevin Danaher (ed.). Boston: South End Press, 1994, pp. 29-30.
14. As reported in the *New York Times*, October 7, 1998.
15. Stackhouse, John, "Knowledge key to progress, World Bank report says", in the *Globe and Mail*, October 5, 1998, A14. Reprinted by permission.

Chapter 5: The MAI — Globalization Gone Mad

1. Yeutter, Clayton, quoted in the *Toronto Star*, October 6, 1987.
2. "U.S.-Canada Free Trade Agreement Briefing Paper for Secretary Baker and Ambassador Yeutter". (Confidential Appraisal of U.S.-Canada Pact presented to Treasury Secretary James Baker and Trade Ambassador Clayton Yeutter) (Washington, September 1987). Photocopy of document obtained by Inside U.S. Trade, pp. 12, 18.
3. The New Democratic Government of Premier Robert Keith Rae, Q.C., was sworn in October 1, 1990.
4. As reported in the *Globe and Mail*, November 25, 1998.
5. *Ibid.*
6. "The Metalclad Case", update prepared by Michelle Sforza, Public Citizen's Global Trade Watch. Reprinted by permission.
7. *Ibid.*
8. *Ibid.*
9. *Ibid.*
10. Millman, Joel, "Metalclad Suit is First Against Mexico Under NAFTA Foreign Investment Rules", in the *Wall Street Journal*, October 14, 1997, P. A2, A11. Reprinted by permission.
11. "The Metalclad Case", op. cit.
12. Appleton, Barry, Appleton & Associates International Lawyers, in a paper "Municipalities and the MAI", February 6, 1998.
13. *Ibid.*
14. Henwood, Doug, "Whatever Happened to Third World Debt?", in *50 Years is Enough: The Case Against the World Bank and the International Monetary Fund*, Kevin Danaher (ed.), Boston: South End Press, 1994, p. 41.
15. As reported in the *New York Times*, December 10, 1998.
16. Daly, Herman E., "The Perils of Free Trade", in the *Scientific American*, November 1993, p. 50. Reprinted by permission.

Chapter 6: Economists Never Learn

1. Elected June 27, 1949, as the Liberal member of parliament for the federal riding of Davenport in west-central Toronto.

2.   Keynes, John Maynard, *General Theory of Employment, Interest and Money*, New York, 1936.

3.   The Reverend Tom Skinner was President of Tom Skinner Associates and former Chaplain of the Washington Redskins.

4.   National Labor Committee in Support of Worker and Human Rights Press Release, "18 months after the Kathie Lee Gifford scandal, sweatshop conditions are worse than ever: Top American companies exposed", New York, November 13, 1997.

5.   *Ibid.*, p. 2.

6.   *Ibid.*

7.   *Ibid.*

8.   As reported in the *Toronto Star*, April 17, 1998.

9.   As reported in the *Globe and Mail*, July 8, 1998.

10.   A view often expressed by C.D. Howe when he was a minister of the crown in the governments of Mackenzie King and Louis S. St.Laurent.

11.   Friedman, Milton, "A Second Industrial Revolution", speech given at the 9th Dr. Harold Walter Siebens Lecture, The Fraser Institute, Vancouver, B.C., May 18, 1994.

12.   The OECD Jobs Study, "Facts-Analysis-Strategies, Unemployment in the OECD Area 1950-1995", Organization for Economic Cooperation and Development, 1994, p.10.

13.   As reported in the *Toronto Star*, September 24, 1998.

Chapter 7: The First Commandment

1.   Chairman Alan Greenspan addressed the Annual Convention of the American Society of Newspaper Editors, Washington, April 2, 1998.

2.   From the 4th of a series of columns submitted to the *Financial Post*, February 14, 1995, by Paul Hellyer at the request of *Post* editor Diane Francis.

3.   Eichenwald, Kurt, "3 Ex-Executives of Archer Daniels Are Found Guilty of Price Fixing", in the *New York Times*, September 18, 1998, A1. Copyright © 1998 by The New York Times. Reprinted by permission.

4.   Pierson, Ransdell, "Drug giants settle price-fixing lawsuit", reported in *The Toronto Star*, July 15, 1998, E3, based on a Reuters News Agency dispatch from New York. Reprinted by permission.

5.   Korten, David, "When Corporations Rule the World", October 12, 1996.

6.   *Ibid.*

7.   As reported in the *Toronto Star*, July 10, 1998.

8. Drohan, Madelaine, "Rice defends hardball tactics of capitalism", in the *Globe & Mail*, February 5, 1997, p. B10. Reprinted with permission from The Globe and Mail.
9. As reported in the *Toronto Star*, September 18, 1998.
10. As reported in the *Financial Post*, April 3 and 25, 1998.
11. As reported in the *Globe and Mail*, December 23, 1998.
12. As reported in the *Globe and Mail*, August 28, 1998.
13. As reported in the *Globe and Mail*, January 9, 1999.
14. Foss, Krista, and Taylor, Paul, "Volatile mix meant trouble at hospital", in the *Globe and Mail*, August 22, 1998, p. A4. Reprinted with permission from The Globe and Mail.
15. Shankman, Neil, "Whistleblowing Can Be a Loser Move", appearing in *Management Ethics*, a publication of the Canadian Centre for Ethics & Corporate Policy, September/October, 1998.
16. As reported in the *Toronto Star*, May 4, 1998.
17. *Ibid*.
18. Noonan, Erica, "U.S. economic boom leaves the homeless, working poor behind", in the *Globe and Mail*, July 22, 1998, p. B9. Reprinted with permission from The Associated Press.
19. Declaration of G7 Finance Ministers and Central Bank Governors, in Washington, October 3, 1998.
20. Mokhiber, Russell, and Weissman, Robert, "Boom and Bailout", in their weekly column Focus on the Corporation, October 9, 1998.
21. As reported in the *Toronto Star*, October 22, 1998.
22. Johnston, David Cay, "American-Style Pay Moves Abroad", in the *New York Times*, September 3, 1998, C1. Copyright © 1998 by The New York Times. Reprinted by permission.
23. *Ibid*.
24. As reported in the *Globe and Mail*, September 5, 1998.

Chapter 8: Where Does Money Come From?

1. Chaffers, William, *Gilda Aurifabrorum: A History of English Goldsmiths and Plateworkers, and Their Marks Stamped on Plate*, London: Reeves & Turner, [1800], p. 210.
2. *Ibid*.
3. Hixson, William F., *Triumph of the Bankers: Money and Banking in the Eighteenth and Nineteenth Centuries*, Westport: Praeger Publishers, 1993, p. 46. Reprinted by permission.
4. *Ibid*., p. 60.
5. Nettles, Curtis P., *The Money Supply of the American Colonies before 1720*, New York: Augustus M. Kelley, 1964, p. 169.
6. Powell, Ellis T., *The Evolution of the Money Market — 1385-1915*, New York: Augustus M. Kelley, 1966, p. 197.

7.   Innis, Mary Quayle, *An Economic History of Canada*, Toronto: The Ryerson Press, 1935, p. 28.

8.   Lester, Richard A, "Currency Issues to Overcome Depression in Pennsylvania, 1723 and 1938, *The Journal of Political Economy*, Vol. 46, June 1938, p. 326.

9.   Hixson, William F., *Triumph of the Bankers*, op. cit., p. 46.

10.   Lester, Richard A., *The Journal of Political Economy*, op. cit., p. 338.

11.   *Ibid.*, p. 341.

12.   Smith, Adam, *Wealth of Nations*, New York: P.F. Collier and Sons, 1909, p. 266.

13.   Nettles, Curtis P., *The Money Supply of the American Colonies before 1720*, op. cit., p. 265.

14.   Ferguson, E. James, *The Power of the Purse: A History of American Public Finance, 1776-1790*, Chapel Hill: University of North Carolina Press, 1961, p. 16.

15.   Hixson, William F., *Triumph of the Bankers*, op. cit., p. 81.

16.   Franklin, Benjamin, *The Writings of Benjamin Franklin*, Smyth, Albert Henry (ed.), New York: Macmillan, 1907, (9), pp. 231-233.

17.   Hixson, William F., *Triumph of the Bankers*, op. cit., p. 80.

18.   *Ibid.*

19.   Morris, Richard B., *The Forging of the Union 1781-1789*, New York: Harper & Row, 1987, p. 155.

20.   Sumner, William Graham, *A History of the American Currency*, New York: Augustus M. Kelley, 1968, p. 123.

21.   Angell, Norman, *The Story of Money*, New York: Frederick A. Stokes Co., 1929, p. 294.

22.   Hixson, William F., *Triumph of the Bankers*, op. cit., p. 150.

23.   Bordo, Michael D., "Gold Standard", *The Fortune Encyclopedia of Economics*, Henderson, David R. (ed.), New York: Warner Books Inc., 1993, p. 360.

24.   *Seventy-Ninth Annual Report of the Board of Governors of the Federal Reserve System*, 1992, p. 281.

25.   Friedman, Milton, in a letter to the author dated October 15, 1998.

26.   Friedman, Milton, in a letter to Professor John H. Hotson, February 3, 1986.

Chapter 9: The Death of Democracy

1.   Metcalf, Jack, *The Two Hundred Years Debate: Who Shall Issue the Nation's Money*, Olymphia: An Honest Money for America Publications, 1986, p. 91.

2.   *Ibid.*

3.   *Ibid.*, p. 92.

4.   Friedman, Milton, and Schwartz, Anna Jacobson, *A Monetary*

History of the United States 1867-1960, Princeton: Princeton University Press, 1963, pp. 327-328.

5. Friedman, Milton, in a letter to the author dated October 15, 1998.
6. Hellyer, Paul, *Surviving the Global Financial Crisis: The Economics of Hope for Generation X*, op. cit., p. 85.
7. As reported in the *Globe and Mail*, September 8, 1998.
8. As reported by the National Alliance of People's Movements, September 1998.
9. Wayne, Leslie, "If No Guarantee of Victory, Money Sure Makes It Easier", in the *New York Times*, November 6, 1998, p. A23. Copyright © 1998 by The New York Times. Reprinted by permission.
10. *Ibid.*
11. Lapham, Lewis, "Pax Iconomica", in *Behind the Headlines*, Vol. 54, No. 2, Winter 1996-97, p. 9, in his 'On Politics, Culture and Media' keynote address to the Canadian Institute of International Affairs national foreign policy conference in October, 1996.
12. *Ibid*, p. 8.
13. Phillips, Kevin, *Arrogant Capital: Washington, Wall Street, and the Frustration of American Politics*, Toronto: Little, Brown & Company (Canada) Limited, 1994.
14. *Ibid.*, p. 43.
15. *Ibid.*, p. 52-53.
16. Lapham, Lewis, op. cit., p. 9-10.
17. Mokhiber, Russell, and Weissman, Robert, "The More You Watch, the Less you Know", in their weekly column Focus on the Corporation, April 17, 1998.
18. Mokhiber, Russell, and Weissman, Robert, "Pulp Non-Fiction: The Ecologist Shredded", op. cit., October 28, 1998.
19. Associated Press dispatch as reported in the *Globe and Mail*, April 4, 1997.
20. As reported in the *Globe and Mail*, October 27, 1998.
21. *Ibid.*
22. Korten, David, "Democracy for Sale", extract of David Korten's Schumacher Lecture in Bristol on October 17, 1998.
23. Reinicke, Wolfgang H., *Global Public Policy: Governing without Government?*, Washington: Brookings Institution Press, 1998.

Chapter 10: World War III — The Banks vs The People

1. Campbell, Alexander, a mining engineer and entrepreneur, elected to Congress from Illinois in 1874 for a single term on a Democrat-Independent ticket.
2. As reported in the *New York Times*, July 31, 1998, and the *World Street Journal*, August 27, 1998.

3.   As reported in the *Wall Street Journal*, October 1998.

4.   As reported in the *Financial Post*, October 3, 1998.

5.   As reported in the *Independent*, London, November 30, 1998.

6.   Campbell, Alexander, *The True Greenback*, Chicago: Republican Books, 1868, p. 31.

7.   McPherson, Edward (ed.), *A Handbook of Politics*, New York: Da Capo Publishing Corp., 1972, p. 271.

8.   Friedman, Milton and Schwartz, Anna Jacobson, *A Monetary History of the United States 1867-1960*, Princeton: Princeton University Press, 1962.

9.   Day, Donald, *Will Rogers: A Biography*, New York: David McKay Company, Inc., 1962, p. 285.

10.   Friedman, Milton and Schwartz, Anna Jacobson, *A Monetary History of the United States 1867-1960*, op. cit., p. 322. Reprinted by permission.

11.   Phillips, Ronnie J., *The Chicago Plan & New Deal Banking Reform*, New York: M.E. Sharpe, Inc., 1995, pp. 47-48.

12.   Simons, Henry C., *Economic Policy for a Free Society*, Chicago, University of Chicago Press, 1948, p. 80.

13.   Taken from an unpublished manuscript entitled "Double-Crossed by the Invisible Hand: Essays on the Behaviour of Money, the Public Interest and the Crash-Test Economy, by Keith Helmuth, Debec, New Brunswick, 1997.

14.   Phillips, Kevin, *Arrogant Capital: Washington, Wall Street, and the Frustration of American Politics*, Toronto: Little, Brown & Company (Canada) Limited, 1994, p. 114.

Chapter 11: Y2K — Year of the Jubilee

1.   Adams, Patricia, "The Doctrine of Odious Debts", Interview by Juliette Majot, in *50 Years is Enough: The Case Against the World Bank and the International Monetary Fund*, Kevin Danaher (ed.), Boston: South End Press, 1994, p. 36.

2.   Declaration of G7 Finance Ministers and Central Bank Governors, in Washington, October 3, 1998.

3.   As reported on the Canadian Broadcasting Corporation Show "Metro Morning", November 1998.

4.   *The Public Good: Lessons for the 3rd Millennium*, A Conference in honor of Hon. Allan J. MacEachen, St. Francis Xavier University, Antigonish, Nova Scotia, Canada, July 4-6, 1996.

5.   Passell, Peter, "Has This War Been Won?", in the *New York Times*, October 25, 1995.

6.   Simulations based on Sources: Laurence H. Meyer & Associates, Limited, and Informetrica Limited.

7.   Tobin, James, "A Proposal for International Monetary Reform",

Eastern Economic Journal, 1978, Vol. 4, pp. 154-155.
8. Felix, David, *Challenge*, May/June, 1995.
9. Halifax Summit, *Communiqué*, June 15-17, p. 1, 1995.

Chapter 12: Democracy and Hope Restored

1. As reported in the *New York Times*, December 23, 1998.
2. Estimate of Informetrica Ltd., "A Macroeconomic Policy Package for the 1990s" by Mike McCracken.
3. As reported in the *Globe and Mail*, October 27, 1998.
4. Excerpt from an article by Carol Goar originally appearing in the *Toronto Star*, October 31, 1998. Reprinted by permission.
5. Feature Article, "Rx for the Health Care System", in the *Wall Street Journal*, October 18, 1998. Reprinted by permission.
6. *Ibid.*, A18
7. *Ibid.*

8. *Ibid.*
9. From an article by Brad Lavigne, national chairperson of the Canadian Federation of Students.
10. See Ministry of Education, UNDP, UNESCO (National Project Education Sector Review and Human Resources Sector Analysis), *Vietnam Education and Human Resources Analysis*, Vol. 1, Hanoi, 1992, p. 39, in *The Globalisation of Poverty: Impacts of IMF and World Bank Reforms*, by Michel Chossudovsky, Malaysia: Third World Network, 1997, p. 165-166.
11. Based on a report released October 7, 1998, by the Commission for Environmental Co-operation, the Montréal-based watchdog created under NAFTA.
12. *Ibid.*, as reported in the *Toronto Star*, October 7, 1998.
13. As reported in a *New York Times* editorial, September 29, 1998.
14. As reported in the *Toronto Star*, May 7, 1998.
15. The Ninth Biennial Report of the International Joint Commission on Great Lakes Water Quality, 1998.
16. *Ibid.*, p. 7.
17. As reported in the *Financial Post*, June 12, 1998.
18. As reported by the Canadian Broadcasting Corporation on "Ideas", April 29, 1998.
19. As reported in the *Globe and Mail*, September 14, 1998.

ABBREVIATIONS

BIS   Bank for International Settlements
BUS   Bank of the United States
CPI   Consumer Price Index
EPA   Environmental Protection Agency
FCC   Federal Communications Commission
FDA   Food and Drug Administration
FED   U.S. Federal Reserve Board
FIRA   The Foreign Investment Review Act
FTA   Free Trade Agreement
G7   The World's Seven Largest Industrial Economies
GATT   General Agreement on Tariffs and Trade
GCM   Government-Created Money
GDP   Gross Domestic Product
GNP   Gross National Product
HMOs   Health Maintenance Organizations
IBRD   International Bank for Reconstruction and Development
IJC   International Joint Commission
IMF   International Monetary Fund
ICSID   International Centre for the Settlement of Investment Disputes
LDCs   Less Developed Countries
MAI   Multilateral Agreement on Investment
MMT   Methylcyclopentadienyl manganese tricarbonyl
NAFTA   North American Free Trade Agreement
NDP   New Democratic Party
NEP   National Energy Program
NGOs   Non-Governmental Organizations
OECD   Organization for Economic Cooperation and Development
OPEC   Organization of Petroleum Exporting Countries
PCBs   Polychlorinated biphenyls
rBST   Recombinant Bovine Somatotropin
SALs   Strategic Adjustment Loans
WTO   World Trade Organization

BIBLIOGRAPHY

Angell, Norman, *The Story of Money*. New York: Frederick A. Stokes Co., 1929.

Campbell, Alexander, *The True Greenback*. Chicago: Republican Books, 1868.

Caufield, Catherine, *Masters of Illusion: The World Bank and the Poverty of Nations*, New York: Henry Holt and Company, Inc., 1996.

Chaffers, William, *Gilda Aurifabrorum: A History of English Goldsmiths and Plateworkers, and Their Marks Stamped on Plate*. London: Reeves & Turner, [1800].

Chossudovsky, Michel, *The Globalisation of Poverty: Impacts of IMF and World Bank Reforms*. Penang: Third World Network, 1997.

Danaher, Kevin (ed.), *50 Years is Enough: The Case Against the World Bank and the International Monetary Fund*. Boston: South End Press, 1994.

Day, Donald, *Will Rogers: A Biography*. New York: David McKay Company, Inc., 1962.

Deane, Marjorie, and Pringle, Robert, *The Central Banks*. London: Hamish Hamilton Ltd., 1994.

Ferguson, E. James, *The Power of the Purse: A History of American Public Finance, 1776-1790*. Chapel Hill: University of North Carolina Press, 1961. and Company, 1992.

Fisher, Irving, *100% Money*. New York: The Adelphi Company, 1935.

Franklin, Benjamin, *The Writings of Benjamin Franklin*, Smyth, Albert Henry (ed.). New York: Macmillan, 1907.

Friedman, Milton, *Monetarist Economics*. Oxford: Basil Blackwell Ltd., 1991.

Friedman, Milton, *A Program for Monetary Stability*. New York: Fordham University Press, 1959.

Friedman, Milton, and Friedman, Rose D., *Free to Choose: A Personal Statement*. New York: Harcourt Brace Jovanovich, Inc., 1981.

Friedman, Milton and Schwartz, Anna Jacobson, *A Monetary History of the United States 1867-1960*. Princeton: Princeton University Press, 1963.

Galbraith, John Kenneth, *Money, Whence it Came, Where it Went*. Boston: Houghton Mifflin Company, 1975.

Gouge, William M., *A Short History of Paper Money and Banking in the United States*. New York: Augustus M. Kelley, 1968.

Gray, John, *False Dawn: The Delusions of Global Capitalism*. London: Granta Publications, 1998.

Handy, Charles, *The Hungry Spirit: Beyond Capitalism — A Quest for Purpose in the Modern World*. London: Random House, 1997.

Hellyer, Paul, *The Evil Empire: Globalization's Darker Side*. Toronto: Chimo Media Limited, 1997.

Hellyer, Paul, *Surviving the Global Financial Crisis: The Economics of Hope for Generation X.* Toronto: Chimo Media Limited, 1996.

Henderson, David R. (ed.), *The Fortune Encyclopedia of Economics* New York: Warner Books, Inc., 1993.

Hixson, William F., *Triumph of the Bankers: Money and Banking in the Eighteenth and Nineteenth Centuries.* Westport: Praeger Publishers, 1993.

Innis, Mary Quayle, *An Economic History of Canada*, Toronto: The Ryerson Press, 1935.

Jones, Aubrey, *The New Inflation: The Politics of Prices and Incomes.* London: Andre Deutsch, 1973.

Kapur, Devesh, Lewis, John P., and Webb, Richard, *The World Bank: Its First Half Century.* Washington: Brookings Institution, 1997.

Keynes, John Maynard, *General Theory of Employment, Interest and Money.* New York: Harcourt, Brace, 1935.

Korten, David D., *When Corporations Rule the World.* West Hartford: Kumarian Press, Inc., 1995.

Lekachman, Robert, *Inflation: The Permanent Problem of Boom and Bust.* New York: Vintage Books, 1973.

Lester, Richard A., "Currency Issues to Overcome Depression in Pennsylvania, 1723 and 1938, *The Journal of Political Economy*, Vol. 46, June 1938, p. 326.

Lux, Kenneth, *Adam Smith's Mistake: How a Moral Philosopher Invented Economics and Ended Morality.* Boston: Shambhala Publications Inc., 1990.

McCarthy, W.E.J., O'Brien, J.F., and V.G. Dowd, *Wage Inflation and Wage Leadership: A Study of the Role of Key Wage Bargains in the Irish System of Collective Bargaining.* Dublin: Cahill & Co. Ltd., 1975.

McPherson, Edward (ed.) *A Handbook of Politics.* New York: Da Capo Publishing Corp., 1972.

McQuaig, Linda, *The Cult of Impotence: Selling the Myth of Powerlessness in the Global Economy.* Toronto: Penguin Books Canada Ltd., 1998.

Metcalf, Jack, *The Two Hundred Year Debate: Who Shall Issue the Nation's Money.* Olympia: An Honest Money for America Publication, 1986.

Mill, John Stuart, *Principles of Political Economy with some of their Applications to Social Philosophy.* New York: Augustus M. Kelley, 1909.

Millman, Gregory J., *The Valdals' Crown: How Rebel Currency Traders Overthrew the World's Central Banks.* New York: The Free Press, 1995.

Mitchell, Broadus, *The Price of Independence.* New York: Oxford University Press, 1974.

Morris, Richard B., *The Forging of the Union 1781-1789*. New York: Harper & Row, 1987.

Munkirs, John R., *The Transformation of American Capitalism From Competitive Market Structures to Centralized Private Sector Planning*. New York: M.E. Sharpe, Inc., 1985.

Myers, Margaret G., *A Financial History of the United States*. New York: Columbia University Press, 1970.

Nettles, Curtis P., *The Money Supply of the American Colonies before 1720*. New York: Augustus M. Kelley, 1964.

Nicolay, John G., and Hay, John (eds.), *Abraham Lincoln: Complete Works*. New York: The Century Co., 1907.

Orchard, David, *The Fight for Canada: Four Centuries of Resistance to American Expansionism*. Toronto: Stoddard Publishing Co. Limited, 1993.

Phillips, Kevin, *Arrogant Capital: Washington, Wall Street, and the Frustration of American Politics*. Toronto: Little, Brown & Company (Canada) Limited, 1994.

Phillips, Ronnie, J., *The Chicago Plan & New Deal Banking Reform*. New York: M.E. Sharpe, Inc., 1995.

Powell, Ellis T., *The Evolution of the Money Market – 1385-1915*. New York: Augustus M. Kelley, 1966.

Reinicke, Wolfgang H., *Global Public Policy: Governing without Government*. *Washington: Brookings Institution Press, 1998*.

Russell, Marcia, *Revolution: New Zealand from Fortress to Free Market*, Auckland: Hodder Moa Beckett Publishers Limited, 1996, p. 7.

Samuelson, Paul A., *Economics*, 9th ed. New York: McGraw-Hill Book Co., 1973.

Schumacher, Ernst F., *Small is Beautiful: Economics as if People Mattered*. New York: Harper & Row, Publishers, Inc., 1989.

Simons, Henry C., *Economic Policy for a Free Society*. Chicago: University of Chicago Press, 1948.

Solomon, Steven, *The Confidence Game: How Unelected Central Bankers Are Governing the Changed Global Economy*. New York: Simon & Schuster, 1995.

Smith, Adam, *The Wealth of Nations*, Cannan, Edwin (ed.). New York: Modern Library, 1937.

Smith, Adam, *Wealth of Nations*. New York: P.F. Collier & Son, 1909.

Sumner, William Graham, *A History of American Currency*. New York: Augustus M. Kelley, 1968.

Thoren, Theodore R., and Warner, Richard F., *The Truth in Money Book*. Chagrin Falls: Truth in Money, Inc., 1994.

INDEX